CULTURAL HERITAGE AND CONTEMPORARY CHANGE
SERIES VII, SEMINARS, VOLUME 12
General Editor
George F. McLean

FREEDOM AND CHOICE IN A DEMOCRACY

Volume II

THE DIFFICULT PASSAGE TO FREEDOM

Edited by

Robert Magliola
Richard Khuri

THE COUNCIL FOR RESEARCH IN VALUES AND PHILOSOPHY

Copyright © 2004 by
The Council for Research in Values and Philosophy

Box 261
Cardinal Station
Washington, D.C. 20064

Library of Congress Cataloging-in-Publication

Freedom and choice in a democracy: the difficult passage to freedom.
  p. cm. — (Cultural heritage and contemporary change. Series
VII, Seminars on cultures and values ; v. 11-12)
    Includes bibliographical references and indexes.
    1. Liberty. 2. Democracy. I. Magliola, Robert R. II. Khuri, Richard
K. III. Title. V. Series.
JC585.F734 2003   2003011240
  320'.01'1—dc21   CIP

ISBN 1-56518-186-7 (pbk.: v. 1) -- ISBN 1-56518-185-9 (pbk.: v. 2)

CONTENTS

INTRODUCTION

The dramatic pace of change in recent times manifests the power of the basic human drive to be free. Often, freedom movements have defined themselves in terms of "liberation from"—from colonialism, from totalitarian, from prejudice. This evokes passion and upon success triggers explosive joy. The achievements of the last 50 years have been marked by three such celebrations of hard fought freedom: the end of the Second World War, the establishment of newly independent nations and the opening of the Berlin Wall.

Each such victory, however, brings with it new and even greater challenges. Surviving oppression required noble fortitude and forbearance, but "freedom for" a life that is fully human requires a yet broader and deeper range of virtues. To live freedom requires forgoing blind self-affirmation which, in the name of privacy and choices, disregard their effects upon others. The building of a truly human community cannot be achieved without truth and justice, love of one's neighbor and magnanimous civic concern, creativity and even genius in the classical sense of that term.

It was thought perhaps naively that upon the end of the highly centralized controls of the Marxist era all would fall easily into a liberal mode in which the new freedom would be exercised socially. What was not expected was the extent to which new freedom could be subverted by private agoism that could now flow into public extortion.

The new challenge raised by freedom in our days is not merely to be free from state, system, and ideology, but to create out *of the very stuff of freedom* itself those structures, traditions and commitments which will enable a people:

(a) to make decisions about their future and their relations with others which mobilize the free efforts of all in a cohesive, subsidiary and creative manner;

(b) to develop local and national policies for the promotion of human life in the spheres of health, education and culture, of employment, business and politics; and

(c) to engage as full and free participants in this process of decision making, implementation and fulfillment all sectors of the population, and indeed all persons, even those presently marginalized.

Such issues of freedom and choice are central to the human challenge at this point of transition. If this century is to experience new levels of democratic life a more rich notion of freedom must itself be elaborated. Philosophy must grow with and through the new and dramatic affirmations of liberation toward the articulation of new modes of human life worthy of free peoples.

To respond to this challenge it is necessary to combine the rich experience of the various cultures and the technical insights of the various sciences in a creative effort to deepen present wisdom and trace out new pathways for this century. This volume attempts to sort out some meanings of freedom especially in the Western tradition.

Part I, "Which Path to Freedom?" pushes to a head the conflicts regarding freedom and the defining differences which this study both marks and attempts to resolve.

Chapter I, by Richard K. Khuri, "Between the Two Domains," analyzes the domain of freedom and that of unfreedom, identifying the former with the 'metaphysical' (the doorway to the infinite, the transcendent) and the latter with the 'physical' (the merely finite world). Khuri sees two contemporary currents as most harmful to the metaphysical: (1) egocentrism, which—with the complicity of corporate governments and the media—generates commercialism and consumerism; and (2) 'nomological rationalism', which, despite some pretensions to the contrary, in fact caters to self-interest.

Chapter II, by Richard A. Graham, "Democratic Communities vs. Democratic Laws," taking the opposite tack from the preceding paper (Khuri), argues that self is the driving force behind reason, passion, and personal identity, and that its ethical regulation is more equitably handled by a nomological, not a communitarian, society. Graham broaches the transcendental in a Kantian way, arguing "that [an individual's] truly autonomous judgement is congruent with the same universalizable principles of highly developed religious faith."

Chapter III, by Ruta Rinkeviciene, "Occupation, Man, and Freedom of Choice," describes the state of psychological paralysis which affected the majority of Lithuanians after the collapse of the totalitarian U.S.S.R. regime. He argues that eager to become like the 'West' but unable to muster either the skills or the courage to change, most Lithuanians have agonized in a no-man's land of "yes" and "no." Lithuanians, she affirms, must re-do the educational system so that critical thinking is taught at an early age; the society at large must learn to accept responsibility and gain self-reliance. But on the other hand, Lithuania should retain and cultivate what is 'good' about its unique tradition, and be forewarned that 'Western' forms of government and economics, have their over defects and pitfalls.

The group discussion of the Chapter III is summarized and reported by G. McLean.

Chapter IV, by Ronald K. L. Collins, "The Tyranny of 'Freedom and Choice in a Democracy'," argues that the terms 'freedom' and 'choice' in the U.S.A. are too often manipulated by neo-liberal capitalism so they collapse into their opposite, as in Aldous Huxley's Brave New World. Whereas R. Rinkeviciene's paper exposes the devastating legacy of a repressive and collectivist Soviet society, Collins shows how 'free choice' can become entrapped within an 'unfree' cycle of consumerist greed in a society dominated by giant corporations.

Part II, "Fates and Futures of Freedom in Eastern Europe: Under Communism and After," focuses specifically on the suppression of freedom during the Soviet era, and the crises—filled with both turmoil and hope—which have followed in the wake of Soviet Communist collapse.

Chapter V, by Alfonsas Andriuskevicius, "Soviet Culture: Hiding Transcendence," demonstrates the strategies the Soviet system used to destroy a population's awareness of the 'metaphysical', the 'transcendent'. Andriuskevicius shows how the more sophisticated strategies involved not so much the prohibition of choice in favor of religion and 'spirituality', as the elimination of all information about them (except under extremely controlled conditions, as in an 'atheist museum'). He lists and explains a range of techniques used to make metaphysical values disappear, especially from the visual arts.

Chapter VI, by Silvia Nagy, "Culture and Popular Culture in Post-Cold War Central Europe," traces the vagaries of culture, especially of literary culture, during this post-totalitarian period. Nagy regards the current mass commercialization of culture as the main threat to Central Europe's small nations, whose cultural life is rooted precisely in their 'small village' and 'uniqueness'. She argues, along with Milan Kundera, that the cultural mission of the smaller nations to 'world culture' should be their resistance to global uniformity.

Chapter VII, by Tomas Sodeika and Arunas Sverdiolas, "Life in the Retort and Soon After," describes the psychology characterizing transition from (Soviet-)totalitarian state to post-totalitarian state. Human life in the Soviet state functioned in an "artificially constructed social life-space" (like life in a chemist's retort), since all values were reduced to 'social physics' engineered by 'cultural technologists'. The problem of the post-totalitarian state becomes that the people's psychology subconsciously retains survival mechanisms developed in the totalitarian period, such as 'daily pragmatism' and 'particular self-interest'. Sodeika and Sverdiolas argue that the solution is to cultivate transcendent ideals in their own right, without material reduction. A summary of this chapter follows.

Chapter VIII, by Rett R. Ludwikowski, "A New Constitutional Model for East-Central Europe," reports in detail on the constitutional restructuring of several East European countries (in particular Poland and Hungary) after the collapse of Russian Soviet domination. He sees Eastern European countries moving in governmental structure towards dual executive format (with President and Prime Minister) rather than the American model; and in economics towards market economies but with some socialist characteristics.

Part III, "Towards Freedom and Choice in Other Venues: Spain, Taiwan, The Philippines," assembles relevant information on other experiments in freedom, past and present.

Chapter IX, by Roberto J. González-Casanovas, "Alfonso X's Image of Enlightened Rule: Nature, Society, and Politics in the Law Prologues," examines the King of Castile's Prologues to four books of law in Castilian, with an eye towards uncovering their notion of natural law and social utopia. As intersections of revised Roman Law, Greek natural philosophy, the Chivalresque Code, and Islamic legal models, the Prologues set the medieval foundation for much subsequent Continental theorizing on justice, equity, and the nature of freedom. To achieve his aims, González-Casanovas studies the Prologues on both rhetorical and ideological levels, and draws upon historicist methodology. An Appendix supplies the four Prologues in Castilian and in English translation.

Chapter X, by Ming-Lee Wen, "Critical Thinking and Democratization in Taiwan," studies what was the pre-democratic phase in Taiwan's development, and the relevance of 'critical thinking' to that phase. Arguing that traditional Chinese concepts such as 'harmony' and 'loyalty' have been exploited by authority in order to force conformity, Wen urges three conceptual markers whereby critical thinking contributes to democratization. The first is emancipation from 'final' authority; the second is 'quasi-universality', or agreement by consensus; and the third is 'reconstruction' by way of new paradigms adopted with the understanding that in turn they can be changed if inadequate.

Chapter XI, by Vivian Ligo, "Variations in Value Orientations: Their Implications for Freedom and Choice in Filipino Democracy," appropriates the socio-empirical methodology of Kluckhohn and Strodtbeck to analyze the Filipino value system. The traditional Filipino Life-World is described,—its notions of nature and supernature, of time, of community, etc. The colonial and post-colonial periods have served to abuse and distort these values, so— for example— utang-na-loob ("mutual gratitude") is often exploited by authority-figures to abet corruption. Ligo contends that 'Western democracy' is not adapting well in The Philippines. She presents five theses accounting for present stress, and making recommendations for improvement in the future.

George F. McLean and Robert Magliola

PART I

WHICH PATH TO FREEDOM?

CHAPTER I

BETWEEN THE TWO DOMAINS

RICHARD K. KHURI

The metaphysical domain has been open to philosophers from the very beginning. The pre-Socratics acknowledged this. And how could they not? For it takes far less insight and depth than the philosopher is gifted with to recognize some among the innumerable things and deeds in the world that point beyond the physical. The philosopher's unique contribution has been not only to articulate this beyondness, not only to highlight the greater reality of the metaphysical, but to discern its unity. As the one philosopher who least got carried away by his peculiar endowment once pointed out, however, *too much* of something is harmful. Philosophers in the past generally drifted towards the sharper and harsher separation of the physical from the metaphysical which is latent in their conceptual approach. As a consequence, nowadays, for many under the sway of contemporary philosophy and the intellectual culture that has nurtured it, metaphysics has either ceased to exist or, at any rate, is incomprehensible to the alleged physical limitations of our inquiries and accounts.

Philosophy has long forgotten to look at the calling of things and deeds to the metaphysical, a calling so common and evident that no shepherd, seafarer or supplicant can fail to notice it. Art is grounded in the exemplification of this calling. Religion constantly celebrates it as it reminds us of the calling's origins. If the physical is indeed other than the metaphysical, the metaphysical nevertheless speaks through the physical. That is how we hear it. So what those philosophers now need is a healthy dose of what is routinely exemplified in art and celebrated in religion. Those philosophers incredibly fail to see this need, and not so incredibly when one considers, as we shall see in the second part of this paper, the extraordinary suppression of the metaphysical at the heart of modernity, immediately preceded by an equally extraordinary suppression (by Western European philosophy) for the supposed sake of the metaphysical. Such philosophers need a good ear for the song of the world.[1]

Freedom is perhaps the quintessential metaphysical state of human beings. No discussion of freedom is true to it without turning to the metaphysical reality that makes it possible. Thus, above all, I shall emphasize the metaphysical domain to which freedom belongs. But given that we in this era are witnesses to the most systematic and insidious suppression of the metaphysical ever known, a suppression that has the darkest consequences for our freedom, I have also furnished an essay in which I explain the moments of this suppression. We need to know where freedom belongs and what threatens it.

THE DOMAIN OF FREEDOM

To begin with, since a venture into the metaphysical is a venture into the significant infinite, let us contrast significant infinities with others.

The Finite and the Infinite

Quantitative and qualitative infinity: The mechanistic view of the universe allowed for infinite quantity (points on a line or point masses in a rigid body), but was finite with regard to its view of the universe as made up of material points and bodies related through mechanical laws. Mechanism upheld the view of the universe as a closed system. The research that had paradoxically supported mechanism has by now resulted in a picture of a universe bounded by qualitative infinities at both of its limits. Particles are now indistinguishable from mathematical entities, and the energy concentrations that allow matter to be identified in discrete terms are spread through vast areas of space. At the limits of the universe, it is widely believed that there are areas where all known (and, within our present framework, *knowable)* laws are inapplicable. The universe, which is more like yarns in a ball of wool than a sphere, appears to fade into the infinite at various points. It is even more widely believed to have emerged from one such point. Thus, science itself, long exploited for its apparent denial of qualitative infinities (the kind that make materialism suspect), accepts their existence well within the frontiers of contemporary theoretical physics. The universe now seems very much an open system. We may also understand the gap between life and its privation, and even that between humans and other creatures, as qualitative infinities that confront biological research.

From the quantitative/qualitative distinction to the insignificant/significant: An insignificant infinity is reached when a magnitude/quantity is stretched to a degree that it becomes *in principle* unmeasurable. For example, it will never be possible to count all possible melodies. This, however, is a trivial fact. But a melody is also something that can sing to us, with or without extra-musical evocations. This is significant. It is a reality to which a different sense of "unmeasurability" applies. Being songlike is *beyond all possible measure.* In general, when a significant infinity is reached, the reality at hand cannot be measured in any way. The sufficient conditions for a significant infinity are far too complex to be formulable. That is why the quantitative/qualitative distinction between infinities does not exactly correspond with the insignificant/ significant. The following section will illustrate significant infinities.

Significant Infinities

Preamble: The appeal to contemporary science for a boundary zone between the finite and the infinite is limited (a) by scientific research and theory remaining largely open to the existence of this zone and (b) to argumentation against those who still appeal to science in their resistance to significant infinities. Science provides neither the most reliable path to significant infinities nor are its paths necessarily those along which significant infinities are most luminous. The minute a scientist pauses to reflect on the significance of a qualitative infinity that obstructs further research and mathematical theorizing, he ceases to act as a scientist. It is therefore best to sample other experiences that we as human beings share.

Music and beyond: We may distinguish between the notes that form a melody, and the melody that they form. The notes are thought of as material components, while their melodic character is rather more elusive. If we think of those melodies that stand out, we can contrast them more effectively with their bare elements. We can hear a melody as a song, just as we recognize certain sequences of words as poetic. There is no conceivable algorithm to cover the transition from musical sequences (like scales or arpeggios) that are not songs to those that are. Nor can we learn to impart poetry to our words systematically. The transition is miraculous. It defies all necessary laws. It appears that notes and words have to be exposed to another world before they can sing. The infinities to which notes, words and colors must be oriented for them to come to life as they do in art, beyond every possible measure, are *significant.* No decree, no theory can ensnare significant infinities. No one who can hear notes as songs and words as lines of poetry can be denied the freedom of the significant infinite. And no one who denies the significant infinite to his freedom can be really free. This is what I seek to emphasize as we go along.

Songs, poems and paintings can be banal and perfunctory. Sequences of notes may be songlike in either a trivial or a serious sense. The sense I am after is that brought out by a performer who successfully imparts the songlike character of an unsentimental, unhackneyed but attractive melody to a listener. We should keep what moves us in mind. Our vast artistic heritage is replete with masterworks whose best moments indicate their origin deep within the significant infinite.

Folkways and religion: Songs need not surge against the backdrop of complex works in order to move us. Simple songs can waft resonant evocations to certain audiences. Folk songs can evoke the memory or history of a culture. Gregorian chants call up a climate of piety and devotion. Both can place the listener, though s/he be unsympathetic to their extra-musical dimensions, in the presence of a rare beauty. Here we come upon the intersection of music with the realms of folk culture and religion.

Folk culture is another way that the finite is thrown open to the significant infinite. An area of land, in the continued presence of those historically bound to it, takes on an *aura*. It begins to echo with the voices of generations who cultivated its soil, enjoyed its landscapes, built the towns it has hosted, and fought wars to keep it. The transition from land to native realm is as unfathomable as that from words to poetry. To fashion a native realm out of land is no less a leap from the material than what the poet fashions from words. This exercise in drawing cultural forms from the bosom of the earth is also inspired by a turn to the significant infinite. Only this turn is collective. Its signposts are partly in poetry and song.

Religion is openness and responsiveness to the significant infinite par excellence. If the artist exposes notes and words to another world, if a group of people tend their land with one eye to the heavens, the religious human being hurls himself entirely into that immensity and lets his existence be thereby progressively dematerialized. To fashion a person, a moral or religious person, from the material point of departure into which we are born is perhaps the most unfathomable transition of them all. That there is much more than survival, that there are benevolence, compassion, grief and envy over and above self- interest, that there is love in addition to lust, that there is faith beyond what the senses and the mind deliver—these all miraculously transcend what might have been, and signify an infinite that it would be ridiculous, if not insane, to contemplate quantifying.

First sketch of freedom and first definition of the boundary zone: The artistic, cultural and religious paths open innumerable byways to us all, in the presence of the significant infinite that imparts song to notes, an aura to the land, and a morality and spirituality to human beings. These innumerable byways stretch into a domain outside of all number, showing the extent and depth of our freedom when we exercise freedom fully. From this point of view, the world appears as so many outlets for our potential to transcend the material, to hear a song at every turn, or grow into the immensity that hovers over the vicinity of our lives.

Where we recognize poetry or song, the dematerialization of land by its natives, or the morality and spirituality of a human being, there lies the boundary zone between the finite and the significant infinite; it is the zone where a variety of experiences are located in which the finite appears, carried over a chasm into possibilities for which no algorithm can account. It is the zone where notes, words, land and human beings leap from their materiality into the unfathomable and turn into songs, poems, native realms and moral or religious persons. This is the external portrait of the zone. Internally, one lies within it whenever one grasps or experiences such dematerializations. Once we enter that boundary zone, we begin to realize our freedom.

There are many ways to enter and cross this boundary zone. These have to do both with its internal possibilities and with our own constitution. Thus we turn to a discussion of style and personality. We shall then have the occasion to come across another view of the boundary zone and other sketches of freedom.

Style and personality: Every composer, like every other human being, has a personality. They differ in the extent to which their music bears their personal stamp. It is fairly easy to recognize the music of Beethoven, Chopin, Schumann, Faure, Ravel or Prokofiev. The power and uniqueness of their personalities are revealed in a distinctive style. Style is another significant infinity. There is no measure for how one forges the elements of a given medium expressively. Style sets us apart from mechanical manipulations through the quantitative infinity of musical or linguistic permutations and possibilities. Computers loom as replacements for humans only because they can potentially sift through a vast number of permutations much more rapidly than their inventors. They can even be programmed to imitate or approximate "given" styles (if we grant that a particular style can be analyzed adequately and completely in terms reducible to a binary logical system). But they are inherently incapable of imparting style to the elements that they combine, least of all in a manner that rivals the accomplishments of a composer like Beethoven in the wake of whose work music could never be the same.

If style reflects the freedom we have within the media for our expression, the elements of the media also embody the freedom of the beings among whom they have evolved. For not only is style resistant to all algorithms, but the mastery of the elements of language or music cannot be taught beyond a certain point. There is a quasi-mechanical nucleus in each, but the further one moves away from the nucleus, the less rule-bound the choices and possiblities are. The mastery of a language is itself an art. All the documented information about each word and grammatical rule can be easily stored in the memory of a computer. But no complete set of rules exists that will enable the computer to use them all correctly and effectively. The reason is our freedom: It is totally unlike us to develop media for all our possible expressions that do not form a seamless whole that accommodates every imaginable turn towards the significant infinite. Language and music, outside of the quasi-mechanical core necessary for their introduction to newcomers and a measure of communicative stability, reflect the continuous will of their users to maintain their freedom in every direction.[2]

If style marks our way through the expressive media into which we are born, then personality marks the individual's way through all that he may possibly encounter. Style is one of the features of personality. Personality therefore reflects the deeper freedom. One way that a personality reveals itself is in the intersection of an individual life and the boundary zone. How one interacts with the significant infinite, the points at which one is open and responsive to it, the character of the openness and the response - there is no end to personal possibility. Not only can all the different intersections between the boundary zone and human beings never be counted, but each given intersection can never be fathomed. The boundary zone is entirely open to the capacity for dwelling within it. "For personality," says Berdyaev, "infinity opens out, it enters into infinity, and admits infinity into itself; in its self-revelation it is directed towards an infinite content."[3] A little later, he goes on:

> Personality must be the exception, no law at all is
> applicable to it. Everything generic and hereditary

is only material for the creative activity of
personality. The whole burden is laid upon man by
nature and society, by history and the demands of
civilization. This burden confronts us in the form of
difficulties which demand resistance and creative
transformation into the personal,—indeed, *uniquely*
the personal. The typical members of a group, a
class, or a profession may be clear individualities
but not clear personalities. Personality in man is the
triumph over the determination of the social group.
Personality is not a substance but an act, a creative
act.[4]

Whatever psychologists and social scientists point out in a
given person, these, far from being constitutive of personality, are
its points of departure. The basic freedom one has as a person
allows the transcendence of any combination of restrictive factors.
The creation of a personality, beyond what one is born into and
grows among, is a leap into the significant infinite. Every religion
that outlines broad spiritual avenues above all the petty differences
between human beings takes the creation of personality for granted
(but suffocates it when institutional pressures engender conformism
and subdue the vibrancy along the avenues preached). However
we may be free, . . . in the end we *are* free as persons and thus
move freely through the boundary between the finite and the infinite,
transcending our hereditary psychological, political, ethnic and
socio-economic limitations, and making the elements of our
expressive media congeal into a distinctive style. Freedom is situated
at both ends: that of personal possibility, and that of the openness of
the domain present to every person.

Second Sketch of Freedom

We can thus also define freedom as that which enables us to
forge ahead with our personality, whatever we may start out with,
into an undefined and undefinable domain, creatively and each time,
originally; or that which enables us, given the language in which
we dwell, to make it congeal around the style that issues from our
personality; or that which enables us, given our experiences, to seek
the root of transcendence. Plato would object to listing sketches of
freedom and would demand, if his method were taken at face value
(and I doubt that it should be, for it is by no means clear that in the

Theaetetus, say, he really sought one definition of "knowledge"), a single unequivocal definition. Perhaps, and above all with freedom, not only is this impossible, but the attempt itself is unwise. It would be fitting for freedom to be defined in a manner that embodies its proper sense.[5]

The Temporal and the Eternal. The foregoing examples are all spatial in some sense. They refer to the transcendence of the finitude or insignificant infinitude of quantity at given moments in time. Time itself is also binding when viewed as physical time. At the limit, if we really lived according to physical time, our lives would proceed in clockwork fashion. Time would pass relentlessly and without meaning, much as it does for Fordism's assembly line worker. In every way that this is actually not the case, we see signs of eternity. The first signs are fairly simple. When we use the word "now," the reference is highly variable. An officer supervising the launching of a missile in combat will say "now" and literally mean the shortest possible moment perceptible to a human being. This "now" comes closest to a moment in physical time. The moments of a clockwork existence would ideally be describable by a sequence of such "nows." If, however, I am now thinking about the problem of time, the "now" only superficially refers to the moment in physical time when I write this. In reality, it refers to the unified segment of physical time during which this problem continuously engages me. With the "now" that describes this segment, many other "now"s might coincide - the "now"s which fix the moment when a plane flies overhead, the telephone rings or a passing car backfires, for example. The present can "stretch" and overlap with other more ephemeral presents. This elasticity has been noticed for a very long time and was written about by St. Augustine.[6] Next comes the matter of the direction of the stretch. The present not only broadens within physical time, but may leave it altogether. Any moment that we experience as timeless, in love, prayer or aesthetic contemplation, is called timeless because it is experienced as a moment outside of time. The "now" that fixes such moments in physical time not only refers in reality to a present that stretches across a segment of that time, but to a breach with it.

The most accessible breach with physical time is the involuntary return of past moments many years after their "real" location in physical time. A fragrance or a musical fragment can draw forth a whole slice of one's life without the slightest loss of detail or freshness long after it was "actually" lived. Such memories differ substantially from the voluntary memory of having done something. Involuntary memory is not the mere revelation that certain facts were registered. It is the retention of an event or a period of one's life as *it was lived*. One remembers not only that one stayed in a certain house one summer and that certain events took place there—one remembers what it felt like to be in that house that summer amid those events. For a moment, this is not even experienced as a memory, but as a genuine return of the past. When such experiences are finally recognized as remembrances, they have already faded back into the past (understood in its straightforward physical sense). For a while, in other words, the past, even the distant past, seems more like the present than the past. That one can, however briefly, relive the past is remarkable. It means that we have the capacity to retain the inner dimensions of our past in addition to its external features.

That something is past is final only in the physical sense. Psychologically and spiritually, the past can potentially merge with the present and inform it in ways far richer than is possible when the life of a person is narrated and assessed according to a strictly linear temporal sequence. This atemporal feature of a person's past gives it duration into the present and beyond. The moments that endure in this way are in some sense still present. Thus, points that are separate in physical time merge on the psychological-spiritual plane. Time is no longer a straight arrow, but a rolled-up yarn, where several segments intersect at a single point.

To the extent that Proust's massive documentation of involuntary memory and the living past is representative in *Remembrance of Things Past,* and to the extent that I can confirm it myself, it appears that what endures characteristically lies within the boundary zone. The thread that holds together a period of one's life which remains alive is, at the very least, an aesthetic transcendence of the finite. It is a moment first, and authentically experienced as timeless. We may then wonder whether what endures has reason to endure from the beginning, in particular since it makes a breach with physical time because it had transcended time in the first place. Thus, what was first experienced as timeless will show its true nature by living on and momentarily rising to the forefront of one's consciousness to fill it up unpredictably, in complete defiance of the standard measure of time.

Thus there are intimations of being in touch with the timeless, so that havoc is played with the physical time-frame of one's life.

The timeless causes the points and segments of physical time to criss-cross. It changes our entire perception of finitude because of the direct experience that something dead has been resurrected. If this is not yet eternity religiously understood, it is nevertheless a clear sign that we dwell on the boundaries of such eternity.

We not only read a summary of the account just adumbrated in the following passage from Berdyaev's *Slavery and Freedom*, but an extension of the living past to include the memory of those who are physically dead as well as an extension of the effect of the living past on our present to include the possibility of transfiguration (By his expression "existential time," we may understand "time in the boundary zone between the temporal and the eternal," and then interpret "the existential order" accordingly, given that it obtains among those who live in existential time):

> Memory of the past is spiritual; it conquers historical time. This however is not a conserving, but a creatively transfiguring memory. It wishes to carry forward into eternal life not that which is dead in the past but what is alive, not that which is static in the past but what is dynamic. This spiritual memory reminds man, engulfed in his historical time, that in the past there have been great creative movements of the spirit and that they ought to inherit eternity. It reminds him also of the fact that in the past there lived concrete beings, living personalities, with whom we ought in existential time to have a link no less than with those who are living now. Society is always a society not only of the living but also of the dead; and this memory of the dead which the usual theory of progress lacks, is by no means a conservatively static memory, it is a creative dynamic memory. The last word belongs not to death but to resurrection. But resurrection is not a restoration of the past in its evil and untruth, but transfiguration. We are linked with the creatively transfigured past, and it cannot be a burden of enslaving determination for us. We desire to enter with the past and with the departed people of the past into a new transfigured order, into the existential order.[7]

We can follow the meeting place of time with the timeless, from the living past in a person's life, through that of communion with the living dead, to its endpoint, taking our cue from Berdyaev's vision of transfiguration: the intersection of the eternal with the historical. This is the moment when eternity appears in history, so that history itself is turned towards the eternal and transfigured by it. We can point this out, with Kierkegaard, at two different levels: The first is the appearance of God in history, the second the moment when an individual person finds himself in the eternal dimension.[8] For Kierkegaard, this was merely the repetition for the individual of the same event that has occurred universally, which makes perfect sense when one considers the paradox of the meeting between eternity and history: Eternity is indifferent to the succession that defines historical time. The appearance of eternity at a historical moment becomes the appearance of eternity at every moment in history. This appearance, fixed in historical time from one point of view and spread all across it from another, becomes available to every person within his own lifespan.

Third Sketch of Freedom and the Transfiguration Wrought by the Encounter with Eternity

The implication of eternity for our freedom is this: We are not prisoners of the relentless and final passage of the moments that superficially mark our existence. What we do and what we are open to, if it faces the eternal, will so mark our lives as to remain with us and accumulate with other like happenings. We are then free of the nightmare of accomplishments needlessly pursued and a life wasted when we realize that much of what we have lived, if we have lived it in a certain way, never goes to waste. The grinding mechanism of temporal structures that threaten to rule our lives will recede to become the surface that they really are. This does not mean that all efforts to change temporal structures are meaningless; we are simply shown a domain where we are free as we fly over them and less dependent on and wiser about whatever freedoms we may enjoy within them. It is this flight, as well as the actions and attitudes that follow in its wake, that symbolize the transfiguration of which Berdyaev speaks. We can recognize many effects of this transfiguration, all of which take the form of an enhanced capacity to encompass significant infinities. A breach with physical/historical time that plunges one's existence into the eternal eventually translates itself into a deeper poetical view or moral ground for action. For the transcendence of physical time frees one to absorb the vast multiple spaces otherwise pressed into the planar cross-sections that rush through with each moment. The poetical view originates with the freedom to absorb not only how a mute plane speaks through its openness to its neighborhoods, but how a whole neighborhood of spaces is irradiated by the hidden space brought forth by the breach with time. The painter not only moves us with the dialogue between the various subjects of his work, but with the vision that informs this whole dialogue, drawn from another space. The moral ground opens up in an analogous way, with the proviso that one not lapse into the aestheticization of morality; only figuratively can one speak of the space of a specific moral rule or virtue, and another that holds all morality together and animates it. The spatial metaphor is most useful when it comes to providing the phenomenology for the transformation of morality from an external model into an inner reality that animates all particular moral acts and sentiments in a person's life. This surely happens against the backdrop of some breach with time and some subsequent experience of quasi-spatial openings and expansions.

As one wanders further towards the significant infinite after one's existence is touched with the eternal, the separation no longer makes sense. The eternal and the significant infinite come together. Space and time fade into one another in the timeless. An existence blessed with the timeless can thus enter wider spaces as it reaches into significant infinities. This is what at once informs the best art as well as the authentic assimilation of morality into one's personality (That is morality not as obedience to rules, but as the outflow of living interaction with its spiritual origin or, in a nutshell, action in the spirit of the law). The significant infinite and the eternal, now recognized within the same domain, will henceforth be combined into a single expression, the "infinite/eternal".

Fourth Sketch of Freedom and Second Definition of the Boundary Zone: the InFinite/Eternal

The domain of the infinite/eternal is the metaphysical ground for our freedom. It is also the playground in which we freely grow up. Freedom is a metaphysical condition, even though it is often debased to the level of physical choice (as we shall see in the second part of this paper). It is this metaphysical condition that causes languages to form seamless wholes, lands to assume an aura, persons to view all the circumstances into which they were born and raised as but a point of departure and to go on into the domain of the infinite/eternal more vigorously. The metaphysical condition has the dual aspect of the tendency towards a metaphysical domain and the domain itself. Where freedom comes from is where it flows best.

We cannot prove the existence of God. If we could, what would it mean to have faith in Him? The world, however, is full of things and happenings that point beyond the physical. We can therefore portray the zone where the (physical) world flows into another, with the shape of the boundary visible and ever present to the senses and the soul, and in works of art and human deeds. Few have portrayed this boundary zone with greater skill and conviction than Proust. All the more noteworthy is the occurrence of this following passage in a work that continuously displays the aesthete's worst excesses, so infuriating are the detail and self-absorption at times. These exercises in aesthetic self-indulgence lend credence to the author's titanic struggle to overcome them and steep the morass of his labyrinthine art in the domain of the infinite/eternal. This passage comes across with great force because it appears just when the reader is near despair over the possibility of deliverance. It reads:

> Certainly, experiments in spiritualism offer us no more proof than the dogmas of religion that the soul survives death. All that we can say is that everything is arranged in this life as though we entered it carrying a burden of obligations contracted in a former life; there is no reason inherent in the conditions of life on this earth that can make us consider ourselves obliged to do good, to be kind and thoughtful, even to be polite, nor for an atheist artist to consider himself obliged to begin over again a score of times a piece of work the admiration aroused by which will matter little to his worm-eaten body, like the patch of yellow wall [in "View of Delft"] painted with so much skill and refinement by an artist destined to be forever unknown and barely identified under the name Vermeer. All these obligations, which have no sanction in our present life, seem to belong to a different world, a world based on kindness, scrupulousness, self-sacrifice, a world entirely different from this one and which we

leave in order to be born on this earth, before perhaps returning there to live once again beneath the sway of those unknown laws begins to unfold in the life of a person, the finite/temporal does not which we obeyed because we bore their precepts in our hearts, not knowing whose hand had traced them there - those laws to which every profound work of the intellect brings us nearer and which are invisible only—if then!—to fools.[9]

The exact manner of Proust's portrayal of the boundary zone is not beyond dispute. But the perception of works and deeds way in excess of what a physical view of the world and a functional view of life suggest, which lies at the heart of the passage just quoted, signifies a genuine encounter with the infinite/eternal by way of its most accessible presences. Such an impassioned turn to excess—and the very idea of the metaphysical ever present in our neighborhood is an excess—is also a sign of transfiguration. The perception of the metaphysical as an excess is related to that of the metaphysical as a gift. And the world takes on a radically different aspect in the souls of those who behold its metaphysical dimension as a gift in song. The freedom to experience the world as shot through with the infinite/eternal with which it resounds is the return to the metaphysical essence of freedom. The free person is one free to ground his relationships with others in that different world eulogized by Proust, "based on kindness, scrupulousness, self-sacrifice," and, we may add, untold love and generosity. A world dead to its other becomes a domain for slaves.

Our transfiguration, that through which we become free, passes through the boundary zone where the physical becomes porous to the metaphysical. The extent to which the metaphysical permeates the physical varies a great deal, between the faintest glint on one hand and effulgence on the other. Physicists have recently described the universe as seamless. That would be fitting if it withstands the test of time. For the world is metaphysically seamless; any physical limits fade into the metaphysical.

Thus, the finite/temporal domain is not separated from the infinite/eternal by a sharp frontier. Between the two lies a boundary zone. We have just noted the general interaction of the physical with the metaphysical. The sphere of this interaction defines the boundary zone. The particular case reflects the wide variance of the degree and quality of this interaction. Thus, as the infinite/eternal shrink instantly into a well-bounded domain now viewed from the outside, but gradually gives way as one becomes increasingly immersed in the infinite/eternal. The edges of the finite/temporal, always cracked because of the relentless run of everyday experiences that point beyond them, eventually develop the crevices through which one's existence intermingles more easily with the infinite/eternal.

The omnipresence of cracks at the edges of the finite/temporal, always ready to become crevices, has important implications for our intellectual heritage as well. We begin with the ease in pointing out those cracks and crevices. All we need to undercut any denial that we can expressively scale the noumenal is the perception that our world, after all, could have been one where snow had the texture and color of crude oil and human life consisted in the mechanical pursuit of a handful of quantifiable desires. All we need is the recognition of the simplest natural phenomenon that poeticizes our world, the simplest act of compassion. Already so, the boundary zone is well marked and the infinite/eternal has come to the fore.

That it takes so little to invalidate the positions taken by Kant in the *Critique of Pure Reason* and Wittgenstein in the *Tractatus,* that it was possible to claim the existence of an impregnable wall between the phenomenal and the noumenal, speaks volumes of the conditions under which Kant and Wittgenstein in his youth philosophized. These conditions—so powerful that intellectuals since Kant have generally disowned the noumenal and willingly ignored its presence in his work as well as Wittgenstein's—will be featured in the second part of this paper. For now, we may note either the will to deny the noumenal entry into philosophical discussion or, far worse, the will to deny the noumenal *altogether.* And there has been a will to deny it, an incredibly strong one, for all the ease and frequency with which we are reminded of the noumenal. It is the strangest thing that European civilization should first suppress freedom for the sake of the noumenal and then, for the sake of freedom, suppress the noumenal. Freedom is now wanting of its true origins. For what is left of a metaphysical condition when metaphysics is stripped of a domain and reduced to empty conceptual hairsplitting within the academies and existential apathy outside?

Freedom and the Mystery or Identity of the Significant Infinite

What does the calling to the infinite/eternal signify when we begin to dwell within it on the side of the zone nearer the finite/temporal? It suggests a further point at every level—in art, in life on a land sacred to its people, and in moral and religious experience. And these intimations of a further point to reach, wherever one may be, describe a state of utter freedom: One grows towards the furthest reaches of humanity and always feels the surrounding immensity, at times as if there were too much! This freedom would be absurd were it not for the possibility to divine direction in this growth—a direction which is not automatic, not formulaic, not necessary, built only on the ineffable conviction that one moves through the immensity as if guided by an invisible hand. (Even total insensitivity to this free guidance, however, is not an abnegation of freedom. It is only an acceptance that the ends posited within it are arbitrary and that the overall state one is in is itself absurd.)

Our first intimation of the invisible hand that guides us through the immensity where our freedom fully comes into its own will again traverse the work of Proust. I have briefly mentioned composers, with regard to their style and personality, and music, with regard to the openness of its signification, in the foregoing discussions. The time has come to consider the direction of the unified work of a great composer, indeed the source of its unity. Much as the simplest melody already signifies the metaphysical, the vast reach of an oeuvre such as Beethoven's last string quartets (or Bach's *St Matthew Passion)* into the metaphysical underlines the depth and extent to which Beethoven was really at home in the domain of freedom. But Beethoven's expression of this was not the same as, say, Schubert's or Faure's. Nor was it possible for him to explicitly lay out the features of that domain (If anything, his late quartets are shocking in their defiance of the infinite/eternal's alleged impermeability to finite/temporal expression). Every time the infinite/eternal is present in a work, in a life, in a life's work, it is present anew and uniquely. This is the consequence of its elusiveness to final expression. The Word must ever remain open. The one domain seems as many.

Thus Proust speaks of the composer Vinteuil, one of the fictional characters in his novel probably modelled on a cross between Franck and Faure, as a

> . . . native of an unknown country, which he himself has forgotten, and which is different from that whence another great artist, setting sail for the earth, will eventually emerge . . . .

Composers do not actually remember this lost fatherland, but each of them remains all his life unconsciously attuned to it; he is delirious with joy when he sings in harmony with his native land, betrays it at times in his thirst for fame, but then, in seeking fame, turns his back on it, and it is only by scorning fame that he finds it when he breaks out into that distinctive strain the sameness of which— for whatever its subject it remains identical with itself—proves the permanence of the elements that compose the soul. . . . A pair of wings, a different respiratory system, which enabled us to travel through space, would in no way help us, for if we visited Mars or Venus while keeping the same senses, they would clothe everything that we saw in the same aspect as the things of Earth. The only true voyage of discovery, the only really rejuvenating experience, would be not to visit strange lands but to possess other eyes, to see the universe through the eyes of another, of a hundred eyes, to see the hundred universes that each of them sees, that each of them is; and this we can do with an Elstir [the painter], with a Vinteuil; with men like these we do really fly from star to star.[10]

There is a tension in these marvelous passages between the transcendent world that draws the work of a great artist ever closer to itself, and the world of the individual artist which appears to fall back upon itself. This tension is characteristic of Proust's struggle to leap out of his narcissism. For our purposes, we should concentrate on the sense of an *oeuvre*, especially when expressed in a symbolic medium as potent as music, wandering deeper into the infinite/ eternal. We should try to empathize with the moment when a composer feels in harmony with that domain, as if his music issued directly from it and he grasped that this were so. We therefore have before us another instance of the moment when the eternal and the historical intersect, and we may read Proust's phenomenology as a detailed and empirically reproducible introduction to the ultimate encounter between eternity and history at the core of the great monotheistic faiths.

The invisible hand is present, then, in the composer's sense of return to his "native country" deep within the domain of freedom.

It is present as well in the sense of being in touch or in tune with the regions within that domain to which one has access. And what is true for the great composer like Beethoven, what is true for all great art, is potentially true in the lives of persons, for whom great art has its ultimate worth because it holds up a "measure" for one's own transcendence. But this is not the only way for there to be a "measure" (and here we must leave Proust's overdependence on art behind). We can transpose Proust's celebration of great art directly to the realm of religious experience, equally for the anonymous person who reaches into the infinite/eternal and for those whose mystically gained freedoms have become the summit of our religious lore.

We have been told many things about God. Whatever God may be, the eternal/infinite is infused with His presence. The infinite/eternal stretches between our world and God, we lie at the edge of the domain where we can therefore be infinitely free and, if we so choose or are so graced, be open to His presence and allow it to become the invisible hand that guides us through its simultaneous presence and withdrawal. God's presence gives meaning to the infinite/eternal, while His withdrawal gives us the freedom to extend our existence within that domain as far as it can go *and in a manner unique to it.* The traditional word for this ineffable, unfathomable presence-at-once-withdrawn is "mystery." This is how Berdyaev leads into his phrase "God is Mystery" in the context of his attacks on those who have held the ultimate giver of freedom within the prisons of their conceptual limitations and thus unwittingly surrendered their freedom on the threshold of its fulfillment:

> God is not to be thought of on the analogy of what takes place in society or on the analogy of what takes place in nature. We cannot think in determinist terms in relation to God. He determines nothing. Nor can we think of causality. He is not the cause of anything.

> Here we stand face to face with Mystery and to this Mystery are applicable no analogies with necessity, with causality, with domination; with causality in natural phenomena, with domination in social phenomena. Analogy is only possible with the very life of the spirit. God is certainly not the cause of the work. He certainly does not act upon the

human spirit as necessity. He certainly does not pass judgment as judgment is in the social life of man. He certainly is not a master, nor authority in the life of the world and of man. None of these socio-morphic and cosmo-morphic categories are applicable to God. God is Mystery, a Mystery towards which man transcends and with which he enters into communion.[11]

I for one am reluctant to insist that God must be this or that. But there is the intuition of divine mystery as freedom for those drawn towards it (in addition to the natural convergence of divinity and mystery). For how can we be free before a transparent divinity? We must, if we feel God's presence, realize how essential for our freedom and very being the mystery of this presence is. Our freedom and being finally consist in being drawn to a definitely present but mysterious divinity. This is not a logical argument. It is an existential affirmation, not of how something must be, but of how it is; and that, given how it is, the mystery is as clear as its source elusive.

Rahner knew this and wrote about it. I quote, without further comment, this sublime passage, which begins with God as mystery and ends with a heartfelt affirmation that the mystery is at once present to us and caring; and as we read it in light of the foregoing, we should be able to recognize the infinite freedom with which we are graced in the caring presence of this mystery, a freedom that need only be guided by awareness of its origins as it fully realizes itself:

The God of the philosophers is no "Father," but the incomprehensible ground of all reality which escapes every comprehensive notion because he is a radical mystery. This is always only the beyond, the inaccessibly distant horizon bounding the small sphere we are able to measure. He certainly exists for us also in this way, as the unanswered question that makes possible any answerable one, as the distance which makes room for our never-ending journey in thought and deed. But does this ineffable being which we call God exist only in this way? That is the question. True, the distance which philosophical theology establishes between God and ourselves is still necessary to prevent us from

confusing God with our own idols, and thus it is
perhaps more than philosophy, it is a hidden grace.
But the question whether God is only unapproach-
able ineffability must be answered in the negative.
He is more, and we realize this in the ultimate
experience of our existence, when we accept it
without rejecting or denying it under the pretext of
its being too good to be true. For there is the experience that the abyss protects, that pure silence is
tender, that the distance is home and that the ultimate
question brings its own answer, that the very mystery
communicates itself as pure blessedness. And then
we call the mystery whose customary cipher is
"God,"—Father. For what else are we to call it?[12]

Throughout this paper, I have emphasized the entry into the
infinite/eternal through the myriad ways that things and deeds point
beyond the physical, as I think I should in our ecumenical and secular
environment. I would like the agnostic or atheist reader in particular
to at least reflect on the metaphysical excess so easy to start out
with. With faith in God as the caring, ever-present mystery at the
heart of the metaphysical, however, the perception changes, for we
now no longer look at a tendency towards a vaguely metaphysical
origin, but a definite origin that animates the tendency and sustains
metaphysical space. And so I close this section with Chesterton's
inspired literary portrayal of the saint's moment of conversion as a
paradigm for this changed perception, the saint here being Francis
of Assisi:

The transition from the good man to the saint is a
sort of revolution; by which one for whom all things
illustrate and illuminate God becomes one for whom
God illustrates and illuminates all things. It is rather
like the reversal whereby a lover might say at first
sight that a lady looked like a flower, and say
afterwards that all flowers reminded him of his lady.
A saint and a poet standing by the same flower might
seem to say the same thing; but indeed though they
would both be telling the truth, they would be telling
different truths. For one the joy of life is a cause of
faith, for the other a result of faith. But one effect
of the difference is that the sense of a divine

dependence, which for the artist is like the brilliant levin-blaze, for the saint is like the broad daylight. Being in some mystical sense on the other side of things, he sees things go forth from the divine as children going forth from a familiar and accepted home, instead of meeting them as they come out, as most of us do, upon the roads of this world.[13]

THE DOMAIN OF UNFREEDOM

Here again, I shall begin with observations culled from our lifestyle, in settings familiar to us all. The domain of unfreedom will gradually become manifest. Once it does, I shall extract and highlight the two greatest currents that run through this domain.

What the Buildings Say

Many lessons can be learned by looking at the buildings each civilization leaves behind as its symbol. Among the many ways that the buildings most characteristic and symbolic of the twentieth century differ from their predecessors is their lack of reference to what lies beyond their confines. Houses, whole towns, used to be one side of a friendly dialogue with the surrounding landscape. The main square earned its centrality because around it lay the chief centers of worship and government for that locale. The buildings that stood out did so because of their eminence in the political structure or in the spiritual lives of the people who frequented them. But with the simultaneous rise of factories and slums, this began to change. There is no need to dwell on how much the factory denies, above all in the early industrial era. Externally, its design typically spurns the landscape and the materials spewed out add insult to injury. Internally, the activities that it houses are an affront to the dignity and humanity of those employed by it. Overall, the factory points towards nothing outside of its severely material existence and purpose. Slums speak for themselves in the various privations that they symbolize. For the first time in history, and for many in what now is the "First World," the workplace and the hearth denied the freedom to be *human* to a great degree.

That duet of factories and slums has now largely been transferred to places like Sao Paolo, Lagos, Cairo, Bombay and Jakarta. But their less starkly inhumane successors in the West remain noted for their lack of outside reference. Corporate headquarters and shopping malls are far and away the most prominent buildings rising here. Their size, height or style scorn and mock the landscape. Windowless or without windows that can be opened, they underline the concentration on exclusively material pursuits demanded of those inside. Let us then take stock of the freedoms enjoyed at shopping malls and in corporate life.

For every consumer good that we want to buy, we have lots of choice. If we are interested in a cassette recorder, for instance, there are so many on the market that it is prudent to consult one of several guides that explain their various strengths and weaknesses and rank them accordingly. Once our selection is made, we can shop around until we find the most competitive price. There is a great deal of freedom once it comes to choosing things such as cassette recorders. Even assuming infatuation with the consumer paradise, however, what does this freedom amount to? It is the freedom to move along the *path* of *least resistance*. Given the urge to buy, and a combination of whim and specific needs, the rest is a matter of calculation. Freedom becomes simply the availability of the desired product at the best possible price. Of course, there remain many products whose quality and appropriateness cannot be quantified—loudspeakers and pianos, for instance. But one of the ironic twists of the free market and the technological innovations it has spurred is that the sheer variety and complexity of many goods makes consumers dependent on expert opinions and the published results of various tests in making their choices.

Far more influential than specific consumer goods are the media, the leading members of which are large corporations. We are guaranteed the free flow of information. But how freely is the information flowing when we need it most? All the major television networks (including CNN, PBS and FOX) have been acting more in concert than many state controlled media have during the current war in the Gulf. The reason for this is quite simple: Anyone who dares upset the government, especially the military, will lose access to major stories as they break. The audience will naturally shift to other sources for news, which means that advertisers also stand to lose many of their captives. When a corporation becomes as large as a major television network, it cannot afford to upset its commercial backers. The structure is naturally conservative, more so than state-controlled media that at least can undergo mercurial transformations at the behest and fancy of the authorities. Thus, while those employed by the media corporations are legally guaranteed almost limitless freedom, the laws of the marketplace impose restrictions on them that comprehensively belie what we are led to believe. While this latest war has brought the problem into sharper focus, ever since media organizations became heavily dependent on advertisers (commercial interests in general), and politically important stories could only be broken through personal contact with government employees who usually remain anonymous, the media have been at the mercy of government favor by way of the implicit potential for commercial blackmail (no scoops, less readers, therefore less advertisers, a cycle that in theory can continue until the organization has gone out of business).[14]

The First Current: the Egocentric Turn

The commercial interests that seriously impede the free flow of information—not to mention artistic freedom, ever more driven to submit to producers who must "play it safe" and hold much of what hits the big and small screens to a shrinking least common denominator—and rule the shopping mall are emblematic of a profound current that runs through our civilization. The reason why individualism has, in these respects, not begotten free individuals is that one of two contrary latent tendencies within individualism has prevailed. Individualism, to borrow Berdyaev's distinction, can either be egocentric or personalistic.[15] If the egocentric tendency predominates, then the individual becomes walled up within himself. Given egocentrism, the individual is obliged to view the world in terms of the opportunities for and the obstacles that it presents to the satisfaction of his desires. He sets himself apart from the world. He becomes atomized, an isolated part within the whole in mechanical interaction with other atomized individuals, who see the world as a theater for the execution of plans that revolve around the satisfaction of their desires.[16] We shall presently see how intimately egocentrism is connected to nomological rationalism, the other great current to be extracted. We shall also face the possible root of this egocentric turn.

The rise of commercialism to the degree that we have known it could not occur without mass egocentrism. For there to be shopping malls that mimic the outward appearance of a ziggurat, without a hint of the significance of those awesome Sumerian mounted temples, and pretend to inspire the same awe in those who flock towards them, is a lasting and resounding testimony to what individuals have become. A civilization that, far from recognizing the materialism and arrogance embodied in its architectural centerpieces, takes pride in them, affirms its egocentrism as a natural and fully acceptable tendency. With such affirmation, it becomes possible to dramatically expand the research, development, production and marketing of far too many more products than have long been necessary both with regard to variety and sophistication, and devote far more human energy to this end than people within any other civilizational locus would have deemed desirable or even sane (I politely avoid the subject of what, for the sake of this continuous dinner, has been done to peoples elsewhere now condemned to the crumbs thrown off the gigantic table hosting it). Egocentrism becomes the moral underpinning for the extent to which commerce, technology and bureaucracy dominate our lives (even the production of armaments is for the first time in history driven more by economic than by strategic imperatives).[17]

The freedom of egocentrism is to unabashedly pursue the satisfaction of desires to the greatest degree allowed by the need to allow a reasonable number of other like-souled individuals the same pursuit. It is a freedom that not only presupposes, but *requires* isolation from others and the world. It must deny any transcendence of the techno-bureaucratic consumer culture that is its contemporary progeny. In other words, it is hostile to significant infinity *at its very foundation*. And in its hostility to the wellspring of religious experience and sentiment, it has found an ally in the form of nomological reason.

The Second Current: NomoLogical Reason (or the Rule of Law) and Its Affinity with Egocentrism

There are two ways that the currents of egocentrism and the rule of law have become intertwined. An egocentric attitude towards an otherwise meaningless world it seeks to exploit for the satisfaction of individual desires can make use of discoverable mechanisms that facilitate the exploitation. After all, why not satisfy desires more efficiently, with the use of ever more powerful tools? Natural laws, more than anything else, have nurtured the technologies that overwhelm the exploitable face of the world.[18] That it is only the face does not matter, for what is behind the face means nothing from the standpoint of egocentrism and *nomological rationalism*.

In addition to the psychological affinity between the two currents, there is a historical affinity that goes back to the rebellion against the authority of the Church at the end of the medieval era. The Church had been too extreme in its disregard for the body and unwittingly spawned a culture that would become obsessed with the satisfaction of bodily desire. People dogmatically driven to appalling material conditions could only be driven to create paradises of material comfort. But whatever justification the rebellion needed, given that it could hardly express itself in egocentric terms, perhaps even to itself given the prevailing atmosphere, came in the form of natural reason. The very same natural reason cultivated by Church scholars was turned against its mother when it was found to support arguments contrary to what the Church had taught about nature. The coming together of a powerful critical tool (natural reason) with many levels of disaffection (mostly centered on material privations) was more than the Church could eventually resist, at least at the political level. I present this as a tentative account for the historical alliance of egocentrism and nomological rationalism.

The use of reason that first undermined Church teachings about nature centered on the discovery of laws that can be verified experimentally. From the very beginning, however, there was ample evidence for skepticism about both the horizontal and the vertical reach of a rationality restricted to the discovery of natural laws and other causal relations. On the one hand, there is much in nature that does not lend itself to neat causal structures. While it was not until the latter part of the nineteenth century that the physical and biological sciences, still within the restrictions imposed by causal analysis, confirmed that even a nature strictly objectified does not always conform to law-like behavior, nor are all its relations causal, the phenomena that exposed this have always been there. People were simply *unwilling* to look at them in the right way. On the other hand, what Berdyaev said about the law of universal gravitation, namely that "it is partial and relates to the partial,"[19] applies to the totality of natural laws so far uncovered. They indeed provide the technology to launch missions to Mars, but they tell us a great deal, with a great amount of precision, about very little.

In other words, not only is the nomological rationalist picture incomplete within its own framework, and destined to remain so, but it is *inherently shallow*. It can describe every molecule in a human face, but not how that face lights up with joy, much *less* what joy is. Given that people since Montaigne have pointed these shortcomings out, and given all the resistance with which the phenomena have met the nomological rationalists, it is quite remarkable that reason continued to be almost exclusively mobilized in the search for natural laws. That causal necessity and objectification could have dominated intellectual life for so long bespeaks the desperate need for them. In Nietzschean language, there *was a will to causal necessity,* a will that nature conform to law, that it be ruled by law. No one said this more clearly and explicitly than Kant: "*. . . the understanding does not derive its laws (a priori) from, but prescribes them to, nature"* [Kant's italics].[20] And: ". . . the understanding is the origin of the universal order of nature, in that it comprehends all appearances under its own laws and thereby brings about, in an *a priori* way, experience (as to its form), by means of which whatever is to be cognized only by experience is necessarily subjected to its laws."[21] The amazing thing, in the context of our discussion, is that people who rebelled against Church authority and hierarchy were quite prepared to live in a universe entirely governed by law.

The Rule of Law and Egalitarianism

For all their negation of freedom, the appeal of these laws consisted in their discovery by human beings and their indifferent accessibility to whoever had the mental capacity and the technological tools to make or ascertain these discoveries. The laws of nature may be stifling to our deeper sense of freedom, but they lend themselves to a desperately sought egalitarianism. They do not discriminate against their seekers on any unfair grounds.

Transposed into the social, economic and political spheres, nomological rationalism allowed visionaries to create systems that conformed to their egalitarian outlook. A political order ruled by law does not distinguish between the individuals who pass through its revolving doors. An economy where the jobs are almost completely contingent on impersonal qualifications is theoretically open to whoever has them. And those who wage war only to ensure that such egalitarianism is more consistently applied further reinforce the premises of nomological rationalism. The determinist character of Marxism is therefore no surprise.

The supreme irony of modernity is that in seeking to free individuals from authority and hierarchy and improve the material conditions of life, it has pressured them into submission to a more elaborate structure of laws, many of them invisible to the ordinary person, than has ever held sway among them. An immediate everyday sign of this is the exponential increase in litigation and paperwork in this society. More serious are the psychological restraints on the free growth of personality. The much praised uniformity that cuts across cultural and ethnic diversity in the United States only confirms the power of nomological reason to work its way through society. The extent of conformism in the world's freest society (from a constitutional standpoint) should not baffle us.

Egocentrism and nomological reason have cut us off from significant infinities in comprehensive fashion. At the theoretical limit, modernity leads to self-enclosed, thus self-indulgent, human beings maximizing their desires in a universe entirely governed by causal relations. Why this limit is never in fact reached we shall presently examine. That it is even conceivable is a legacy of the failure of modernity. It is difficult to imagine a greater freedom than that to grow into the fullness of our humanity as persons, a growth that has been made redundant by the very underpinnings of modernity, a redundance that has since worked its way into our institutions at many levels. Modernity, to the extent that the currents of egocentrism and nomological rationalism run through it, which is considerable, inherently subverts our freedom to dwell within the eternal/infinite. Whatever freedoms it has bequeathed unto humanity are well within the temporal and the finite, and appear spurious given the labyrinth of laws through which they now must pass. We exercise the flimsiest of freedoms when we work, vote, shop, or seek entertainment. And even then, all sorts of subtle coercive forces are at work to restrict either our choices or their meaningfulness.[22]

POSTSCRIPTS

Why the Brave New World Will Never Be

Thinkers such as Kierkegaard and Aldous Huxley visualized and seriously entertained the possibility of a world at least externally governed by an all-encompassing surface culture, where everything is either trivialized or fitted into a total hierarchy based on natural laws. These visualizations resulted from extrapolations made under the influence of a great leap forward in the apparent direction of that bleak end state. We are not to fault them, especially Kierkegaard, who lived in the golden age of mechanism, for failing to foresee the barriers that nomological reason itself would run into. In fact Kierkegaard would take great satisfaction in that he inspired, well after his death, a physicist and fellow Dane who would go on to play a pivotal role in opening up the physical sciences to a qualitative understanding of the world even at the *physical level* and thereby rise to eminence. Niels Bohr, together with Einstein, Heisenberg and many others, have bequeathed a view of the physical world that reawakens us to its ambiguity and/or seamlessness and therefore its openness to the metaphysical. The cosmological revival since then shows that it does not take much for human beings, even within the disciplines that had upheld and refined the intellectual tools of suffocation, to break loose and ask questions of the universe as free beings.

Analogous to what in retrospect was the inevitable defeat of mechanism, given the extremely limited reach of its framework, is rampant anomie within the techno-bureaucratic consumer culture. Still so far from complete domination of the world, people have already expressed enough disaffection with it, through open rebellion, apathy or self-destructive behaviour, that it would take a degree of insensitivity and blindness on a mass scale hopefully never to be reached in order to deny the blatant inadequacy of that culture for human beings.

In other words, there have been concrete developments, which historians of science and sociologists among many others can easily survey and document, that tell a story of resistance, by the phenomena and by the people who study and live among them. This, however, is to learn the lesson the hard way. The tortuous path back to freedom can be shortened if we start out with what I have emphasized time and again in this paper: So surrounded are we with things and deeds that point beyond the physical that the call to wonder and act accordingly never really deserts us. This is where freedom begins. And this is where any (metaphysically) closed scientific or socio-cultural enterprise will ultimately run aground.

Freedom as Choice and Freedom as Movement

There are two senses in which we feel our freedom or its lack, one with regard to choice and the other with regard to movement. Movement is more important than choice, for even with very little to choose from, we could nevertheless have lots of room for our (inner) movement. On the other hand, if our existence is (internally) narrowly based, then an infinity of choices will not drive away the sense of constriction. It seems to me that choice is there for the sake of freedom; I mean, even if we are in the end to choose one path to follow, it is crucial for this path to be experienced as *chosen* (It would be odd from the standpoint of freedom to experience the path towards it as though we were on an express train; it must always be possible for the individual to leave the path or proceed at his own pace). In this sense, we follow that path freely. But that is where our freedom begins. Within certain paths, our room for movement expands in breadth and depth, and then we are really free.

For the most part, I use "movement," "room," "expansion," and "constriction," all of which originally refer to physical space, metaphorically, in what we may call psychological or spiritual space. For with a healthy psychological outlook and an active spirituality, the freedom one feels, for instance to detach oneself from the pressures of the domain of unfreedom, does have a spatial character. As human beings, while we lament situations where state authorities physically restrict freedom of movement, what really matters is our psychological and spiritual freedom to move. For even when we enjoy the freedom with which squirrels hop gracefully among treetops using twigs as springboards, they touch our longing to be free in a metaphysical way.

The irony of greater psychological or spiritual freedom under the thumb of states that restrict physical movement must hence not be a cause for consternation. For such restriction unintentionally invites people naturally inclined to their metaphysical condition to channel it through its ultimate paths; whereas a great lack of physical restriction entices others to disperse their freedom among the endless rows of consumer goods and means of escapist entertainment.

Freedom, Choice and Democracy

From what has just been said in section C.2, it seems that the more freedom is exercised within the domain of the physical, the more dependent it is on choice (and the more it therefore needs choice); whereas the more it is exercised within the domain of the metaphysical, the less dependent it is on choice (and the less choice it therefore needs). Given the full metaphysical exercise of freedom, we can go on to note that choice has little to do with it once one has chosen to be open to the infinite/eternal (or at least be open to being graced with it). The essential residue of choice is the freedom to leave whatever path one has chosen to follow and to always experience it as chosen. If so, then the limitations of democratic freedoms are easy to grasp. For democratic freedom can only mean the freedom to choose. Democracy *must be indifferent to what is chosen* (with the proviso that there be a consensual acceptance of necessary functional constraints). Thus all the energies expended on providing democratic freedoms are not, at least ostensibly, oriented to the content of the choices then made and therefore cannot have much to do with freedom when freedom is truly itself far removed from the level of mere choice.

What then happens, given the much greater effort required to scale the metaphysical and therefore be fully free, the enormous pressures exerted by the techno-bureaucratic culture that is inherently hostile to anything metaphysical (a hostility built into its genesis as we have seen), and our proneness to indolence, lassitude and egocentrism, is that democracy, precisely by guaranteeing free *choice,* lopsidedly favors any freedom that *distracts* from its authentic exercise. Without external intervention, this situation in theory can only get worse, for the techno-bureaucratic consumer culture feeds on a system that is neutral to what is chosen and is obsessively devoted to preserving the right to choose. Democracy's metaphysical neutrality is a sham when it is realized that neutrality towards the metaphysical collapses into the anti-metaphysical and then allows free play for all forces hostile to our metaphysical growth. In practice, however, the situation can only get that much worse, given the frequency with which we are called to the metaphysical and the ease with which its beginnings can be recognized, a calling hence perhaps sufficiently pervasive for there to be no need for democracy to be explicitly disposed towards the metaphysical. If democracy's neutrality does not favor the metaphysical, then the phenomena certainly do. For theirs is not a story well told by business and hardnosed science. This natural balance between the physical and the metaphysical, and the freedom from arbitrary arrest or from thugs who break into one's home at the crack of dawn to intimidate or do worse, are enough to temper the temptation to extol totalitarian states for their unwitting favor to their subjects' quest for authentic freedom.

NOTES

1. Heidegger of course diagnosed this problem with philosophy in his last published works (See for example the essays in the collection entitled *Poetry, Language and Thought,* Trans. Albert Hofstadter, New York, San Francisco: Harper Colophon Books, 1975). But his turn to art is restricted to unnecessarily esoteric and cumbersome presentations of superbly chosen poems by Rilke, Trakl

and Holderlin. He also ignored the ease with which religion approaches the openness and unconcealment so central to his reflections. We owe him a great deal, however, not only for the diagnosis, but also for his heroic efforts to animate language through poetical exegesis and thereby throw open the metaphysical domain. From such work, Karl Rahner has drawn a theology of language that greatly enhances our expression for the surge into the metaphysical.

2. In recent decades, linguists have realized that even the preliminary introduction to language is far from exclusive to mechanical methods. These must be augmented with the intangible but indispensable experience of growing up within the language. Plato seems to suggest as much in the argument near the end of the *Theaetetus*, where Socrates and his friends fail to establish a foundational theory for the learning of language. Wittgenstein's enthusiasm about this must owe a lot to his acquaintance with the late Platonic dialogue, which he is known to have read around the time he began to emphasize the slippery elements in the learning of a language.

3. Nikolai Berdyaev, *Slavery and Freedom*, Trans. R. M. French (New York: Charles Scribner's Sons, 1944), p. 22.

4. *Ibid.*, p. 24.

5. We can see the complexity and ambiguity of all key words in our language, like "love," "knowledge," "truth," "beauty," "goodness," and "God," in the light of our freedom. Their elusive meaning is a sign of the room our existence is given in several of its dimensions; and the complaint about their vagueness can be read as the will to dominate (and be dominated by, as we shall see) a narrower domain at the expense of its wider and deeper regions, which truly provide the room we need to come into our own as free intelligent beings.

6. St. Augustine, *Confessions,* Trans. R. S. Pine-Coffin (London: Penguin Classics, 1961), Book XI, Ch. 28, p. 277. The whole of Book XI is a monument to how well (and how *early)* St. Augustine grasped the elasticity of time and time's contrast with eternity. The account of the expanding "now" appears in Heidegger's *Basic Problems of Phenomenology,* Trans. Albert Hofstadter (Bloomington, Indiana: Indiana University Press, 1982), pp. 248-264. And a detailed phenomenology of the enduring present, which draws on the work of St. Augustine, Heidegger and Wittgenstein, appears in the second chapter of my doctoral dissertation, *The Artist-Philosopher's Struggle to Save Appearances* (Ann Arbor, MI: University Microfilms International, 1986), pp. 791 47.

7. Berdyaev, *op. cit., p.* 111.

8. Soren Kierkegaard, *Philosophical Fragments,* Trans. David Swenson, revised by Howard V. Hong (Princeton, NJ: Princeton University Press, 1936, 1962), pp. 30, 79.

9. Marcel Proust, *Remembrance of Things Past,* Vol. 3, Trans. Moncrieff, Kilmartin, and Mayor (New York: Vintage Books, 1982), p. 186.

10. *Ibid.,* Vol. 3, pp. 258-260.

11. Berdyaev, *op. cit., pp.* 82-83.

12. Karl Rahner, *Grace in Freedom,* Trans. Hilda Graef, (New York: Herder and Herder, 1969), pp. 196-197.

13. G. K. Chesterton, *St. Francis of Assisi* (Garden City, NY: Image Books, 1957), p. 76.

14. Walter Karp, "All the Congressmen's Men: How Capitol Hill Controls the Press", *Harper's,* July 1989, pp. 55-63.

15. Berdyaev, op. *cit.,* pp. 36, 42-3.

16. The modern epistemological approach thus goes hand in hand with egocentrism: The subject of knowledge approaches and judges the world in isolation from other subjects of knowledge. As Habermas puts it, there is a *knowing* subject who forms *opinions,* which are capable of being *true,* about something in the objective world, in parallel with an *acting* subject who carries out *purposive activities,* which are capable of being *successful,* to bring about something in the world (See Jürgen Habermas, *The Philosophical Discourse of Modernity,* Trans. Frederick G. Lawrence [Cambridge, Mass.: MIT Press, 1990], e.g., pp.63-4, 245). The book on the whole is a thorough and highly articulate recapitulation of the currents flowing through modernity; it also critically examines the most passionate attacks on these currents that have come from France since Bataille. The main problem with the book is lack of clarity over the nature and purpose of the communicative community that evolves a richer rationality than that rightfully rejected by Habermas for its inadequacy, and excessive venom in his dismissal of Heidegger's conception of Being, which Habermas is also right to complain about because of the vagueness of Heidegger's conception sometimes to the point of near emptiness. Berdyaev for his part makes the intriguing observation that the more valid knowledge is (according to subjects who independently judge its truth according to necessity and the rule of law), the weaker the bond between the subjects who share this knowledge; and vice versa (See Berdyaev, *op. cit., pp.* 114-6).

17. Hermann Broch left us with a brilliant and concise account

of this development. He contrasted the modern era, which has made rampant egocentrism possible, with the restraints imposed by the medieval era according to the following difference: The Middle Ages placed limits on war and business, and gave direction to art, because of *faith*, which provided what Broch termed a "plausibility point" for the logic of each activity. But as a result of the abstraction of God, the plausibility point was pushed so far into the abstract realm that activities previously restrained by it first drifted apart, and thus were granted the conditions under which they could be pursued for their own sake: war, business, art for art's sake, and politics without compunction. He described the overall situation at the outset of the modern era as governed by a "ruthlessly single-minded logic without plausibility points." This in turn allowed one activity to dominate if it were markedly stronger than the others. This one activity, Broch thought, would be *business* (See Hermann Broch, *The Sleepwalkers*, Trans. Willa and Edwin Muir [San Francisco: North Point Press, 1985], pp.445-8).

18. The reader should carefully note that this is not in any way to be understood as the denial of the experimental or theoretical validity of most natural laws. What I find suspect is the grossly disproportionate emphasis on laws that pertain to the shallowest perspective on our world, so much so that intellectuals now routinely appeal to (and abuse) Nietzsche's description of the world exclusively in terms of surfaces and have become allergic to the least mention of words such as "profound" or "deep."

19. Berdyaev, *op. cit.*, p. 99.

20. Immanuel Kant, *Prolegomena to Any Future Metaphysics*, Trans. Paul Carus, Revision James W. Ellington (Indianapolis: Hackett, 1977), p. 62.

21. *Ibid.*, p. 64.

22. We have seen, for example, how our consumer freedoms are channelled along the path of least resistance and how the freedom of information becomes subject to the free market. The primacy of the free market is another icon within the techno-bureaucratic consumer culture. That "freedom" means "free market" so often to so many reflects the starkly physical domain to which freedom has been reduced.

CHAPTER II

DEMOCRATIC COMMUNITIES VS. DEMOCRATIC LAWS

RICHARD A. GRAHAM

The conflict over what kind of democracy best fosters freedom and choice is now being fought out in the streets and in the legislatures of Eastern Europe and the Soviet Republics. Two hundred years ago the same issues were fought over by a small group of generally well-read American planters and businessmen in a Philadelphia meeting house. The fundamental issue now, as then, is whether freedom and justice are best secured in the short term and best fostered in the long term by an ethnically-culturally homogeneous democracy in which factions are subdued by consensus or whether by a culturally heterogeneous democracy in which factions tend to offset one another and are constrained by law.

Underlying the conflict over communitarianism (a society based upon cultural traditions and like-mindedness) vs. nomologicalism (a society based upon laws and diversity) is the great disparity within any society about the meanings of freedom and justice. As thousands of interviews in dozens of societies throughout the world have shown, five distinctly different meanings of justice[1] are held by the members of any society although just two of these underlie the conflict between communtarianism and nomologicalism. The conflict is founded upon other concepts and draws upon other terms: participation vs. distanciation, romanticism vs. enlightenment, *mythos* vs. *logos*, *Gesellschaft* vs. *Gemeinschaft*, particularity vs. universality, subjectivity vs. objectivity, transcendentalism vs. science and materialism, revealed or transmitted values vs. self-constructed values, etc.[2] The cultural-communitarians, at least those in America, find present-day support in MacIntyre[3] and Ricoeur, the nomological-nationalists in Rawls[4] and Frankena.[5]

The conflict has intensified of late. In a report from Eastern Europe two years ago, Sylvia Poggioli of American National Public Radio observed that the solidarity within the nations that had provided the strength they needed to overthrow their governments was splitting apart into ethnic-minded and civic-minded factions. Each ethnic faction had its own test of the legitimacy of a new government and the civic-minded faction had still another standard for legitimacy.

Five standards for legitimacy of a government can be seen to correspond to each of the five meanings of justice. By each of these standards, a government is legitimate[6] when:

1. The power of the police or military is sufficient to impose the will of the ruler.
2. Under the order secured by the government one can expect reward or punishment in rough proportion to one's actions.
3. The government is committed to and able to preserve ethnic-cultural-religious traditions and conventions and adheres to them in judging rights and obligations.
4. The government is able and willing to faithfully execute laws that are enacted by freely elected representatives of the people.
5. The laws are enacted and carried out in accordance with universalizable principles that establish rights and obligations.

There has not yet been rigorous research in a number of societies that would confirm that these standards for legitimacy exist in all societies regardless of culture but the thousands of studies of reasoning about justice make it all but certain that there is a high correspondence between the patterns of reasoning about justice that are found in every society and patterns of reasoning about legitimacy. The research on justice reasoning indicates that an individual will progress in judging the rightness of authority according to these criteria, one after the other, but generally stopping short of universalizable principles. Moreover, individuals do not replace their earlier judgments of legitimacy but often draw upon them to buttress or, at times, to prevail over, the higher standards for legitimacy that they may have consolidated.

Most people in most societies have rejected legitimacy of government on the basis of the first criterion alone that might makes right or on the second criterion of reward and punishment but only a few people in any society have come to judge a government's legitimacy on the basis of universalizable principles. Ever since the Enlightenment, the conflict over legitimacy has centered on the question of whether freedom and justice are best secured by a government that is principally communitarian-traditionalist or whether nomological-rationalist, that is, a nation of laws. The conflict arises not only from differences in the meaning of justice but also from differences in the meaning of freedom. If freedom can be conceived of as both external and internal, as involving both freedom of action and freedom of thought and spirit, then the legitimacy of a government will depend upon the priority assigned to each measure of freedom. For example, Professor Khuri argues that restrictions on freedom of action; of speech, assembly, worship, place of home and work, can have the unintended effect of fostering a higher freedom, a freedom of the spirit that transcends corporeal experience.

To judge which form of government, communitarian-traditionalist or nomological-rationalist fosters freedom of each kind requires some understanding of how each freedom is developed. Assuming that freedom of action in a democratic society is largely governed by customs and by laws that are an expression of the freedom of thought and the strength of character or of the spirit of the individual members of that society, the question becomes that of how and why freedom of thought and freedom to act upon it is developed by an individual.

There is continually growing evidence that bears on the question. Much of it points to a single life force, a drive for preservation and growth of the individual and the species. For higher forms of life, to grow is in large part to know, and for humans the force for preservation and for knowledge is sometimes expressed in terms of the preservation of the soul and the knowledge of God.

Recent studies in developmental psychology examine these two aspects of life force in other terms: the drive for development of self-identity or self-integrity and the drive for development of reason. Much of philosophy has seen this drive for self in opposition to the drive for reason but recent studies seem to support Hume's assertion that "reason is and ought only to be the slave of passion." Hume would seem to be supported if passion can be seen as a manifestation of the drive for the preservation and the growth of the self. For it is the self that gives force to reason. Neither reason nor precepts are acted upon except through a self that sees its own preservation or growth as fostered by the action.

It is passionate sympathy or religious belief, more often than highly developed reason, that accounts for the ethical behavior of most people in most parts of the world. It is self-identification as a caring mother or a sympathetic friend or devout believer rather than a highly rational moral philosopher that most often provides the strength for ethical deeds. When reason appears to prevail, it is because drive for reason and the drive for the preservation of self - indentity are similarly directed. Where cruelty, deceit, greed or lust seem to have overpowered a sense of rightness or good, a perverse drive for self-assurance has overpowered reason.

Recent research indicates that the forces for the development of reason are closely related to those for the development of the sense of self. Studies of infants and of children identify beyond question a force, apparent from birth on, to establish a self-identity, a force that persists throughout life to understand and to secure a place for the self, or the soul, in the cosmos and beyond. Similar studies observe the manifestation of a drive in infants to know and understand the world around them, to categorize and to conceptualize.

In the first twenty years of life, human reason has been found to progress through a series of transformations or re-orderings of knowlege, at much the same time that one's sense of self -identity goes through transformations or re-orderings that are largely driven by physiological changes and the resultant changes in the roles and responsibilities that are assigned by one's society.[16] After twenty, the changes in reason and self-identity tend to slow or cease. Many adults fail to reach the stages of identity and integrity that Erik Erikson sees as part of a well- developed personality or character. Similarly, many adults fail to reach the later stages of reason and of judgment that have been identified by the research of Jean Piaget, Lawrence Kohlberg, and several hundred others.

According to philosophers from Plato to Kant and beyond and to psychologists from Piaget to Kohlberg and beyond, internal freedom is the consequence of a developed ability to reason autonomously and to judge universalizably. If so, how can this seemingly individualistic-rationalistic freedom be reconciled with commutarian freedom and with the religious doctrines to which many communtarians look for solidarity? The answer is that truly autonomous judgment is congruent with the same universalizable principles of highly developed religious faith.[17] It is universalizable in that it is reversible; what is seen as fair for oneself must be seen as fair from the perspectives of others. It is judgment that is consistent with most religious precepts. It is, in the sense of Plato's *Meno*, self-experienced, self-constructed "true knowledge" that agrees with the "right thinking" of traditional or religious precepts and instructed belief. The actions that are guided by "true knowledge" appear much the same as those guided by true belief and true love.

The alleged "rationality" of communism was not rational at all, not in the sense that true rationality requires reversibility wherein rights require obligations of like kind and degree. One's rights entail the obligation to assure the same rights for all others regardless of their beliefs or class or sex or culture. Communitarians should not expect others to conform to the customs and beliefs—not to say the laws—of their community any more than communitarians should be expected to conform to the customs and beliefs of others. The laws in a mature communitarian democracy, as in a mature nomological democracy, will be based to some degree upon fundamental human rights as these are defined both by universalizable principles of justice and by most religious doctrines. But the evidence from research is clear enough that most people in most societies of the world of today, whether these societies are principally communitarian or nomological, hold to concepts of justice that are not universalizable nor even nomological. They will accord to the ethnic and religious minorities within their midst, and to women, equal rights more from sympathy, religious precepts, and fear of punishment than from respect for law or for principle. Laws that guarantee equal protection and equal opportunity regardless of race, religion or sex, if enacted will tend to lack rigorous enforcement. Even religious precepts for equal rights—and they are generally weak with respect to discrimination based upon sex—will tend to give way to the conventions and traditions of a society.

As long as the character of the new democracies in Eastern Europe and the Soviet Republics is established by protests in the streets and by legislatures that are responsive to these protests, communitarian -traditionalist democracy is almost certainly assured. Whether this is right,—whether, for example, communitarian states should be created by secession from the ostensibly nomological Soviet Union, ought to be determined not so much by past history as by whether secession provides reasonable assurance of progress toward freedom and choice. For reasons too complex to be examined fairly in this brief paper, a strong argument can be made that secession would foster progress toward human rights in the Baltic States but it is much less likely that this would be true in more fundamentalist states. A part of the reason for supporting Baltic secession is that the divisions between a communitarian and a nomological society and between communitarians and nomologicalists within a scoeity are seldom neat and clean. There are many nomologicalists in the Baltic States and many Soviet traditionalists still holding power in the Soviet Union. Whatever the rightness of the conflicts of secession, they are likely to be decided more by the power of passion and armed force than by the power of reason. The best hope for justice is that power of sympathy and of religious precept will come to the aid of reason.

The forthcoming decisions for communitarianism will be counter to the American decision 200 years ago in Philadelphia. For almost 200 years the individualistic-factionalistic United States has functioned as melting pot for nationalities. The founders of the United States counted upon factions to offset one another but also counted upon the tempering of faction by a shared faith in the blessings of God and in the freedom and opportunity of the country. This faith in freedom and choice did much to make up for lack of a common ethnic-based cultural and religious faith. This common faith in the blessings of God and the freedom and opportunity of the country now seems less firm and individualism-factionalism seems more intense. The clashes seem to reflect not only a continuing difference between the concepts of freedom and justice that are held by different groups of American people but also a similar internal conflict of reason and identity for individual Americans.

NOTES

1. Lawrence Kohlberg, "Cultural Universality of Moral Judgment Stages" in *The Psychology of Moral Judgment* (San Francisco: Harper and Row, 1984).

2. See, for example, Paul Ricoeur, "Ethics end Culture: Habermas end Gadamer in
Dialogue" in *Social and Political Essays* (Athens, Ohio: Ohio UP, 1974).

3. Alasdair MacIntyre, *After Virtue* (U. of Notre Dame Press, 1981).

4. John Rawls, *A Theory of Justice.*

5. William Frankena, *Ethics* (Englewood Cliffs, N.J., 1973).

6. Jürgen Habermas, "Legitimation Problems in the Modern State" in *Communication and the Evolution of Society* (Boston: Beacon Press, 1976). Habermas says ". . . levels of justification can be ordered hierarchically. The legitimations of a superseded stage no matter what their content are depreciated with the transition to a next higher stage; . . . these depreciatory shifts are connected with social-evolutionary transitions to new learning levels . . ."; and in a footnote he observes, ". . . a collective identity becomes superfluous as soon as the mass of the members of society are socio-structurally forced to lay aside their role identities, however generalized, and to develop ego identities."

CHAPTER III

OCCUPATION, MAN, AND FREEDOM OF CHOICE

RUTA RINKEVICIENE

Before considering human existence and its problems under democracy, in Lithuania we must discuss first the obstacles, both inner (mutilated man) and outer (occupation) impeding the creation of the democracy. Here I shall concentrate on the inner problem, i.e. that of man, because the person is not a result of democracy, but its condition.

In looking to the East the world anticipates democratic change. In Lithuania people are tired of limitations on their existence and a poor way of life. Undoubtedly it is necessary to change the political system and economic structure in order to create a life that will be bearable. But the moment we began to think of the changes to be carried out, we find ourselves in a vicious circle: desiring to change the order, the man must be changed; but to change the man, conditions for stimulating human re-orientation must be created anew.

It is evidently impossible to change social order while retaining the same philosophy of man and making no changes in values, morals and practical provisions, for it can be only the people themselves who reform reality. Most perceive that, although the rules of the old social system are still in force, it is now possible to change the rules. But the old stereotypes still exist in thoughts and characteristics shaped by the totalitarian system.

Considering what to do and how to reform society and one's life, one suddenly understands that s/he lacks some significant qualities. Moments of despair become inevitable when one perceives, acutely and painfully, that one has been forced within the boundaries of fate, that much in him/her has been strangled and that s/he has been 'reduced' and become Lilliputian. The more conscious one is and the more willing to change reality, the more strongly one feel one's limitations and inferiority.

One breaks into the democratic world of the West, desiring to know that forbidden life and its principles, to perceive its way of thinking, feeling and action. At first one is deprived of speech by the very abundance of colors and the range of the possible choices.

But these experiences are fairly superficial and the feeling of surprise grows weaker, and so it should; for the world which has been hidden for so long is rather natural, especially when one understands that it is not without its own shortcomings.

The real shock of civilization strikes when one begins to consider what one can do in the existing reality. When one begins to perceive the everyday thinking of the Western man, his motives, principles of action and characteristics, and tries to take what one lacks, there is an inconceivable leap. One apprehends oneself entirely: not only one's own existence, but even one's non-existence,—the killed potencies. This is not simply the lack of some characteristics which could be compensated for by others in order to live a purposive and valuable life. The gap is all-round and total: one strives to act reasonably as if s/he had been taking part in western civilization for the last 50 years, but in reality one is entirely paralyzed. There is nothing to grasp at except despair, annoyance and shame at one's weakness.

Whenever one tries to take the perspective of Lithuania, one feels very sad. Many are not to be blamed for everything and are not responsible for things. Others endeavor to live, but do not wish to waste their energy for the common good; others do not believe in the possibility of success; while still others support the old system. But the greatest number of people desire to further the reforms promising a better life, but do not know how to act.

All of us who were brought up and educated for slavery desperately desire to be free and are conscious of the right to freedom. But while accepting freedom we remain unwilling to acknowledge responsibility for these 50 years; we do not admit fault for our situation. One cannot separate freedom from responsibility, however. If we want to be free, we must have a sense of responsibility for the worthlessness of society, for the disorder and finally for our inferiority. The first prerequisite for the future changes is a sense of responsibility for everything that happens and a perception of the qualities which are needed but which our people presently lack.

Self-knowledge begins the moment we distinguish ourselves in the world, when we single ourselves out from the other people and compare our "self" with other beings. One's self-understanding as a person of a specific type is possible only if we compare ourselves with one who has been brought up in another culture. Of course, in a sense such cognition is formal because every one is a specific being, but this does not mean that one cannot attempt to define the most characteristic features of the Lithuanian people. In spite of differences of work, origin and attitude, West Europeans and Lithuanians have much in common, and this allows us to situate ourselves culturally and historically.

The mode of life in our country, its material poverty, educational system, legal and moral prohibitions, and the incapacity of making a living from one's own job has formed people's mentality, tastes, value-orientations, motives, stereotypes and self-image.

A description of a person in West Europe (which, of course, would be more or less abstract) would note first his industry or activity. Extended meditation, exaggerated dreaminess or sentimentality are not his characteristics; the main principle of his existence is purposive activity. In contrast there are many inactive, passive people in different offices and institutions in Lithuania. Nobody will be shocked at hearing of utopian plans, long discussions with zero result or a result contrary to the one planned. Thus, compared with Westerners, Lithuanians seem to be dreamers more than active people—though they are more active than Russians who would rather talk than work. Living standards and the material welfare correspond to the aforementioned qualities.

Another complex of closely connected qualities characteristic of Western man is: responsibility, consciousness and freedom (for it is impossible to speak about the responsibility of a man who is not conscious or who cannot act freely). The possibility of acting freely is a necessary condition for any kind of activity: I cannot cooperate with a man who owns nothing because everything is held in common, for such a man is not free in his decisions and thus cannot be held responsible. In the West personal responsibility is felt very deeply because one risks one's job, salary or even entire property. Many in Lithuania either do not feel responsibility or fear it: they are afraid to be free in the sense of making their own decisions for it is much more untroubling and convenient to await directions and instructions. In the West one's welfare depends upon the possibility of making decisions as soon as possible; where the possibility of being bested by competition looms real, lightning quick decisions with full responsibility often become the condition for success.

Courage also is closely related to responsibility: when there is a presentiment that some kind of activity may be profitable, even if the person has no guarantees, he resolves to act. Greater courage and more subtle intuition usually meet with success. The capability of taking a risk, and adapting to the new requirements of a changing reality are developed. Some may change their vocation twice or thrice during their lives, and this is considered ordinary.

In Lithuania the person is relatively inert. In studies knowledge is adopted as if mechanically and for all time. In both schools and universities people are taught according to the same principle, namely, the teacher gives all required knowledge. In contrast, in West Germany students are taught to think and act; no one tries to provide all knowledge. The subjects taught may be on special narrow issues, for they provide only the bases on which one may begin with a view to becoming independent, responsible and free to decide.

Where The West usually looks for matter-of-fact suggestions and concrete activity, in Lithuania people are accustomed to excuse themselves by old habits which were developed during cooperation with Russia. They show their feeling, shed tears and become steeped in a sea of sentiment. At times one hears the epithet,"Lithuanian Spirit," unfortunately with negative connotations. On the other hand, sentiments quickly melt away and sentimentality becomes languor, weeping and dissatisfaction. On the one hand, we pride ourselves in being Lithuanians; on the other hand, we are not content with our situation. Western people seem content with things and more self-confident.

This is not to idealize the Western personality or society. It too has many problems, because even under democratic conditions none is insured against illness, misfortunes, unfortunate love or death, i.e., against everything characteristic of human existence. The 20th century West is industrialized with a high social culture and its own specific problems. Though technological culture is formed by man, the development of engineering and technology has expanded so much that man has become unable to control the results of the process. Our technological culture threatens ecological, genetic and even spiritual catastrophe. The discussions regarding the results of technologization and technocratic ways of thinking begun in the Federal Republic of Germany in the 70s still continue. In searching for solutions no one believes that either the further development or the cessation of technological progress could solve the problems of industrial society. It seems necessary to humanize the scientific-technological attitude, while recognizing technological values and culture. In other words, the way toward solving the problem is seen to lie in changing man's relations between himself and the world in general.

Unforseen consequences for human beings are caused by the "concern for the self" (*Die Sorge für Sich*) which expressed the main characteristic of human existence in the Western philosophy. "Self-concern" makes possible self-creation and finally responsibility for one's own life. But according to G. Böhme, today this "concern for the self" seems to be vanishing. "Schools, the social welfare system of public health and social security have removed self-care from man today, i.e., in the developed industrial countries of the West. A rational plan of life is always decided before one resolves to carry it out" (Böhme). In the developed industrial countries social guarantees of what is personally unattainable become problems for one's responsibility, for one's own existence.

One hears the idea that it is impossible to preserve human dignity or one's sovereignty, if one observes all the social norms and does not resist the social care of doctors, lawyers, teachers, all types of life counsellors, pedagogues, psychologists, sexologists, and organizers of tours, leisure, fashion, etc. This resistance is risky, but allows one to feel responsibility for oneself.

Thinkers of the end of the 20th century see danger not only in the nature of the man and in the facticity of human existence, but in the second level created by man, in this case, the system of social care which converts the feeling of human responsibility for the self and changes man himself as did technological culture. In other words, under the conditions of democracy the problem of man's freedom and choice is still a pressing one.

In describing the essence of the man and his existence, 20th century anthropology notes some negative facts: fear, death, nothingness, etc. In the end it is said that "man is a being, which may utter 'no'" ("der Mensch sei das Wesen, das nein sagen kann," Böhme). Saying-no, resistance, revolt, behavior refusing or denying something, are comprehended as phenomena through which man perceives himself as a man (Böhme). But it is not only a matter of perception, for in saying 'no', man takes responsibility. The challenge in education of arousing a sense of responsibility points to its importance in a society that is characterized by competition, the free market, and democracy. Personal responsibility is the essence and the basis of the problem.

A human being lives in a heterogeneous world: nature and culture constitute the context in which man can develop. Some thinkers supposed natural surroundings to be the most suitable for man and used to call for a return "back to nature" (Rousseau). Other considered nature a chaos and declared culture to be the law; they used to invite man "back to culture" (Gehlen).

These fragmentary notes on the problems existing in Western

society, which we consider an example, demonstrate that even a highly developed culture and a democratic society cannot solve the problems of all mankind. On the one hand, culture performs functions of stabilization (reproduction, nutrition, defense, etc.), i.e., it compensates for difficulties in instincts (Gehlen). On the other hand, performing the function of instincts, culture transforms feelings of care and responsibility for oneself and protects against the dangers to human identity.

At the beginning of this paper we mentioned the fact that in the undeveloped social and material culture of Lithuania, man was depersonalized, deprived of human identity. But this problem exists as well in the countries in which the material, spiritual and political culture is developed to a degree we sometimes consider unattainable. In this sense we may talk about the situation of existence, common both for us and for the West, as of the universal situation of human life in general, without differentiating the physiological, psychological, natural and political aspects of human existence. In answer to the question of what is man and what he looks like, first of all we must notice that a man is never finished, never a stagnant 'givenness', but always in formation and self-creation. Tradition is the ground for this human formation, for human nature is also historical: if one wishes to live in a society, one must act traditionally, i.e. historically. "When denying the future, human development becomes different; in hurrying into the future, the self becomes empty and is denied in time. Identity and continuity (*Identität und Kontinuität*) are the polar limit of existence" (Revers). In other words, the human being usually alternates between constantly saying "Yes" and "No." "Yes" affirms the tradition as the well spring of human existence. "No" ensures the identity of man as such (freedom-responsibility). Describing the situation common to all mankind we may say that there must be a permanent linkage and balance between saying "Yes" and saying "No."

We Lithuanians are often said to be "from the East" (though the fact often insults us). Though in comparison to a person from Western Europe, we do find many differences (a Lithuanian is sentimental, a dreamer, not matter-of-fact, not able to think practically; one from the West is concrete, business-like and practical), we nonetheless reject the notion of being from the East. In fact, features which have become traditional over the last 50 years of our history are the ground of our existence and to avoid denying ourselves means saying "yes" to them. When we say "No" to the present historical reality and that we want to depend on

Western Europe, we testify to our feelings of freedom and responsibility and to our search for our identity. Whereas the West revolts against the material and social welfare it created, we revolt against the conditions pressed upon us by strangers.

At present, reform in Europe has become an urgent issue. The problem is perceived quite clearly, because of the existence of two Europes—two different worlds with different experiences, outlooks, emotional attitudes and systems of values. West Europe feels correct and satisfied; we feel that what we were doing was mistaken. We feel deceived and unsatisfied, and want to become Western Europeans in spite of all the reservations. We conceive (consciously or not) of a *rapprochement* of the two Europes in this manner, namely,—that a hurt and dissatisfied East will go towards the West. What does this "going toward" something mean? Does our historical, cultural situation correspond to the universal human situation, or is it exceptional? One attempts to know what Europe was like two thousands years ago. From the hills of the new Rome through the lush greenness and alluring redness of blossoms, you gaze at the mystery spread out below—the Forum Romanum. As you go down the contour becomes apparent, the obscurity of the past opens with its romance. In the heat and light of the Sun, in the ruins and the dust where you can feel the life of past centuries, you try to imagine the wishes, thoughts and the daily life and feelings of the people. But, if you try to identify with them, you are not successful and say "No." If everything there could receive you, you would feel as a stranger there: as if you came from the street onto a stage decorated with old scenery. "Yes" and "No" are separated by the chasm of two thousand years.

For example, if you live for some time in West Germany and try to identify with its people, mentality and mode of life, there is nothing strange: such should be the life of any normal man. Then if you try to identify with the people of this planet and feel pushed ahead in time for fifty or a hundred years, you are a foreign body— like an actor dressed in another fashion, who went into the streets of Europe at the end of the 20th century. If one's feelings in the heart of Rome testified only to the objective truth, the feelings in West Germany are very painful: in the first case one said "No, I do not want to be what those people were, I want to be myself." Now you say: "I want to be from the past, I would like to be in the same time as those people who, from my standpoint, are a future people." But between the real I and the one that I want to be, or between the time-frames in which I am and want to be, there is an abyss.

One may never catch up with a remote time by normal motion. If, *per impossible*, one were to leap over the abyss at a bound, one would hardly be oneself, the same person. This state corresponds to the common situation of all mankind, our life and transformation go on in spite of signs of the 50 years within us, when we say "Yes," that we nevertheless wish to be Lithuanians, we are saying as well "No," that we do not want to be from the East. This "No" signifies our exceptional situation, because becoming what we want to be and catching up with time means a jump over an abyss which not only promises growth, but threatens deprivation as well.

But what are we ourselves? For fifty years we were what we were forced to be. When a child is unable to satisfy his own needs he smothers them in order to remain alive, and there appear symbolic needs which he is able to satisfy. A little man becomes real because he does not want what he needs and does not want anything he does not need. "Neurosis is nothing else but an attempt to become real in an unreal way" (Arthur Janov, *The Primal Scream*). Because we lived as if our real needs have not existed, we have become a society of neurotics. Now we must not neglect ourselves, but recover from neurosis; this means that we must regain our reality, our nature, ourselves. I do not insist that our illness does not fit within the framework of the universal human situation, for I do not think this is really so. But it is clear, that returning to Europe will mean for us recovering from a neurosis, and this will not be easy: "The way towards neurosis and the way out of it are equally painful" (Janov, *The Primal Scream*).

If we accept that, in being divided between East and West, Europe became alien to itself, we must apply this to ourselves. The root of the alienation is not a difference of outlook or world view. The roots of Europe's alienation are hidden in those in East Europe who are eager to go to West Europe because they are not as they want to be, because they are as they do not want to be. We recognize the challenge but are not confident that we can respond to our own expectations and to the expectations of those who are interested in our situation. The neurotic alone is not able to cure himself: he needs a doctor—a psychotherapist and a healthy one indeed!

A rhetorical question leaps from us: will the free, democratic and sound world present itself to fill the role of a doctor-psychotherapist?

Only when we have recovered will we be able to speak about democracy. It is too early to speak now about freedom and choice under the conditions of democracy because we are not free to choose democracy. We can and really do choose an unarmed struggle for the right to create a democracy. Dancing and singing in front of tanks, like Sartre's heros we choose death. This means we choose ourselves—this means freedom. Otherwise, while the world holds a cowardly silence, we, having become neurotic during the previous 50 years, will become incurable invalids unable to choose anything or to distinguish freedom from slavery under the brutal red fascists. To obey them would mean disavowing one's human essence.

That is why at the moment I would like to speak not about freedom, choice and responsibility under the conditions of democracy, but about the freedom and responsibility, and perhaps about the fear on the part of the democratic world in the presence of the vandalism of the 'Evil Empire'.

DISCUSSION OF CHAPTER III

1. It would seem helpful to distinguish two levels. On the one hand, the theoretical level is not among the concerns of most people and thus people might not object to the substitution of a metaphysics by a quasi-metaphysics. Nevertheless, they may well, on the other hand, become neurotic, that is, when suppressed they may attempt to become real in an unreal or substitute manner. Thus, the resolution of present problems must go beyond unmasking the ideology to a deep personal healing even with new metaphysical basis for a sane life.

In order for this to arise from free creative action man must be healthy, for the attempt to restore killed potencies is not just an attempt to add missing pieces but to face one's despair and shame. Because in the East the psychological tendency is toward contemplation, dissatisfaction leads to immobility. This contrasts to a more practical attitude in the West where problems get worked out through action. Nevertheless, even this is undermined by the spreading net of social welfare programs which deaden a people's sense of self-responsibility and self-consciousness. Since the people's taking of responsibility is the essence of democracy, the loss of this sense is central to the problematic faced in the development of freedom and choice in a democracy.

Lithuanians face a special dilemma due to the past 50 years of their history. For to the degree that they say "yes" and accept responsibility for their recent history of forced absorption by the East they lose their self identity, whereas to the degree that they say "no" and desire to be part of the West they must leap over an abyss of 50 years of identity with what they are not and the many subterfuges by which they attempted nonetheless to be real in unreal ways.

To return now to Europe means recovering from a neurosis. Not only is this very painful, but it requires a psychotherapist who is truly sane. Who can fulfill this task: the west, the philosopher—or are they as well too ailing, fearful or compromised?

Perhaps then in Lithuania it is too soon to speak of making choices in a democracy, for freedom does not yet exist. The leap to this could be the radical negative of Sartre, the concrete negative before the tanks in Vilnius as in Tienanmen. In this light the establishment of freedom may consist not only in a choice of self against the USSR, but in an existential choice of disavowal of self.

2. The psychological dimension of the search for freedom in our day, especially in the Lithuanian context, could have multiple levels. One is the sense of well-being, confidence and ease of life, i.e., of feeling good about oneself and what one does. Another is the move from the level of psychological incapacitation to that of confident self-responsibility, which is itself a process of liberation. A third is the personal character of the choice of saying "no" to what one has become in order to achieve a new freedom: this is the existential process of dying to self in order to be born again in a new life.

Concretely, for Lithuania this implies a choice. On the one hand, there is the option of settling passively into the situation which has been imposed from the East over the last 50 years, and accepting the compromises which weave the net of daily life, from fuel and transportation to medical care and education. On the other hand, there is breaking free from this unsatisfactory situation at the cost of painful disruption.

In this context one may speak of turning toward or rejoining the West. But here both the terms "West" and "East" must have multiple meaning. Beyond its obvious geographical denotation, "West" has a range of additional meanings. More external is the plethora of goods and services produced by its physical industrial capacity. This exercises a real attraction, but one which seems less perduring. Undergirding this is the liberation of the productive capacity of the people in the context of free competition in industry and commerce. This has managed to stimulate creativity and initiative and, relatively without central guidance or government initiative, to constitute the arteries and capillaries for making goods available and maintaining them in serviceable condition.

At a second level "West" signifies a *topos* of ideas—an open space for creative thought. Here pluralism is at least tolerated and even promoted. Schooling is considered to be at its best when the young are encouraged to think for themselves, to raise questions in class, to suggest new approaches and to test them out critically. The free market is not only a fact of economics, but an attitude of mind. Behind this are the values of the enlightenment with their emphasis upon personal autonomy and hence equality, with standing before the state, and hence with freedom in thought and action.

At a third level "West" hearkens back to a longer heritage from Greece and Rome and of Christianity—together these constitute a Mediterranean culture with its deep sense of human meaning, its balance in responding to the problem of the one and the many, and its transcendent vision of the purpose and goals of human life and action. The resulting complex is not only a system of production or of political life, but a rich and integral culture.

When Lithuania looks to the "West," it looks at these many levels. What is more, this is not only a world that is beyond its borders: it is its own heritage and soul for its own culture is Western. For this reason its situation of these last 50 years (and of the last century as well) of separation from that culture constitutes special and painful violence.

On the other hand, some noted that the symbolically indicated "East" is itself the bearer of a great culture. Reference was made to the enormous richness of the Islamic tradition which so amazed the Western crusaders. Further, attention to feelings, especially when oriented to one's family, people and religion, are rich and integrating factors. Without these, to limit one's motivations and responses to clear rational calculations after the manner of a science constitutes an impoverished quasi-metaphysics as noted in the paper of T. Sodeika and A. Sverdiolas. The need to surpass this was seen by Kant in moving beyond his first critique to the second critique and to the dimensions of aesthetics and teleology in his third critique.

The potentialities for conflict between East and West have a long history. This can be traced to the split in the Roman Empire between Rome and Byzantium and to the accumulation of unresolved tensions this entailed. More remotely it is found in the early division between the Judeo-Christian and Islamic cultures and the conflict entailed in the expansion of Islam not only across Northern Africa, but into Europe from the East through the Balkans and from the West through Spain. The crusades are but one sign of this conflict, however. The present movements toward dividing Yugoslavia and tensions between North and South in Czechoslovakia bespeak the perduring tensions between the enlightenment and the Ottoman Empire with their two cultures and their respective senses of person and order.

Even beyond this it is important also to be cautious in turning to the potentialities of a culture, for these never delineate actual life. In reality everyone is but at some point in the realization of their potentialities which are intermixed with multiple modes of excess, imperfection and even contradiction. Thus, the Western material accomplishment can become consumerism, its sense of individuality too easily slips into individualism, its emphasis on rationality veers toward a depersonalizing bureaucratic formalism, freedom of competition can become exploitative and destructive, utopias from Plato to Skinner have become contexts for elitist control. In a parallel manner, the sense of unity and symmetry in the East can become autocratic and overbearing. This has been manifest in the old Russian aristocrat in the new guise of a party leader, and in the deadening aspects of the Chinese conception of harmony (see the paper of S. Wen).

Hence, one needs always to be ready to take account of the negative forces in a person or a people. A blueprint for the North American effort to recognize this, provide for it, and even convert its energy from anti-social to social goals is found in the *Federalist Papers.*

Whatever be the examples and pressures from without, some suggest that the essential direction in which to look is within, though this was diversely understood. Some considered the impact of the other nations to be external and no reason for shame or discouragement. Others recognized the damaging impact of colonialism and saw the need to repair the damage to self-identity and self-confidence. Still others saw the need to look into one's own degree of compromise and complicity, after the suggestion of Pres. V. Havel and certain African thinkers, as a first essential step in establishing self-responsibility and thereby restoring self-identity.

In any case, it was suggested, to measure oneself by another is always a losing proposition for one can never be as good in those terms as they are in that other. Nor is there any need to. One's own cultural traditions are rich and deep. As one's own history and present situation have their own uniqueness, in order to be appropriate one's response must be uniquely and creatively crafted. It is in these terms that success in identity, collaboration, and even competition, must finally be measured.

George F. McLean

CHAPTER IV

THE TYRANNY OF "FREEDOM AND CHOICE IN A DEMOCRACY"

RONALD K. L. COLLINS

> [I]sn't the [democratic] city full of freedom . . . ?
> And isn't there license in it to do whatever one
> wants? . . . And where there's license, it's plain
> that each man would organize his life in it privately
> just as it pleases him.
> —Plato[1]

> [F]reedom is not the answer to everything.
> —Camus[2]

I. Freedom. Choice. Democracy. These three words are the vernacular icons of modern America. They are the terms of our times. They are largely synonymous in much the same way that enslavement, oppression and tyranny are. As pseudo-synonyms and pseudo-antonyms, the use of both sets of terms exploits language to the point of redundancy. But there is more here than a schoolboy's lesson in language. There is a redundancy in the former that reveals a certain craving, at one and the same time personal, psychological and political. In its contemporary and pathological form, this craving culminates in its archetypal[3] opposite—tyranny. Thus, freedom is enslavement; choice, oppression; and democracy, tyranny. Orwellian newspeak is not my objective. Rather, the phenomenon of such opposites collapsing into one another is distinctly Huxleyan and therefore particularly apropos to what is called mass culture in late-twentieth-century America.* Pleasure, in all its rapacious forms, is one of the key components of the modern American order. '[T]he problem of happiness . . ., the problem of making people love their servitude"[4] is the real totalitarianism confronting Western capitalism. The goal, obsessive by definition, of this regime is to fill the gap between desire and its fulfillment. And as the culture's advertising captains (the new popular rulers) understand, the goal is as well to *create* a forever new consciousness of desire. This is the *Id*-world of immediate 'gratification, trivialization, atomism, and ceaseless distraction. It is the brave new world where the "citizenry" euphorically digests "soma tablets" and where a surfeit of "stuff" (material or mortal) is held out for consumption. Today, the very idea of *citizen* has become synonymous with *consumer*—the ones who devour all. Thus viewed, consumer government institutionalizes the collective and "systematic exploitation of all the possibilities of pleasure."[5] This, then, is the portrait of the new culture: human nature reduced to a narcotized population feeding on nihilistic materialism.[6] Above all, it is a culture steeped in "freedom, choice and democracy."

Maximizing "more" is the credo[7] of this regime. But it is a credo that at some point turns on its followers; it is Judas Iscariot-like in its betrayal but Sigmund Freud-like in its pursuit. The latter diminishes the moral significance of choice, while the former holds out choice as the indispensable condition of a newfound freedom. Endless choices ("[e]verything must be tried"[8]), free of normative shackles, translate into the political or constitutional regime we call Democracy. The effects dialogical, political and psychological tend to escape us to the point that to contest the Huxleyan tyranny is seen as synonymous with condoning its Orwellian counterpart.

II. The concept of limit is not really a part of our constitutional, political and cultural vocabulary. We stress Rights not responsibilities; we idolize Liberty not virtue; we fancy Freedom over justice; and we favor Buying over voting. If we are a community at all, we are a community not civic but consumptive. (Advertisers and romantic constitutionalists would have us think we can be both.) The very notion of rights as we know them, Simone Weil once observed, "has a commercial flavour, essentially evocative of legal claims and arguments."[9] Should it then be any surprise that the constitutional calculus of our era equates the "rights" of commercial advertisers with political activists or likens poor people's pleas for sustenance to property? Once we embraced the idea of a consumers' constitution, the corresponding emergence of an economic analysis of law was inevitable. From this linguistic and economic vantage point, a "constitutional bill of duties"[10] is plainly absurd.

In one sense, the paradigm of modern discourse is the "discourse" of unending amusement and its economic kin the "discourse" of unending commerce. Both forms of "discourse" serve the pleasure principle in pursuit of a kind of satisfaction with no definable objective. "But when there is no objective there is no longer any common measure or proportion."[11] Consequently, the absence of a cultural mass-vocabulary of self-restraint mimics the absence of a similar idea in mass culture's pursuit of happiness. In quantity and variety, such pursuits are indeed "democratic" and therefore free of the nagging constraints of any principle of moderation.

A few words about Television (the pleasure medium) should suffice for this occasion. Essentially, the point is this: today, the forces of advanced American capitalism encourage the exploitation of highly advanced electronic technology to accelerate the age-old human drive for self-gratification. The consumptive thrust of such unchecked capitalism affects all public discourse. This phenomenon is most apparent in the *culture* of commercial television, a culture in which America's most beloved toy provides unceasing mass amusement. Basically, "the predicament of American television is the predicament of American culture and politics as a whole."[12] Public discourse is increasingly taking a distinctive and aestheticized form consistent with the look and feel of commercial television. The aestheticization of public discourse is essential to the effective marketing of ideas and commercial goods in a highly consumptive economy: marketing has become, after all, a selling of images. The business of television trades in the economy of such images and has pulled other discourse into that economy.[13] With entertainment as the paradigm for most public discourse,[14] traditional Madisonian values—which stress civic restraint and civic dialogue—are overshadowed. This, then, is part of the picture of the Huxleyan nightmare. Madison's First Amendment is ill-equipped to deal with Huxleyan tyranny. In the brave new world, the antiquated First Amendment is eclipsed. Its fear of the tyranny of terror is overshadowed by a tyranny of pleasure. As Huxley noted

> [T]he early advocates of . . . a free press envisage only two possibilities: [that] propaganda might be true, or it might be false. They did not foresee what in fact has happened, above all in our Western capitalist democracies—the development of a vast communications industry, concerned in the main with neither the true nor the false, but with the *unreal*, the more or less totally irrelevant. In a word, they failed to take into account man's almost infinite appetite for distractions. [15]

III. Of course, people still choose to converse. They still value freedom. And they still wholeheartedly support democracy. But how they chose to converse, exactly why they value freedom, and precisely *what* they understand democracy to be are all greatly colored by the mass pleasure medium of commercial television. The medium does not so much create, as it reflects, this mass hedonistic experience. That is, the medium does not force: rather, it feeds an all too voracious "mass."

The "mass" neither knows nor cares much about things rational; it is a creature charmed by ever-changing images of plenty. Like the "great beast," the "mass" expresses only its urges. It equates "creative communion" with a secular and profane eucharist. Aside from criminal sanctions, the freedom of the "mass" is restricted primarily by its capacity to devour. Its sense of choice is dictated by the magnitude of its appetite. And its freedom is checked, if ever, only by what the market can feed to it. Life by impulse, language by image, and learning by appetite—these are the earmarks of contemporary "freedom."

Consumers need to have their world commercialized. They crave the association of the "lowest passions with the highest ideals."[16] Mass consumption demands mass appeal.[17] This in turn means that the dichotomy between the high and the popular cultures disappears into a leveling mass of commercial images, forever trading back and forth between two cultures. Hence the preeminence of advertising, on which last year alone $130 billion was spent. The commercial message is ubiquitous. It is on our clothes and in our minds. Mass advertising has conquered much of the modern world with a power greater than that wielded by Rome when it conquered much of the ancient world.

Mass "[a]dvertising," wrote Jules Henry, "is an expression of an irrational economy that has depended for survival on a fantastically high standard of living incorporated into the American mind as a moral imperative."[18] This irrational tendency, perpetuated constantly by image advertising, fosters pecuniary truths, pecuniary logic, and a pecuniary psychology all in one form or another illusory. Truth is image, is what sells, is whatever people believe. Again, Huxley:

> The principles underlying [commercial] propaganda
> are extremely simple. Find some common desire,
> some widespread unconscious fear or anxiety; think
> out some way to relate this wish or fear to the
> product you have to sell; then build a bridge of verbal
> or pictorial symbols over which your customer can

pass from fact to compensatory dream. . . .[19]

Seen against this backdrop, freedom becomes first and foremost the freedom to buy, to spend irrationally. Thus, environmentally concerned young people buy Toyotas often because of the *feel* that comes with the car company's "environmental" advertisements. Inner-city kids similarly exercise their freedom to buy $130 Nike hightop sneakers. Convenience stores, such as 7-11, sell hot dogs with an ad tag-line borrowed from the Declaration of Independence. Bloomingdale's Department stores market appliances and bubble gum tins with "stars and stripes," this to urge people to buy and thereby show their support for the war effort. Boy scouts' merit badges now carry commercial messages, suggesting that good deeds be repaid by turning children into walking billboards. Thanks to Whittle Communications, advertising Levi jeans and Snickers candy has come to take its place as a regular part of the mandatory grade school curriculum. Even religious symbols are commercially transformed into graven images, as exemplified by the popularity of "Madonna," the "material girl." (A recent Good Friday print advertisement for extravagant jewelry urged readers to "Share Our Passion"[20] and purchase diamond-studded crosses.) In these and countless other instances, image redefines both reality and symbols, be they cultural, political or religious. Image is even held out as reality; it is the inducement for realizing a pseudo reality premised on materialism.

America is a nation infatuated with veneers. "[T]he powers of appearance have come to overshadow, or to shape, the way we comprehend matters of substance."[21] We have commercialized information, politics, culture and art. This commercialization of the culture affects our notion of core values—such as "freedom, choice and democracy"—in much the same way that a droplet of colored dye affects a glass of clear water. The danger here is this: "as the world encourages us to accept the autonomy of images, the 'given facts that appear' imply that substance is unimportant, not worth pursuing. . . . In the midst of such charades, the chasm between surface and reality widens. Our own experiences are of little consequence, unless they are substantiated and validated by the world of style."[23]

The commercial culture generates new belief systems. It does this not by renunciation but rather by redefinition. Since the culture speaks to us primarily in the language of commerce, we have come to listen in the same manner and to frame much of our world accordingly. If indeed "the power of advertising comes from ... the need for meaning,"[24] then that need is transformed into a kind of fetishistic consumption. "Material meaning" is the result. And in the process, essential needs are transformed into endless desires. In this culture the impulsive side of our psyche controls. The values of Mammon govern. Yet we do not see this as an evil for two reasons: we have no collective understanding of Mammon; and we have transformed any such notion of evil into a positive good. We are, after all, Americans wed to "freedom, choice and democracy."

This marriage of commerce and values has produced its own offspring. For one thing, civic-mindedness is an alien concept to a people mesmerized by the consumptive life. The soul of a community cannot thrive in a commercialism-run-wild environment. This is the "me only" world, the world where politicians feed the great hungry beast with disingenuous promises of "no new taxes." Likewise, egalitarian values are placed in jeopardy. The materialism promoted by Madison Avenue tends to accentuate class differences. This is because the differences between the commercial haves and have-nots become synonymous with one's rank in society. My point is *not* that material wealth be the same for all segments of the population. Rather, the concern is that at some point excessive consumption exacerbates social disparities of the kind linked to class conflicts, especially along racial lines. Additionally, the commercial culture promotes envy, creates anxiety, and fosters insecurity. The tragic end-product of this is kids killing kids in Baltimore and elsewhere in order to walk in their playmates' $130 Nike sneakers.

In an era of excess, the dominant precept is instant maximization. No desire is deferred. Thus, we strive to maximize *pleasure* (in forms ranging from gluttony to pornography), *rights* (in forms ranging from reproduction[25] to abortion), *violence* (in forms ranging from cinematic to serial murder), and, of course, we maximize our *purchasing power* (in forms ranging from multiple credit cards to second home mortgages). Traditional notions of freedom and choice take on new meaning in this world. At one level, there is a peculiar psychological twist to the commercial culture which operates to redefine (yet again) the phenomenon of pleasure. The commercial life intensifies the pleasure principle to a numbing degree. That is, just as over-stimulation deadens nerve endings, so likewise consumerist culture replays this occurrence in mass form. The obsessive side of commercialist society (namely, its repetitive buying behavior) produces this dulling effect. At some point, then, one may wonder exactly *why* one is consuming. But absent such reflective wonder, consumption becomes tautological. Put another way, consumption becomes an act in itself, devoid even of pleasure. Accordingly, in capitalist terms consumption is *ultimately* linked more to production than to pleasure. The culture consumes primarily because it produces! To fail to understand this requires a quantum leap of faith—a leap consistent with the commercial credo.

Not surprisingly, freedom and choice take on still other meanings consonant with this larger culture, meanings which feed the culture of excess. For example, in such an era the idea of "choice" translates into something approximating an unlimited (pathological) freedom to buy. Yet this prized freedom depends on a culture premised on waste. Consider, for example, the end-product of this freedom of choice—the more than 300 billion pounds (over 1,000 pounds per person) of solid waste dumped into our landfills annually. Such "freedom" is a way of life designed for disposal, if only because the consumptive imperative demands forever new commodities.

IV. From the parched plains of this moral, psychological and ecological wasteland Habib Malik rhapsodizes about "dialogical communion."[26] Admittedly, this is a worthy objective for a worthy people. So too with concepts such as "freedom, choice and democracy." But as Professor Malik also stresses, these ideals must be rooted within a particular value context. Put another way, they cannot be context-free. Yet American commercial culture, which is rapidly becoming the cultural paradigm for the world, lacks any real value context beyond material value. At least two things, pertinent to our discussion, follow from this striking fact.

First, attempts to communicate values, such as those we have been discussing, may well prove Sisyphean, or nearly so. Thus, when we speak in the language of, say, "freedom," we may well convey a message radically different than one rooted in some value context. Similarly, when we mouth the word "choice," the idea that may fill the ears of the mass of our fellow people might be one premised on the power to consume. Moreover, when we say "democracy" what may most likely to occur to our listeners is a government dedicated to safeguarding the "RIGHT" to live without context and to consume without limit. Tersely put, the commercial culture seems to have captured much, if not nearly all, of our language. If so, the consequence has been to redefine that language into its opposite and/or to transform word-based language into image-based language, replete with all the accompanying consequences. In this sense then, the Huxleyan brand of tyranny has produced its own version of "newspeak."[27] Second, to the extent that the language of such messages is understood, it will fall on the ears of "antagonistic others"—the American "mass." Those others do not imagine the Huxleyan evil as a threat to "freedom, choice and democracy." If anything, they view the latter in a positive rather than negative light. For them, portraying the Huxleyan life as a threat is itself the real threat. Those "intolerant" few who speak out against unfettered consumption, against nihilistic hedonism, against the objectification of reality, and against the conversion of values, will themselves be depicted as tyrants. In the modem commercial culture, then, the very possibility of actually fighting tyranny seems doomed.[28]

    In light of all of this, is it possible, is it prudent, to speak of "freedom, choice and democracy"? Or should we abandon these words and speak a new language? What does this problem of language portend for mass education? Lastly, *if* it is possible to develop a new language of value, what are the *conditions* for such a new language?

    V. We have yet to consider and confront the epistemology of commercialism. Given this failure, it is near impossible for Americans to talk and think about concepts such as freedom, choice and democracy. Either such concepts collapse into an ideology of images (and therefore lack even a basic syntax), or such concepts actually foster a mindless materialism rooted in consumptive nihilism. Alternatively, there is romanticism—the escape hatch for a lost generation of liberals. But the rhetoric of the latter can do no more than obscure a disturbing truth, namely, the corruption of value, meaning, and existence itself. Additionally, this critique necessarily extends *as a conceptual point* beyond the geographical and temporal boundaries of the United States. That is, if there is any real measure of truth in the preceding account, then the dilemma of contemporary America may well be one and the same for *all* capitalist or similar regimes that have attained a certain level of economic prosperity and technological advancement. This problem, if we chose to view it as such, is even more onerous in a post-*Glasnost*, "global village" age insofar as America's cultural credo begins to take "root"[29] in Europe and Eastern bloc countries, among others. After *Glasnost*, when world prospects are cautiously promising, why would decent-minded people ever want to export

American images of "freedom, choice, and democracy"? To do so would be no more than to replace one form of tyranny with another.

NOTES

    * What follows are constructive provocations intended to induce critical thought about ideas central to the *modern* American way. Several points made in this short essay are discussed further in Collins & Skover, "The First Amendment in an Age of Para-troopers," *Texas Law Review*, 68 (1990), p. 1087; Collins & Skover, *Commerce & Communication* (publication forthcoming); and in Collins & Jacobson, "Commercialism versus Culture," *Christian Science Monitor*, Sept. 19, 1990, p. 19.

    1. Plato, *The Republic*, trans. A. Bloom (New York: Basic Books, 1968), p. 235.
    2. Albert Camus, *Resistance, Rebellion, and Death*, trans. Justin O'Brien (New York: Modern Library, 1963), p. 74.
    3. I use the term in its Jungian sense, namely, an unconscious image present in individual psyches.
    4. Aldous Huxley, *Brave New World* and *Brave New World Revisited*, Intro. Martin Green (Perennial Library, 1965), p. xix.
    5. Jean Baudrillard, *Jean Baudrillard: Selected Writings*, ed. Martin Poster (Stanfor, Cal.: Stanford U.P., 1988), p. 48.
    6. See Robert S. Baker, *History, Science, and Dystopia* (Twayne Publishers, 1990), pp. 128, 138.
    7. I use this word in an ironic sense, duly mindful of its religious connotations.
    8. Jean Baudrillard, p. 49.
    9. Simone Weil, "Human Personality," in *Selected Essays : 1934*, trans. Richard Rees (London: Oxford U.P., 1962), p. 18.
    10. For examples of such playful talk, see "Who Owes What to Whom?: Drafting a Constitutional Bill of Duties," *Harpers Magazine.*, Feb. 1991, pp. 43-54 (contributions by Gerald Marzorati, Benjamin Barber, Mary Ann Glendon, Dan Kemmis, Christopher Lasch and Christopher Stone).
    11. SimoneWeil, "The Power of Words," in *Selected Essays: 1934*, p. 155.
    12. Todd Gitlin, *Inside Prime Time* (New York: Pantheon Press, 1983), p. 355.
    13. Consider, in this regard, the following point made by broadcast journalist Bill Moyers: Running campaigns in a nation on

the pleasure principle is wrecking the polity of America, destroying our ability as a cooperative society to face reality and solve our problems. Behind the charm and smiles, behind the one-liners [andj pretty pictures, . . . the government rots, its costs soar, its failures mount. But, on the bridge of the ship of state, no one's on watch and below deck no one can see the iceberg but everyone is feeling good." See "The Public Mind: Leading Questions," PBS television broadcast, Nov. 15, 1989.

14. President Ronald Reagan once observed that "[p]olitics is just like show business." Quoted in E. Drew, *Portrait of an Election* (1981), p. 263.

15. Aldous Huxley, *Brave New World Revisited* (1958), p. 44 [emphasis added].

16. Huxley, *Brave New World* and *Brave New World Revisited* [as in note 4, above], p. 26.

17. I say this mindful of the commercial phenomenon known as "market segmentation." See Sut Jhally, *The Codes of Advertising* (London: Routledge, 1987), pp. 109-110, 128.

18. Jules Henry, *Culture Against Man* (New York: Random House, 1963), p. 45.

19. Huxley, *Brave New World* and *Brave New World Revisited*, p. 41.

20. See Mayor's advertisement in *Sun-Sentinel* (Palm Beach, Fla.), March 29, 1991, sect. A, page 4, col. 1. Above the statement quoted in the text, the advertisement in part reads: "This Easter, faith shines bright with Mayor' s unique crosses of semi-precious gems surrounded with diamonds. Gifts as beautiful as they are meaningful . . . Blue Topaz cross, $1,650. . . . Large rubelite cross, $6,300. Also available in blue topaz, $4,995; peridot, $5,250; green tourmaline, $7,300." Not to be outdone, Tiffany & Co. advertised its own diamond, 18-karat gold cross for $17,500. See *NewYorkTimes*, March 24, 1991, p. 3.

21. Stuart Ewen, *All Consuming Images* (New York: Basic Books, 1988), p. 259.

22. See Neil Postman, *Conscientious Objections* (New York: Knopf, 1988), p. 66.

23. Stuart Ewen, p. 271.

24. Sut Jhally, p. 196.

25. For example, see William Wagner, "The Contractual Reallocation of Procreative Resources and Parental Rights: The National Endowment Critique," 41 *Case Western Law Review*, 1, 5 (1990) [footnote omitted]: "Today, the instinct for commercial

exploitation now extends to the most profound biological process, human reproduction."

26. In Habib Malik, "Freedom & Pluralism: An Essay on the Human Condition" (unpublished paper presented to the participants in the Research in Values and Philosophy Seminar, Catholic University of America, March, 1991).

27. I wonder whether Republican Party political theorists may be placing too much emphasis on diversity as the essential ingredient in the kind of dialogical process they find so basic to political freedom. Similarly, intolerance may *not* be the only viewpoint that really threatens the republican process. In a Huxleyan regime diversity would probably only compound the problem of the tyranny endemic to that way of existence. For an account of Republicanism, albeit in its older form, which emphasizes values well beyond diversity, see David Shi, "The Simple Life: Plain Living and High Thinking in American Culture (Oxford Univ. Press, 1965), pp. 74-99: "Equally disturbing to the classical Republican sensibilities was the raging materialism that seemed to energize all ranks." See also *In Search of the Simple Life*, ed. David Shi (Gibbs Smith, Utah, 1986), pp. 79-80, 90, 96.

28. Of course, the rule of Fate—acting by way of natural, political or economic disasters—may change things. Consider Shi, *The Simple Life*, pp. 264-65, 280. A recent issue of *Time Magazine*, for example, noted: "In place of materialism, many Americans are embracing simpler pleasures and homier values" (Janice Castro, "The Simple Life," cover story, *Time Magazine*, April 8, 1991, p. 58.) Beyond antidotal accounts, the reasons given for this purported new trend were the stock market crash of 1987, higher unemployment, the recession, and the Gulf War. Whatever the accuracy of the magazine account, it is noteworthy that the same story also mentioned a new advertising campaign (by a major ad agency) designed to tap the market potential of this alleged trend in American life. See Castro, *Time,* p. 63.

29. In a very basic sense, there is no rootedness in the "global village." When technology (like industrialization) works to obliterate boundaries, as television does, then there is a corresponding loss of identity in, for example, one's ethnic culture and the development of a "sameness" sort of consciousness. Cf. *Letters of Marshall McLuhan*, eds. Matie Molinaro, Corinne McLuhan and William Toye (London: Oxford Univ. Press, 1987), p.253. Uprootedness in more modern times is the result of technological "conquest" as much as it is the consequence of military conquests of the ancient Roman and

World War II German varieties. For an insightful discussion of the general problem of uprootedness, see SimoneWeil, *The Need for Roots* (New York: G.P. Putman and Sons, 1952), especially pp. 43, 44, 99-184.

PART II

FATES AND FUTURES OF FREEDOM
IN EASTERN EUROPE:
UNDER COMMUNISM AND AFTER

CHAPTER V

SOVIET CULTURE:
HIDING TRANSCENDENCE

ALFONSAS ANDRIUSKEVICIUS

To be free must mean at least to have the opportunity to choose. This supposes knowledge of the existence of the phenomena you are going to prefer one over the other. Accordingly, eliminating choice does not mean necessarily prohibiting one's taking this way or another, selecting this thing or that. People can be barred from making choices (i.e. from being free) simply by not letting them know of the existence of relevant phenomena. In some sense this means destroying their very ability to choose. This method of preventing freedom to people by suppressing their opportunities is more sophisticated than that of simply not allowing them to choose among visible phenomena. The method was widely used in the Soviet system. Along with concealing many facts of social life (for example, it was announced there were no political prisoners in the USSR) and certain ideas (for example, it was impossible to obtain access to certain books of the present and past), Soviet ideologists tried to hide the transcendental aspect itself of Being in order to prevent people from making their own choice in its regard.

This report deals with the employment of these methods. Its main purpose is to show how Soviet ideologists tried to hide the transcendental aspect of Being by treating religion, nature and art in a particular manner. Attention will be paid primarily to the visual arts, namely, to painting.

RELIGION WITHOUT METAPHYSICS

In Soviet society religion was declared to be of no value, "the opium of the people," the instrument of the former ruling classes for manipulating the working people. But it was not destroyed entirely; religious life continued. Being conscious that religious aspirations are deeply rooted in human nature Soviet ideologists, instead of trying to prohibit religious life totally, chose another way of dealing with it. They strove to discredit religion by presenting it as a phenomenon of everydayness, i.e. as an expression of material interests. Thereby they attempted to deprive it of metaphysics, that is, of its function in revealing the transcendental aspect of Being. As a result, in spite of the continuing practice of religious life, the transcendental aspect of Being was to be forgotten and the possibility of making choice between the physical and the metaphysical was to be destroyed.

On the theoretical level they attempted to realize this plan by treating religion in the manner of some Enlightenment thinkers as a set of prejudices which, besides fulfilling the above mentioned social functions, had arisen in order to explain for the people the strange phenomena in nature. Now, they said, science could do this better.

On the practical level exaggerated attention was focused upon the behavior of priests and religious people, concentrating, of course, on past and present negative examples.

THE MATERIALISTIC INTERPRETATION OF NATURE

The ancient Greeks were astonished by the order they observed in nature. This provoked philosophical thought which led to acknowledging the transcendental as the foundation of this order and to revealing the metaphysical aspect of nature. Not to allow nature itself to remind people of its connection with the transcendent and not to allow scientists to speak about it, such was the task of Soviet ideologists. They fulfilled this on both the theoretical and the practical level.

In theory an ancient idea of man being superior to nature and of nature being merely material for man's practical purposes was accentuated. In Michurin's words it took the following shape: "We must not wait for gifts from nature; to take them by ourselves is our task." (Michurin was regarded as the best specialist on nature in Stalin's era and his somewhat surrealistic ideas for forcing nature to produce something against its own laws were notorious. For example, he announced the idea of crossing potato and tomato plants in order to get the benefits of both at once, as well as a plan to grow pears near the North pole.) The ideas of present and past scientists concerning the metaphysical aspect of nature were carefully concealed: their theories were falsified and their biographies censored. In other words, the natural sciences were stripped of their metaphysical dimension.

In practice, various plans for reconstructing nature—of "doing it over again"—were enthusiastically welcomed by Soviet ideologists. These plans had a specific role of which the planners themselves and their supporters were perhaps never clearly conscious, namely, not only to use nature (frequently against its laws) in order to satisfy current needs of the people, but also to make the face of nature as ugly as possible. Otherwise what could be the reason for those polluted lakes (including Baikal, in the past one of the purest lakes in the world) and rivers, for those dried seas (like Aral sea), for those tractor stations in former parks, for those livestock farms in the most beautiful hills, etc. Thanks to the effort at "doing nature over again," distortion, ugliness and disorder became the most visible features of the face of nature. Could these remind man of "the music of the planets" or stimulate him to think of the transcendental aspect of Being? It should be noted also that some of the giant plans for "doing nature over again" when fulfilled resulted in enormous ecological disasters. This could be seen as an emergence of nature's metaphysical aspect in its negative form.

SOCIALIST REALISM AS THE THEORY AND PRACTICE OF ART

The theory of socialist realism as the conscious principles of soviet art was designed to guarantee the implementation of the interests of the "working class" (and in reality those of the Communist Party) in social life by means of art. The widely known formula that in art the artist showed the world *sub specie aeternitatis* was replaced by the formula of showing it *sub specie hominis fabris*. Classical ideas of aesthetic values having nothing in common with practical interests were discouraged in art, whereas certain political values were promoted. The theory of socialist realism was totally utilitarian. Moreover, it defended 'particular interests'. Both these principles, utilitarianism and particularism, led to depriving art of its metaphysical dimension, thus to the impossibility of revealing by the means of art the transcendental aspect of Being, and finally towards forgetting it.

For art to have its metaphysical level means to be able to provide the observer with experience which:

(a) suggests some ideals connected with the highest human values;

(b) suggests fundamental questions regarding human existence; and

(c) helps one see the world and oneself *sub specie aeternitatis*.

On the contrary, art without a metaphysical dimension is able to provide only experience which suggests ideals and questions (or, often, such art merely declares them) connected with particular interests and with values of a lower rank. If the metaphysical level is essential it can be concluded immediately that no great piece of art can be created relying on principles of socialist realism.

To put the art of the past on the physical level served its interpretation as a reflection of class struggle. The examples suited to such an interpretation were declared to be milestones in the history of art; while those which were unsuitable for this purpose frequently were simply omitted, no matter what their degree of importance. This became,. for example, the fate of most of the medieval art.

Placing present art on the physical level facilitated the development of various regulations concerning its subject matter and specific language. First of all, art was stripped of all the subjects and images related to metaphysical thought, especially religious images. In the 1940s and 1950s special lists of subject matters for painting were approved by ideologists and distributed through the Artists' Union. These included scenes of battle between Soviet and German troops, of rebuilding the country, of work on the collective farms, etc. Representatives of the Soviet Army, workers and peasants were to be shown as heroes, fulfilling the tasks laid out for them by the Communist Party. An optimistic, heroic mood was to prevail.

Secondly, art was forbidden from using its specific language in its full range. Not only was the main attention paid to the subject matter (and not to, say, color, space or light), but along with this, a superficial likeness to nature was demanded. As a result, all those tendencies in art dealing with the distortion of nature for art's sake (namely, Expressionism, Abstract Art, etc.) were forbidden.

There can be two explanations of this suspicion of the specific language of art. First, this language was not understandable by the ideologists who therefore feared artists using it on purpose to say something illegal. Second, there was some feeling among party bureaucrats that the language of the arts itself, if used properly by a gifted artist, could say something more than the party considered appropriate. In other words, among Soviet ideologists there always was in one form or another the idea formulated by Heidegger that language is the home of Being. To block all the connections with the foundation of Being, to force people to forget its transcendental aspect, was for them a task of the greatest importance.

THREE RECENT STAGES OF LITHUANIAN PAINTING

In view of this it is of some interest to show how the situation in the visual arts in Lithuania changed from the end of the 1950s till now. It must be emphasized that during those years (and until recently) many artists worked as if on two levels producing both pictures to be shown at official exhibitions and others which were supposed to remain in their studios. My notes concern above all the first or official level.

The first step toward restoring painting to its normal situation was an unspoken permission to use its specific language on a broader scale than earlier, though restrictions regarding subject matter remained mainly in force except for some minor concessions. During this period, which began at the end of the 1950s, a number of strange pictures were created. The language of painting attempted to say something important, to speak about deeper problems. Paintings by more gifted artists tended towards the metaphysical level (because as a phenomenon of culture the language of art itself had a potential metaphysical dimension which it tended to express somehow through works of art). But the subject matter forced them to remain on the physical level, i.e. to proclaim shallow political slogans, to praise the politics of the Communist Party and to represent the world *sub specie hominis fabris*. It was as if trying to run with weights tied to one's legs.

The second stage in Lithuanian painting began with a substantial easing of the restrictions on the subject matter as well (this took place at the end of the 1970s and the beginning of the 1980s). During the period that follows, some drastic images—often fantastic and with strong symbolic meaning—emerge. Also a strange phenomenon can be observed: most of those images express the dark side of life; they are in some relation to the forces of evil, chaos and death. Distorted, crippled creatures, resembling human beings, replace in paintings the happy workers and peasants as well as their wise leaders. Those creatures are engaged in some sinister ritual. The colors of pictures, sometimes those connected in our consciousness with religious painting (for example, gold, red and blue), are arranged in such a way and provided with such extra tones that they speak of something devilish. The ominous darkness is close to defeating the light. The whole atmosphere sometimes is akin to that of the paintings of Bosch or Brueghel. For the most part this art speaks of destruction and ugliness. But it is very significant from our point of view that the art provide the spectator with experience (and it does so) suggesting problems of human destiny, the essence of man, the struggle between good and evil. By this experience, for the first time in the Soviet era Lithuanian art on a broad scale has returned to its metaphysical level and begun to reveal the transcendental aspect of Being, even though this was through revealing the forces of Darkness rather than of Light.

From another point of view the imagery of this stage of Lithuanian painting is also notable. During the Soviet period the representation of God, the Saints, angels, etc., was strictly forbidden in any kind of art including folk art. But representations of the devil and witches, especially in folk art, were permitted and widely used by some folk artists (for example, in Kaunas for several decades there was a Museum of Devils, containing a large collection of works by folk artists). But it must be emphasized that the image of the devil was reduced to the everyday, physical level; it was not represented as a transcendental force. So, on the one hand, though the painters of this period did not represent the devil or witches *in sensu strictu*, the imagery of this second phase had some roots in the past; nevertheless, on the other hand, it was an entirely new phase in art. For through this particular imagery plus the freedom of the specific language of painting, the metaphysical level of art returned.

It should be noted also that these unpleasant pictures urge the spectator to ask what is the source of evil, and then these pictures provide some immediate answers which vary according to the subject matter, style and individuality of the author. Four kinds of answers are to be found there: a) the existing social system, b) the fate of man, c) some dark external (transcendental) forces, or d) subconsciousness.

A third stage of Lithuanian painting is distinguished by the appearance in public of metaphysically-oriented pictures representing in one way or another the bright side of life. They move one deeply, providing the experience which also suggests questions regarding human destiny and the essence of man, as well as those of eternity, God, etc., though by other means. The ritual which appears there is the right one; the colors have their sacral meaning again; light prevails (at times dissolving the objects) and provides the soul with joyful relief. Such pictures speak about harmony, beauty and cosmos. The pictures suggest the following answers to the question of the source of good: a) the principles of some mythical society, which has existed "before the beginning of time," b) faith, religious life, c) some bright external (transcendental) forces, or d) super-consciousness. Their public appearance is the result of the removal of all restrictions on subject matter and on specific language, though a significant portion of them was created during the period when those restrictions were still in force. Various sub-languages of painting are used by the authors, varying from the realistic to the abstract. But from our point of view the most important thing is that this painting expresses (or attempts to express) in an evident manner the metaphysical level. Thus, Lithuanian painting returns to metaphysics once again.

CONCLUSIONS

The social and cultural life in the Soviet system, a system which was anxious above all to reproduce itself, i.e., to assure the interests of those who run it, were so organized and directed as to destroy the normal hierarchy of human values at the top of which are those of metaphysics. In achieving these aims Soviet ideologists frequently preferred not to fight metaphysical values openly by criticizing them or simply prohibiting people from attending to them. They chose the more sophisticated method of forcing the population to forget metaphysical values and the transcendental aspect of Being by treating various phenomena of culture in a specific way. Religion, the natural sciences, and art were thus deprived of their metaphysical level.

To forget something or not to know of its existence means that it is excluded from one's field of choices. By forcing people to forget or not to know of the transcendental aspect of Being and the values representing it, Soviet ideologists deprived the population of the opportunity of basic choice, the fundamental option without which no real freedom is possible.

Returning to democracy means among other things returning to freedom of choice and above all to the fundamental option. But this supposes a knowledge of the existence of the two aspects or levels of Being and of culture: the physical and the metaphysical. This is possible only on condition that various phenomena of culture function freely without any restrictions either in theory or in practice.

CHAPTER VI

CULTURE AND POPULAR CULTURE IN POST-COLD WAR CENTRAL EUROPE

SILVIA NAGY

> *Tout est bu, tout est mangé. Plus rien à dire*
> —Paul Verlaine

Culture is, of course, a highly elusive thing. Elusive, not because it fails to be experienced concretely, but rather because its experience is so pervasive that we are hard-pressed to identify or delineate it. It is like trying to seize air: One finds that it is everywhere, except within one's grasp. Mercifully, my concern is not culture, but popular culture. Yet, even thus qualified, it is a bafflingly complex amalgam of human creativity, and human convention, in which deliberation and intended purpose play their part along with accidents of habit, custom, and the sundry imponderables of fortune and sheer mystery.

Popular culture, as opposed to high culture, developed side by side throughout history. Bakhtin describes popular culture as a deep underlying current based on magic, which draws its incessant energies from the depth of instinct. Popular culture is manifested in the "official culture" and vice-versa: it incorporates some elements left behind by the same "official culture."[1] Nevertheless, the development of civilization caused a bifurcation in this parallel development. In the increasingly complicated condition of the division of labor the reproduction of knowledge is more and more at the hands of different groups of specialists. The definition of knowledge, and the determination of things to know are very important factors in a power structure. In fact, they are so important, that in almost all societies (in some more, in some less; in some overtly, in some in disguise) the elite holds the privilege of formation of all intellectual margins, within which one might acquire a sense of reality based on a collective experience of knowledge. Consequently, the "official culture" always appears to have the image of universality and it is a sole monopoly of a very narrow segment of the society. The popular culture—historically declared to be low-class or unworthy—has been curtailed, even persecuted, which did not result in the reduction of its popularity; it survives in certain segments of the society. This is particularly true in case of an ethnic or cultural minority, which has been torn away from its own original high culture.

Today's popular culture is increasingly widespread, and seems to condemn us to a certain uniformity. As ironic as it may appear, all the different forms of media constitute one commercial system; even the aesthetic manifestations of opposing political views are quite the same by provoking similar psychological reactions, and by using similar artistic/literary resources as stimuli. Adorno, and other members of the Frankfurt school of philosophy, represent a rather pessimistic view of today's cultural expressions, which— according to them—is often substituted by commercial efforts of mere entertainment.

Entertainment is a prolongation of work in late capitalism.[2] The individual seeks entertainment in order to disconnect himself from the mechanized work process, so that later he will be able to participate in it again. The same mechanization which produces more and more articles used for entertainment, and has acquired such a power over the life of the individual, even causes that the indiviudal, in his free time, must simulate parts of the work process. The content is a pretext, there is a need for the repetition of a series of mechanical acts. The joy of entertainment freezes into boredom, because it is disassociated from intellectual effort and is based on old mechanized stereotypies. The spectator must not have his or her own thoughts; the product used for entertainment prescribes all reactions. These are not caused by the recognition of relations of cause and effect, but by signs which suppose certain psychological response without serious intellectual involvement.

We must add to this, that entertainment as a need is an abstract need; it is an activity which reproduces unchanged the societal relations, and it provokes only a reproduction of the individual's intellectual capacity, because of its deliberate exclusion from the different entertainment practices. These practices confine themselves to compensate for psychological lacks through amusement, but these feelings will not add to the personal and intellectual growth of the individual.

In a general sense, the commercialization of art and culture (be noted that the terms "art" and "culture" are used in their broadest sense) has been a hard blow to humanity, particularly in those countries, where in the recent past cultural expression has been oppressed, and other restrictions have been imposed.

According to Polish writer Jan Blonski,[3] the intellectuals of

Central Europe (*Mitteleuropa*)[4] are just recovering their right to their own history, which was monopolized by the government during the Socialist era. On the other hand, a German writer Hans Christoph Buch[5] suggests that literature coming from Central Europe is better, because dictatorship produces better stories, and censorship sharpens the style. This is to be added to the ever existing cultural dichotomy of the Central European nations, whose culture is mainly Western, yet their lives are shaped by the East. According to Hungarian writer Péter Esterházy:

> We are the East Europeans:
> Our nerves are rugged,
> our toilet paper is rough.[6]

This duality, together with the dictatorial regimes and the consequent censorship, produced a fragmented and splintered literature in which no dialogue takes place, but merely a series of parallel monologues. As a result there is not one, but three literatures in these countries: The officially published and approved literature; and the one that generally became known as *samizdat*, that is: writings produced unofficially and circulated inside of the country; and finally what the Russians called *tamizdat*, or literature published outside of the country, and often imported afterwards.

In spite of the officially imposed "norms," some writers in this century, when a moral indignation pushes them to take the floor and speak up, do so. (Morality is the sex appeal of literature— according to Witold Gombrowicz.) According to the view shared by some less politically and more aesthetically oriented intellectuals, martial law in Poland was a disaster for literature not because of censorship, not because of an oppressive regime, but because all literature moved to the noble-minded side, namely that to be against dictatorship, to be against crushing the Solidarity movement by tanks, was a noble cause. As Czeslaw Milosz, a Polish poet suggests, these ideas are very dangerous for literature.

> I realized it very early, and tried not to contribute— with some exception, I should say —to that atmosphere of high style morality. Many times I was inclined to say *non_serviam*, as young James Joyce said about the Irish cause, and I was torn internally between a desire to practice what I consider perfection in literature and a cry of anger.[7]

In Eastern Europe the moral and historical dimensions of literature go back to the 19th century and beyond. In Western Europe, however, writers were not interested in historical situations. Flaubert did not care so much for the history of France: he cared for Madame Bovary, and for the beauty of the sentence. He had, in fact, a greater interest in the history of Carthage, than in the history of France. The strength of Western literature rested in the interest in the metaphysical and the aesthetic. Now it seems that the situation has been reversed, because the West also experienced a taste of defeat, the taste of history. Eastern Europe was always regarded as provincial. Now everybody seems provincial in cultural terms, because high cultures have been over-run by the popular media, which has been possible by the technical advances of our era. The limitations in accessing high culture seem voluntary, rather than imposed.

The criteria for the definition of products belonging to high culture as such, is the recognition, or merely the acknowledgement of their existence. One of the problems of literary works in Eastern Europe is that they are not widely read because of the language-barrier. The literature of countries whose languages are not well-known is often ignored, slighted or filtered through a third language. On the other hand, is it necessary for a work to be translated into a well-known language to become part of the world culture? Should the intellectuals worry about their writing being translated right away? Is it just a matter of finding a translator and a sponsor who will undertake the marketing efforts? The criterion for becoming part of world literature must be based on other principles. Nobody knows which book will eventually become an element of world culture, and when or if it might happen. For instance, the ancient Greek literature is clearly part of world culture, we have all been raised on it—yet no Greek ever worried whether his books will be translated to other languages. Furthermore, Sumerian literature is certainly considered part of world culture, and no one has ever read it. The Sumerians invented the wheel, and did not worry whether people were going to use it—and yet—the whole ancient world was built on the wheel. But the world changed (fortunately or unfortunately?) since the Sumerians, even since the Greeks, and Milan Kundera might be right in suggesting that

> . . . the great mission of the small nations which in today's world have been delivered to the tender mercies of the Great Powers and squelched and

flattened by their measures[:]—By their incessant
search for their own identity and by their fight for
survival, the small nations resist the terrifying push
toward uniformity on earth, making it glitter with a
wealth of traditions and customs, so that human
individualism, marvel, and originality can find a home
in this world. . . . I am convinced that the world
would be better and less gloomy if the voices of
Guatemalans, Estonians, Vietnamese, and Danes had
a weight equal to the voices of Americans, Chinese
or Russians.[8]

It is evident that translation is not the only point for
discussion. (Susan Sontag lived two years in Sweden, she loves the
art of Ingmar Bergman, but was to discover that the Swedes do not
consider Bergman a Swedish artist.) What will become of world
literature once the linguistic barrier is no longer a problem?
Translation—which is very rapid and widespread today—helps us
to convey our own national identities, but the linguistic factor is lost;
not only that, but also the very context in which the work was created.
The translator can only reproduce the form, of what remains of the
form, but he cannot give life to the soil in which this form grew or to
the spirit which motivates it. Nor can he translate the context, the
group, the readership for which a work was produced. Does a world
culture exist? One might say that it is an empirical fact that such a
culture does exist, but one cannot feel it. Each individual exists as
part of humanity, yet every one lives within his own reference group,
which is much smaller. So, how might one combine this enormous
variety and these continuous changes within this totally real but
hardly palpable, absolutely necessary, but not necessarily useful
category, which is called world culture?

Once again, it must be stressed that in the development of a
world culture and world art—without which humanity cannot exist—
there is an increase in qualitative differentiation. It is a dialectic
process without which there would be no development at all. There
are different mass-culture products which day after day inundate
our lives, and the pressure for using them is increasing. As the
industrial production develops to a capability never heard of, the
powerful means of production and marketing do not fit within a
small enterprise. The publishing industry is not independent from
the other forms of media. The commercially controlled mass-culture
slowly substitutes real culture, that which is born freely, inspired by

the creative powers of a human group. Thus tradition loses its validity, its raison d'être, and culture loses its creative capacity: it can no longer express the very essence of humans belonging to the same cultural group, and it can no longer confirm their cultural identity. Consequently, these groups become vulnerable to the aggressiveness of commercialized mass-culture. This danger seems very real in Central European countries where several decades of government controlled media have produced a void in the cultural continuity of those nations.

NOTES

1. Mikhail Bakhtin, *François Rabelais müvészete, a középkor és a reneszánsz népi kulturája* (Budapest: Mérleg Könyvek, 1982).

2. Horkheimer and Adorno: *Dialektik der Aufklarung* (Frankfurt, 1969).

3. Jan Blonski, at the Lisbon Conference on Literature, a Round Table of Central European and Russian Writers sponsored by the Wheatland Foundation of New York, under the auspices of Dr. Mario Soarez, the president of Portugal, in 1990.

4. Central Europe and Eastern Europe will be used as equal terms, given the fact that they are not used in the geographical, but rather in a political sense. It seems that during the Cold War in an effort at political polarization the term "Eastern Europe" was used. Now that the Cold War is over, these same countries rapidly have become "Central Europe."

5. Hans Christoph Buch, The Lisbon Conference, 1990.

6. Péter Esterházy, *Kis magyar irodalomtörténet* (Budapest: Szépirodalmi Könyvkiadó, 1987).

7. Czeslaw Milosz, *Hazátlan költészet* (Budapest: Magvetö, 1990). Translation is my own.

8. Milan Kundera, "Introduction to a Variation" in *Jacques and his Master,* translated by M.H. Heim (New York, 1980).

CHAPTER VII

LIFE IN THE RETORT AND SOON AFTER

TOMAS SODEIKA AND ARUNAS SVERDIOLAS

In this seminar on freedom and choice in democracy I would like to propose an analysis of some post-totalitarian conditions for thinking about society in my country, Lithuania, and some other East European countries. A second title for my paper could be "freedom and choice in a post-totalitarian situation." This situation can be characterized by two main features: first, society has chosen the democratic way; it has accepted the principles of democracy as right and desirable. Second, this choice is an *idea* which has not yet been accomplished in the concrete, everyday life of this society. This second circumstance obliges us to pay special attention to the heritage of actual thought which characterizes this society and effects our present. For the people who live the reality of liberal democracy this description may clarify the negative and nihilistic experience of non-democracy, and in this way help their thinking get to the roots of freedom and choice.

One of the most fundamental factors forming the conscious-ness of post-totalitarian society is Marxist-Leninist philosophy whose influences is felt on two levels: as a monopolistic ideology of the state and as a constitutive principle of the society itself.

SALTO VITALE—SALTO MORTALE

In considering any social phenomena and social life as a whole, we find two different kinds of connections. On the one hand the thinking and acting of a people is determined by their *interests*. As man cannot live without food, clothes and home these elementary needs form something that might be called social physics. This is the level of social reality linked by causal connections of the interests. On the other hand, most human acts are directed by purposes; they are directly or indirectly linked with some ideals, i.e. they are value-oriented. This bring to light another level of social reality which transcends the limits of the material, physical being of the society and in this sense can be named social metaphysics. Social life takes place on both planes at once: the level of social physics formed by the causal connections of interests, and the level of social metaphysics formed by the teleological connections of ideals.

Marxist social theory appears as a kind of anti-metaphysical program. Classically, Marxism considered its main theoretical aim to be the creation of a materialistic view of history which makes it possible to see the development of the society as an objective process determined by reason without dependence on the human will. Engels wrote: "As Darwin discovered the law of the development of the organic world, so Marx discovered the law of the development of human history: the simple fact, covered till now by ideological layers, that the people first of all have to eat, to drink, to have home and clothes and only after this will they be able to deal with politics, science, art, religion, and so on". This materialistic theory of history qualifies all other conceptions of society as ideologies, consciously or unconsciously, naively or cynically presenting a distorted view of social reality.

According to Marxism, these ideologies search out the fundamentals of human actions (or conceal them—the two opposites coincide) in the field of moral, religious, political and other ideals. The materialistic or scientific theory of the society considers the real ground of human actions to be not "ideal motivational forces," but "the moving causes of these ideal motivational forces" (Engels). This conception aspires "to trace behind any moral, religious, political or social phrases, declarations or promises the interests of one or another class"(Lenin), and usually it succeeded. In other words, in dealing with concepts or ideals it immediately searches behind the interests, asking the question: "whom does it profit?"

Generally speaking, the question *cui bono* is not at all new or unusual; it belongs to the storehouse of traditional European concepts. But until now techniques of suspicion were applied locally and empirically as a mean for searching out criminals. The work of the courts was based upon a presumption of innocence of the accused. Here the technique becomes universal and *a priori*. The theorist judges all the social reality, not only tracing, but even punishing criminals and indeed each person, group or class who thinks about or acts in society. This technique of suspicion allows one to explain and evaluate every socially significant truth or value in a very special way—as a function of interest. The small merchant's mistrust of the words of his clients becomes the example for the theorist in researching social reality: "although in everyday life even each *shopkeeper* can perfectly distinguish what a man feigns and what he really is, our historiography does not reach this trivial knowledge. It believes the words of each epoch, believes all that is said or imagined about itself" (Marx and Engels).

What happens when suspicion is universalized and ideas and values are reduced to interests? The answer seems clear. Interests as elements of social physics can be discovered and fixed in objective terms much easier then ideals which are disclosed in the space of social metaphysics. Social theory, grounded on an analysis of interests, becomes more definitive and concrete; it approaches the criteria of rationality of natural sciences and according to the estimation of the authors becomes the first non-metaphysical, scientific theory of society.

But this is not the most important point. Marxists adhere to the Baconian orientation of the knowledge: to know an object means to master it. Knowledge of the laws ruling social reality becomes a force for the active reconstruction of this reality. Equating the materialistic theory of history with the natural sciences, the authors of this theory were convinced, that if we could have knowledge of the laws which rule society, we could construct a corresponding social technology and shape society in a desirable fashion. Lenin wrote: "Engels obviously applies the 'saltovital' method in philosophy, that is, he makes a jump from theory to practice." Materialistic social theory is "saltovital," which means that it permits us to pass from theory to practice. Knowing the regularity of the interests hidden "behind all the phrases," that is, behind every discourse on values and formed in the process of production, one can control, regulate and coordinate these interests and so improve society.

This trick of theoretical-practical acrobatics determined the actual situation of our society. Marxist social theory was applied practically: an experiment on an unprecedented scale was carried out according to a reductive anti-metaphysical social theory; thereby society was created.

IN VITRO

In a society grounded on these reductive principles generally speaking there would be no social metaphysics. In classical society ideals have a regulative function: they permit the realization of the aims of human actions and guarantee the stability of social life. Based on their ideals, for example, confidence between people becomes possible. When social metaphysics is qualified as ideology, unmasked as illusion and perfidy, we pass on to "reality," where stability is guaranteed by physical means alone. In a concentration camp there is no need to explain or to argue the correctness of this or that command: the order is based on pure force and fear.

Whereas the ideals or elements of a social metaphysics are essentially universal, the interests or elements of a social physics are essentially particular. In the scientifically organized society the particular interests of its members must be coordinated by social technologists who through permissions and prohibitions guarantee the stable and unified structure of society. There is no need for confidence in such a society; it is quite enough that social technologists on the base of a social theory disposing of correspondingly constructed means guarantee the balance of particular interests (these interests are not "declared" by their subjects, but are "real," that is, scientifically ascertained).

For the functioning of this society there is not only no need of a metaphysics conceptualizing and constituting the systems of values, but, as we will see later, metaphysics is dangerous for this society. Nevertheless, it is impossible to destroy metaphysics completely. As Kant said, metaphysics always exists "if not as a science (or systematic whole), still as a natural inclination." Man is a metaphysical being searching for ideals that cannot be contained on the physical level of interests. In the nature of man lies hidden the seeds of human solidarity and the search for freedom, heroism and sacrifice. But there must be a sort of metaphysical space in social life for these seeds to open and to become regulative or constitutive elements of the social reality. Mutual confidence between people is born in their hearts, but it can be realized definitively only on condition that people confess publicly the ideals which unite them.

Let us take as an example the ideal of love of our neighbor. The very word indicates the origin of this ideal: *neighbor* is a man who is *near by*. But neighborhood is not only physical or psychological nearness, for people crowded in a bus or metro are not neighbors, although they are very near one to another. We can speak about the love of our neighbor only if by means of a corresponding metaphysics the direct feeling of nearness is transferred to the level of universal principles. In this case the notion of neighbor has not a physical, but a metaphysical sense. The very important and very complicated task of metaphysics is to connect the universality of the principle and the particularity of our actual feeling. If we read in the paper news about a catastrophe experienced anywhere by an immense number of people, we can understand and feel this as part of our common human destiny only if we have metaphysics. By developing and grounding values metaphysics enables us to go beyond feelings of physical nearness and psychological attachment to the love of neighbor as a principle which grounds the confidence and solidarity between a people.

Metaphysics as a natural inclination of man is manifest also in the case where we have to live in a retort or artificially constituted social life-space. When the social experimenter pours in the broth and adds culture (the human material), the development of both the physical and metaphysical possibilities of human nature begin. The artificial circumstances of human life cannot change this nature, just as the artificial pseudo-Renaissance or pseudo-Barocco styles of the Moscow metro cannot change its nature as architecture or organization of human space. But this artificiality can deform and degrade human life. The walls of a retort limit the cultural and mental horizon of the inhabitants. Metaphysical possibilities can be realized within only "de-metaphysisized," reduced forms. Growing children can become only either "pioneers" (members of the super-ideologized soviet youth organization) or hooligans; either they squeeze themselves into the given forms or became antisocial.

If metaphysical energy (conscience, sense aspiration, etc.) turn against these inadequate forms, it can became only pure negative protest—self-destruction (as with the Lithuanian teenager, Romas Kalanta, who burned himself to death some years ago). The heroes of the very popular earlier novel *Timur and His Detachment* by Russian children's writer, Arkadij Gajdar, cared for old people and protected the weak. Human solidarity was realized within the framework of the pioneer ideology, but the deeper Christian roots of this ideology remain quite unknown to the readers.

Much more important is the fact that the solidarity and confidence proclaimed here remains within the framework of the local group (in our case, in some age group). In the retort these principles cannot articulate public life. It is impossible to universalize them; they remain hidden within the personal privacy or the particularity of the group. Public life is both technologically and ideologically articulated by another kind of law, namely, the scientifically fixed law of class interests. In this sense society lives not in just one retort, but in a system of retorts. The supposed real, that is the physical life of this society freed from metaphysical illusions, is not developing, and interests do not exercise their mutual influence. In the many retorts and test-tubes of the social laboratory, life is "bubbling up." Glass walls divide one process from another; only the laboratory assistant can change anything, and then simply by moving retorts from one place to another, transfusing or pouring out their content. The life, restricted within the glass, can fill almost the whole laboratory, but it is impossible to say that the laboratory is a live organism.

THE SQUARE CIRCLE

In the scientifically organized society, though metaphysics is proclaimed to be a dying remnant, it constantly threatens this society. The danger is rooted in the metaphysical nature of each man enclosed in the retort, in the seeds of ideals which cannot be effectively scientifically controlled and which at any moment can begin to open. There always remains the danger that the values, reduced to interests, might begin to regenerate and destroy the mosaic of the retorts. In order to prevent that it is not enough to reject metaphysics and proclaim that values are only a cover for interests. Nor is it enough to construct and launch an engine based on the principles of social physics. Something else, a quasi-meta-physics , is needed to occupy the place of metaphysics. The role of that quasi-metaphysics is played by the so-called scientific ideology.

The concept of a scientific ideology is self-contradictory. Were the ideals theoretically reduced to interests, there would be nothing for the ideologist to do except to criticize other ideologies beyond the glass. Actually, Marxist ideologists live, like Vikings, on their prey, for almost the entire positive content of their statements is stolen from their ideological opponents. This militant production only obscures the paradox of reductive, de-ideologizing ideology, but does not destroy its paradox.

In spite of this paradox, besides the social theorist and technologist, we always discover an ideologist. It is by his efforts that a special kind of ideology, namely de-ideologizing ideology or so-called common Marxism, functions in social consciousness. Social theory, adopting the trivial knowledge of the shopkeeper, asking "whom does it profit?", has lost the character of an open question and become a rhetorical figure. Asking this question one does not aspire to learn something new, because all was clear and known long ago: the suspicious stare discerns interests everywhere. Every idea, every ideal, every action is received in terms of this question, which points out behind the mind, word or act one who thinks, speaks or acts this way because he is interested, because it is profitable for him. Where classical ideology introduces and protects social values, reductive ideology destroys them, introducing a nihilistic view of values.

On the other hand, this reductive ideology is not at all critical: nihilism is not criticism. Official ideologists give birth to positive ideological substance which is a quasi-metaphysics because its purpose is to occupy the place of authentic social metaphysics. The task of ideologist is to occupy the place in the social consciousness and so to preserve reductive thinking about the society and acting in the society. The content and the quality of the produced ideology is not important.

The real political structure of this society, the real mechanism of power is not reflected in this ideology and remains hidden. Ideology reproduces another picture: seeming democracy, seeming elections, seeming common approval of the system, and so on. No one believes in these surreal things, but no one doubts them either. How is it possible to doubt the slogan: "The party leads us to communism!"? What can we contrast to this statement? Perhaps: "The party leads not us (that means someone else) to communism!"? Or: "Some non party (that means someone else) lead us to communism!"? Or: "The party leads us not to communism!" (which means that it holds us in the same place or leads us elsewhere)? Amateurs in logical permutations could compose more alternative slogans ("Not us," "not party . . .," etc.), but all these variations, in spite of their logical radicality (negation), nevertheless remain on the same plane, where we find: "we," "party," "communism," and "leading," no matter how we combine these things. The space of these possible permutations is the space of reformism and revisionism of this ideology. But all such attempts at reformation cannot achieve what is most important, namely, to discover the fictitious character of all these realities.

On the other hand, for a long time only a very small number of people were deceived by these fictions. Slogans usually were perceived not as texts, but as ornaments. Everyone knew also that it was nonsense to try to utilize the mechanism of elections, because the real way governmental institutions were formed was quite different. Thus, the consciousness of irreality of the most important mechanisms of social life became the last refuge for reason, conscience and taste.

Nevertheless this consciousness participated in the life of this society and even supported it. Under the conditions of ideological monopoly this consciousness of irreality of fundamental mechanisms of democratic society fed the same mechanism of reduction of values, nihilism and the view that each ideological text is absurd. The genuine task of ideology was not to show that this picture of social reality was true, but to paralyze real thinking and acting. The people did not protest the fictitious realities not because they consented to them, but because they were resigned to think on and act in a society. In the social consciousness ideology preempted the space where the socially significant ideas, ideals and acts can spread.

VITALITY OF THE REMNANTS AND THE END OF MECHANISM

There are things whose significance is apprehended completely only when they are lost. This is true of the revolutionary idea of improving man by performing an appendectomy on newborn children in order to prevent this illness in their adult years; it had to be rejected when it turned out that the appendix is necessary for the normal development and functioning of the organism. The same thing happens with the attempts to eliminate the remnants of ideals. It may seem that the society itself does not change in accordance with concepts used to describe it; that it would not matter if we considered the ultimate explanation of social life to be ideals and values or the interests which are hidden behind them—in any case the social reality would be the same and its features do not depend upon the standpoint of the subject.

But society is a very particular thing—not only are there direct relations, but there is also play-back between the object and subject. *Perestroika* would hardly have begun except for something that cannot be explained scientifically, namely, in a society where all illusions about the origin of "ideal motivational forces" supposedly had been dissipated and the significance of interests to the life of the society had been clarified, those interests themselves began to vanish. For the man who had been liberated from illusions and scientifically enlightened, it began to cease to matter what and how he worked and even how much he gained from his work! It became clear that even the material interests transplanted into the retort had atrophied, for it began to be supposed that it was better to work less and get less than to work more and get more. Of course, it would be wrong to ignore the fact that interest in earning depends upon the possibility of buying, so that if the shops are empty it makes no sense to work. But we should not omit what can be called the metaphysical dimension of work. It appears that if work is perceived on the level of social physics alone and is treated as an activity directed to production only, it loses its intrinsic sense and value.

It would seem that after performing a social appendectomy,

eliminating the seat of illusory images about social life and explaining the real mechanisms of social processes, and after using this knowledge for the ordering of society, society would move rapidly forward. But that did not happen. On the contrary, social processes slowed down and the social structures began to disintegrate. This paradox appeared even on the level of economics where, it seems, only objective processes take place. It became clear that it was possible to destroy even the elementary structures of social life just by treating them physically, as if the material were the most real or even the only real thing.

We would seem to be going in the direction of consistent rationalization, but quite the reverse takes place: society becomes an unconscious element. It would seem that if we know the laws ruling society we can create and use effectively a social technology, but quite the contrary takes place: technological knowledge in practice destroys the very thing it treats as fundamental, namely, interest. In the same way that reflection paralyzes the physiological processes of a person (eating or sex), so reflection on anatomy and physiology paralyzes social life. Where it would seem that if we know reality, we could use our own discretion in seeking the maximum of happiness, the contrary takes place—when illusions are dissipated we see that the things treated as illusions really are a form of play-back. Objective explanations do not reveal the reality, but break off the play-back channel.

The crisis of a scientifically ordered society makes manifest the insufficiency of social physics. What appears is that for the normal life of society there are required ideals and values which are hidden in the heart of every man. These are indestructible metaphysical inclinations which give men confidence in one another. The fundamental principle of every social system, the free association of people, proclaims: *pacta sunt servanda*. But it is impossible to create or even expect that deception become physically impossible and the suspicion not arise. Universal human ideals cannot ignore the particular interests of individuals, groups and classes, which always exist, but they must overcome them by creating common interest, as it is problematically called, in the political philosophy of Enlightenment. Accord, solidarity and confidence on the part of the people are possible not due to the credulous who do not suspect anything or anybody. For this we need conscious, metaphysical "naïveté."

REVERSE *SALTO* AND WHAT THEN

This collision determined the past of our social consciousness. Must we worry about it today when the retort, if not completely broken, at least is slightly cracked? With the fall of its monopoly the Marxist ideology at once collapsed. The main principles of Marxist-Leninist philosophy were proclaimed openly and without much explanation as out-of-use dogmas. However, in speaking about renewal we must not forget that in the life of society nothing dies once and for all. Of especially great vitality are the structures of consciousness. Seen from this specific perspective, the radical novelty of our present time promises to be the next episode of the 'collision' already discussed.

Soviet ideology has been revised and a new version created, which could be characterized first of all as an attempt to find a substitute for universal ideals in the context of a reductionist social theory and the ideology based upon it. For example, the so-called acknowledgement of the priority of universal human values is an attempt to formulate the supposedly new but certainly classical or pre-reductionist type of ideological programme, using reductionist theory as a means. "The world is a boat and we cannot steer it, as we are inside" (Gorbachev). This "boat of the world" is exactly the pre-image of the common interest, seemingly coinciding with a universal ideal. The form of the statement is universal ("what I must do to protect the existence of the human race") as concerning a value-oriented imperative, but its content is particular as an interest-oriented maxim ("what I have to do in order not to drown with all the others"). But to acknowledge universal human values means the same as to acknowledge a universal interest, which was considered to be the greatest illusion and lie of an ideology. Holding to the logic of Marxist conception, we would come to the conclusion that when the common interests spring up, class struggle and history itself must cease. Not only is the building up of communism impossible; it is dangerous even to change anything—or in the simile of the boat, to move at all—for this may be fatal to the equilibrium of world forces.

Recently Marxist-Leninist historiosophy, as essentially turned to the future and providing for world-wide social changes, reveals a great contrast. The ideological programme of *perestroika* is not situated within the context of world history, but is designed only as an episode in the "development" of local socialism, fitting all into the present. Indeed we can call it a programme only conditionally, because now the long text of socialist ideology has been reduced to a name or label placed on another's product: "socialist" market, "socialist" pluralism, national communist party. Today the ideological project of socialism seems to be minimalized—the future perspective of humanity is not considered, the construction of communism is shyly passed over in silence. Only concrete daily tasks, most of all economic, are spoken of. The project vanishes; only a daily pragmatism remains.

It seems that the ballast occupying the space of the social consciousness has now been removed and that this empty space must somehow be filled. The former, Marxist ideologists try to perform a rare trick—reverse saltation. As if having forgotten the scientificity of their ideology, they look for eternal values and spirituality. They feel no repugnance even to religion, which up to now was considered as the paradigmatic illusion, the illusion *par excellence*. Now they are going to cooperate with the Church in sustaining and restoring ruined morality.

The longing for universal human ideals and values flows from the metaphysical nature of the human person. However, the long time spent in the retort cannot pass without its traces. It is not easy to get rid of the reductionism implanted by the materialistic interpretation of social reality. It perdures in the creation of new social projects introduced as the opposite of the materialistic treatment of the society—for instance, in choosing democracy and confessing the ideal of freedom.

In the attempt to rebuild a reduced level of social metaphysics, ideals and values become the means for seeking other aims. One says: if we want to have the good life, we must work honestly, we must have honesty. But is conscience a means for the good life? Must the man be honest in order to reach the good life? Is not conscience that for which we have to sacrifice, if necessary, not only prosperity but much more as well? Or it is said: since our political situation now is so difficult, do not become liberals now; temporarily, until gaining independence, let us be nationalists in order to save our unity. But liberalism or nationalism are matters of fundamental choice. Those who think we can change those things according to the present moment are treating them simply as means.

Reductionist thinking makes a jumble of values and neglects their hierarchy. In this way truth, good and beauty become the means used to protect society against antisocial behaviour. The ideal of self-sacrifice becomes the means for solving problems of medical care, the attachment of farmer to the land the means for supplying food, maternal love the means for insuring a favorable demographics. Social consciousness must be stocked with ideals and values in the same manner shops must be stocked with goods. Man must become spiritual so that the goods can be of perfect quality.

After all the destructive heritage of our social thinking, the vacuum left by reductive ideology influences also the theoretical interpretation of the present situation. Here and now in attempting to think over the ideals and values and their function in social consciousness our mind inevitably slips on the plain surfaces of pragmatism and vain desire. One of the effects of the longtime influence of reductive ideology on society is that everyone who aspires to think over the present situation of ideals finds himself in a reflective position. Certainly we can ask: Is the ambivalence of reflection not a characteristic feature of any philosophical work? Does not philosophical work always take place at the boundary of nihilism? This is true, but our present situation is particular because not only the professional philosopher, but everyone finds himself in such a situation. That is why philosophy becomes for us an almost daily necessity.

What can a philosopher tell people today, when the life of society is coming out of the retort? One thing is clear enough—in sketching the future we must not reduce ideals to interests and social metaphysics to social physics. It does not matter whether these reductions are carried on as they were in the past, by a theoretical and technological reordering of society, or in "today's" manner, by trying to bring back values in order to motivate the desired thinking and behavior of citizens.

The positive aim is metaphysical reflection: thinking over ideals and values in such a way that questions about their benefits do not arise. The human person, truth, freedom, conscience and other things must be perceived as self-evident values. If questions about their utility nevertheless arise, it is clear that we have not yet perceived the ideal as ideal, have not yet reached the level of metaphysics: all our considerations remain then on the level of social physics and social technology.

Also we cannot design the ideals according to given parameters. The philosopher cannot set for himself the task of "making" and presenting for social use one or another ideal. His task is more modest and more difficult: using the critical intellect to unmask all quasi-metaphysics and quasi-ideals, the philosopher must keep such a distance that the ideal can be seen clearly. The philosopher has to control his reflection and keep ideals in focus in order to clarify them.

Nothing more can be said responsibly here. Even the task of creating metaphysics cannot be advanced. Metaphysics can arise only by itself in free creative act; to foresee this is impossible. What is possible to perceive only reflectively is that metaphysics means *to be*. A "foreseeing reflection" is a contradiction in terms; what is foreseen therein could only be empty and infected by pragmatism. It is possible to give only minimal and negative indications, to outline the limits of positive philosophical work. Metaphysics must be or exist. If it does not, it is impossible to indicate its traits. Nevertheless, an authentic consciousness of values, solidarity and confidence by the people can be supported only on the basis of an existing metaphysics.

DISCUSSION OF CHAPTER VII

1. We are presently in a post-totalitarian situation. That is, society has accepted the principles of democracy but this remains for now an idea; it has yet to be integrated into the circumstances of our life. Hence, in order to prepare positively for the future we need to look at the negative remnants of totalitarianism in our society. This is important not only for practical goals in Eastern Europe, but for all people to help them deepen their choice for democracy.

To do this one can distinguish between what might be termed "social physics" and "social metaphysics." Whereas the latter expresses the value-oriented character of society, the former expresses the concerns for food, clothing and shelter. This is the level of interests about which it is always necessary to ask: whom does it profit? This is not a new question, but Marxism has radicalized it into a philosophy of suspicion in which all is seen as a function of interests. In this attitude knowledge is seen as power (Bacon) which is to be used for reconstructing society. Classically ideals were universal and regulative, and contributed to the stability of social life. Since interests are particular, however, there is need for a social technology to coordinate the multiple particular interests. Hence, stability comes only from force.

It is important to note that metaphysics cannot be destroyed. Kant noted its double character, i.e., both as science and as natural inclination. Both require social space in order to open and regulate social reality. Thus, when society is restricted solely by the laws of class interests it becomes a kind of laboratory, test tube or retort, which seeks the articulation of its ideals via scientific laws as a quasi-metaphysics—which, indeed, is a contradiction in terms. When metaphysics is thus attacked so that its values cannot be universalized to public life, it reemerges at the local level in small private groups.

In our post-totalitarian period the insufficiency of "social physics" is clear, as is the indestructible character of the metaphysical inclinations. Indeed, the very impossibility of doing without interests imposes the need to overcome their limited particularity and to develop common interests as the sole basis for human life together.

This is manifest now in the Soviet's recognition of the primacy of human values. From within the ideology, however, this is as impossible as it is to steer a boat entirely from within. Hence, in looking to other sources, such as religion, for values, it remains an ideology and considers the ideals and universal values merely as ways of solving particular problems or of filling up the depleted social consciousness—the reductionism continues!

Hence, it is important to look for a new ground for understanding, i.e., to surpass "social physics" by looking again to what had previously been seen as the basic error, namely, to a metaphysics. This looks at values not as means for the resolution of particular problems, but, beyond utility, precisely as that for which all particular goods would be sacrificed. Its task is to enable things to be considered in themselves, not in terms of their utility to something else.

Such a metaphysics then consists not in the elaboration of a useful ideal or a pragmatic policy. Its content is, rather, the free creative action of a person or a people; this content must exist, it cannot merely be manufactured by thought. The mode of metaphysics then is not the generation of utopias, but reflection upon our exercise of freedom. This means returning to the life of our people, to its cultural heritage and tradition, and particularly to its religious content as transcending the level of utility and expressing the values in terms of which human society can be built.

2. The intent of the paper under discussion is not to provide a detailed analysis of the concrete situation or its historical account, but rather to provide a model of relationships between different levels of knowledge in order to locate the roots of the present problematic of post-totalitarian freedom and democracy. In this sense it provides a basis for recognizing the need for a distinctive level of thought, namely a metaphysics, beyond any set of social interests or any technique for their manipulation and implementation. It provides as well a caution against being too sanguine in looking to metaphysics for the pragmatic purpose of creating a new world. It suggests rather that the proper mode of metaphysics is reflection on being as expressed in the actual exercise of freedom.

Some would suggest that situating the experience of this century allows one to direct one's modeling between the Scylla of collectivism and Charybdis of individualism, toward an as yet elusive third way. But it may be seen to do more if it is noted that both of these extremes as extremes reflect the same radical reductionism or loss of metaphysical depth, namely, that both reflect the reduction of being to what is clear and distinct to mankind and subject to its manipulation. If that be the case then the added significance of this attempt at abstract modeling is to point the way for philosophical work, i.e., to identify the need and method for a metaphysics that is ever contemporary.

As one explores this path questions arise about the availability of resources; specifically whether it is possible to look toward the West for that content. At first, to turn to the West might appear to call for an abandonment of any metaphysical commitments. In North America the multiple metaphysical sources in the pluralism of the cultural and religious backgrounds of its peoples seem to have induced a tendency to bracket such commitments and to live social life as an adventure in indeterminacy. Decisions then are made simply on the pragmatic basis of "what works"; it is the triumph of pragmatism.

Or is it? Some would note that Dewey's attempt to translate metaphysical ideals into "progress" as the theme of "social physics" seems successful only as long as one does not look too closely at what constitutes progress. The best he could do was to define "progress" self-referentially by saying that it consists in improving the conditions which promote "progress." His attempt to translate this into "action" involved a set of ideals such as "boundless possibility, indefinite progress, free movement, equal opportunity" (*Reconstruction in Philosophy*, pp. 53ff) for which his empirical epistemology left no room. The result was the philosophical abandonment of pragmatism by the 1950s.

In fact, in the West pragmatic efforts are grounded in a set of presupposed and commonly held values. Personal profit is not looked upon as class exploitation, but it is subject to norms. Thus, profit is reprehensible when achieved by dishonest and inequitable means, but is praiseworthy when achieved in open competition by fair means and with respect for personal and social welfare. These commonly held values reflect a long heritage with deep cultural and religious roots. Though imperfectly, this orients debates, legislation and policy decision.

But at another level it should be recognized that modernization in the West has had a notable anti-metaphysical bias corrosive of these values. Nominalism of the late middle ages reflected a loss of confidence in the ability to grasp the nature of things and hence the loss of a basis not only for universal terms, but for ethical norms. The result is a conception of each person and thing as a single atomic entity without inherent relations to others. Such relations must then be externally determined by contract or judicial decision.

In one reading, the fascination of the Renaissance with things ancient was also a not uncalculated effort to break from the

Christian tradition as reflecting the accumulated wisdom of over a thousand years of lived freedom. The result was a radically new mode of human relations. Not incidentally at this point, to substitute for this rejection of an acquired metaphysical understanding of reality, Machiavelli outlined a set of relations based on power and domination. Correspondingly, at the end of this period the nihilism of Nietzsche remains the persistent note.

More positively, others would note the resources at hand. One is the turn from abstract or technical manipulation to creative participation in the concrete through a redevelopment of the crafts. Another is the perdurance of the religious heritage in the inescapable effort to realize a life that consists not only in tactical manipulation of means, environment, and people, but in a deeper sense of the reality and dignity of the human person and community. There can be no human vacuum and that a value horizon is always present, even when intentionally attacked. It is present in the ancient traditions of a people, which in the West is the Christian heritage developed over the last two thousand years. This religious perspective reaches intentionally beyond "social physics" with its pragmatic interests, to the dimensions of meaning which provide for the respect, unity, concern and love between people in terms of which truly human life can be lived.

Is this only ancient, however? Can it be found in the concrete experience of our day? It seems not coincidental that those who have most suffered the repression of freedom are the most alert to its roots, nature and significance. If this be the case then the tradition is not something affirmed in the past and solely remembered. On the contrary, if it concerns metaphysics and if for a living thing to be is to live, then to be for a human being is to exercise his or her freedom or at least to struggle to do so. It is in this struggle, with its dramatic challenges and new opportunities, that the content of metaphysics emerges. In this light the full range of the events of '89, from the triumph in Central and Eastern Europe to the tragedy in Tiananmen, constitute a new, spectacular stage in the life of human freedom. This is a new emergence of being, experienced both positively and negatively. If this be the case, then the prospective work of metaphysics can be not merely temporally sequential or after the fact, but contemporaneously foundational. That is, an appreciation *in* and *through* the act of freedom so that the life of freedom itself becomes at once manifestive of the being which it realizes. This is the effort to act *with* or even *from* an understanding of the truth of being, and to live in the commitment, enjoyment and celebration of goodness, which is love.

George F. McLean

CHAPTER VIII

A NEW CONSTITUTIONAL MODEL FOR EAST-CENTRAL EUROPE

RETT R. LUDWIKOWSKI

INTRODUCTION

Even the most enthusiastic commentators of Gorbachev's attempts to restructure the Soviet economy admit that the system does not show many symptoms of a quick economic recovery. Gorbachev's *glasnost* and *perestroika* are tested in an atmosphere that resembles the Sisyphean Labors rather than the noisy hurrah-enthusiasm of the Khrushchev era. Until recently, only an internal reform of the Soviet Communist Party and a heralded shift of power from the political to the legislative and executive bodies, were generally received in the West as significant symptoms of a structural transformation within the Soviet Constitutional System. The assessment of these constitutional changes, however, requires a careful study of the Soviet post-revolution constitutional development and an examination of the question whether they are a true reform, or only a deception conceived to divert attention from internal distresses of the system.

At this moment, it is also quite apparent that constitutional transformation in Eastern Europe is imminent as the Eastern European leadership continues to change. Now is the most appropriate time to consider what will be the future constitutional model, if any. Obviously it will not continue to be the Soviet model. Will it be, however, based to any extent on American, British, East or West European liberal traditions? Will it be an amalgam of any, or all, of these? These questions have not yet received adequate attention.

Experts studying the process of political transformation observe that the successful transfer of power or the emergence of new centers of political responsibility requires a vast knowledge of the social, economic, cultural and geopolitical circumstances in which the new institutions are to be installed. Successful constitutional or legal engineering also requires advanced comparative technique to help locate political devices applicable to unique combinations of local factors. The success of the constitutional works is largely attributable to the mature intellectual background of the constitutional drafters, and to their ability to draw from the experience of other nations. It requires the appropriate channels of information that facilitate the exchange of political ideas.

The dissemination of the constitutional experience currently makes possible the quick adoption of well-tested constitutional principles. One may argue that the time factor has become less important with the growth of a world-wide constitutional experience. In the conditions of significant political isolation, however, the development of constitutional movements requires more time than in the conditions conducive to the transfer of constitutional experience.

For years, free access to constitutional experience was blocked for the socialist countries. Because of the lack of significant interflow of opinions between the West and East and Soviet control, the societies of Eastern Europe had either to adopt blindly the Soviet constitutional model or to try to draw from their own constitutional traditions. Today, the East Europeans face an exciting and challenging prospect of developing a new constitutional model. With discussion of new laws many questions naturally arise. It is necessary to evaluate the legacy of socialist constitutional structures and to determine the applicability of the Western models and the East European constitutional traditions and experiences. This may need both insight into the inner dynamics of the East-Central European politics and the Western perspective.

The purpose of this article is to supply observations upon the process of formation of a new constitutional model in East-Central Europe. The focus of this study will be on the current constitutional development in the two Central European countries most advanced in the process of constitutional transformation (Poland, Hungary) and in the Soviet Union. The wider version of this paper, comprising the review of the liberal and democratic constitutional traditions of the East-Central European states as confronted with the common core of the socialist constitutions, is published in Vol. 17/1990 of the *Syracuse Journal of International Law and Commerce.*

GORBACHEV'S LAW ON CONSTITUTIONAL AMENDMENTS

There is some routine in the process of making constitutional changes in the socialist system. The initiative usually stems from the Politburo or Secretary General himself.[1] It is typical that the process begins after the initial period of solidification of power of the Party leader. Each transitory period in the Soviet Union may be characterized, however, by the tendency to set up a more collective leadership of the Party, and this period was usually followed by the emergence of a single leader who successfully reduced the number of rivals and introduced his clients to the highest Party bodies. The tendency may be traced through Stalin's triumvirates,[2] Khrushchev's temporary readiness to share power with Tanastas Mikoyan and Brezhnev's coalition with Aleksey Kosygin.[3] The tendency to purge the Politburo and the Central Committee of potential rivals was not only typical of the pre-*glasnost* era: the full Politburo members and a substantial part of the Central Committee are Gorbachev's appointees. Gorbachev's position as *primus inter pares* (first among equals) was clearly confirmed, although it by no means signifies the inevitable success of his reforms.

In this situation, the will to amend the constitutional law in the direction that would reflect innovations in political philosophy of the new leader is natural. According to the Soviet tradition, the constitutional changes were to crown the Party leader's victory over his rivals. It is paradoxical, however, that the process of consolidation of power was always accompanied by the declarations of the democratic evolution of the system. Each new Constitution was portrayed as an apex in the long-lasting process of democratization. Gorbachev's constitutional reform is no exception to this principle.

On October 22, 1988, drafts of the Law on Constitutional amendments were submitted for nationwide discussion. Similar to the period preceding the adoption of the Stalin Constitution and the Constitution of 1977, the media announced enormous involvement of the readers whose political maturity was assessed very highly. *Pravda* reported:

> The most distinctive feature of today's stage in our society's renewal is that millions of Soviet people have emerged from a state of political apathy and are adopting active civic stances. The reform of the political system should be the most important lever for further boosting this activeness of the people and directing it into a single creative channel.[4]

On December 1, 1988, the Supreme Soviet unanimously approved, by separate vote in the two chambers, the USSR Law on

Elections of USSR People's Deputies and approved the USSR Draft Laws on Changes and Amendments to the USSR Constitution by 1344 deputy votes for, five against and twenty-seven abstentions. [5]

Widely heralded changes of the electoral system are quite vague and must be examined with cool skepticism. Article 95 of the Law on Constitutional Amendments provides that "[e]lections of people's deputies take place in single-seat and multi-seat electoral districts on the basis of universal, equal, and direct suffrage by secret ballot.[6] Amended Article 100 provides for multiple nominations; it reads, "Ballot papers can include any number of candidates."[7]

The reform inspires several observations. At first, the extent to which multi-seat electoral districts were introduced is not clear. The elections of People's Deputies took place in single-seat electoral districts.[8] One USSR people's deputy was elected per electoral *okrug*.[9] Multi-seat electoral districts were most likely tested in elections of local Soviet people's deputies.[10] Secondly, multi-seat elections are not Gorbachev's innovation. It was confirmed that Stalin spoke favorably about them to Roy Howard in 1936 although this concept did not materialize in his Constitution of 1936.[11] Until recently, however, only one person would run for each seat in an uncontested election with a high electorate participation. Vyshinsky wrote:

> Under the Stalin Constitution elections to the Supreme Soviet of the USSR and to the Supreme Soviets of Union and Autonomous Republics have shown that the entire population of the land of the Soviets are completely united in spirit, have demonstrated an unprecedented democracy. The days of elections have actually been festive days of the entire people, when the bloc of Party and non-Party Bolsheviks have elected their best people to the Supreme Soviets. The call of the Bolshevik Party to the Soviet People, to all the electors, the vote for candidates of the bloc of the Communists and the non-Party members, had exceptional results. In the voting for the candidates to the Supreme Soviet of the USSR, 91,113,153 electors out of 94,138,159 took part--96.8 percent of the entire number of citizens having the right to vote.[12]

The multi-seat districts were tested in other socialist countries.

They were introduced in Poland where usually between four and six representatives are elected in one district, and in the German Democratic Republic where four to ten representatives may be elected from one list. The 1983 Reform of the Hungarian electoral system also introduced the system of double or multiple nominations confirming at the same time the primacy of individual districts.[13] The multi-seat system or system of multiple nominations did not democratize the electoral law of these countries *ipso facto*. It is well-known that the democratic electoral system of the socialist countries broke down as a result of a combination of a few major elements: defective nomination process, defective secrecy, and lack of adequate and reliable public control of the election's results.

The nomination phase, one of the most sensitive and important elements of the democratic electoral process, was seriously affected by the system, which granted the right to nominate candidates to branches and organizations of the Communist Party (the "CPSU"), trade unions, Young Communist League, co-operatives, and other public organizations, work collectives, and meetings of servicemen.[14] So far, an average citizen was intimidated rather than encouraged to take part in this process The new Law on Elections of People's Deputies provides that new representatives would be nominated by labor collectives, social organizations and servicemen's meetings.[15] Pravda notes:

> Now the situation is changing, although this is not happening everywhere or all at once. This is facilitated by the tremendous preparatory work that has preceded the reports of election meetings and conferences. Lists of [P]arty committees for bureau candidates have been published in advance to that they could be discussed comprehensively. Use has been made of questionnaires in order to discover people's opinion of the possible candidates. Non-[P]arty members have been invited to the conferences which also helps stimulate collective discussion.[16]

This report sounds promising. However, it again resembles Vyshinky's report on the electoral activity under Stalin's Constitution:

> Never in a single country did the people manifest such activity in elections as did the Soviet people.

Never has any capitalist country known, nor can it know, such a high percentage of those participating in voting as did the USSR. The Soviet election system under [the] Stalin Constitution and the elections of Supreme Soviets have shown the entire world once again that Soviet democracy is the authentic sovereignty of the people of which the best minds of mankind have dreamed.[17]

In reality, the reports from the ten-week election campaign that commenced on January 10, 1989, confirmed the reservations drawn from the initial examination of the text of the Law on Elections.[18] In light of the new laws at least one-third of the people's deputies had to be elected from the CPSU and organizations associated with the party. The rule which was dropped later still determined the results of 1989 elections. The 10 seats allocated to the Soviet communist Party were filled by decision of the Politburo, which was endorsed by the Central Committee.[19] The process of "election" of the representatives from the Komsomol, trade unions, labor veterans, and associations of women, were conducted in similar fashion. Western observers reported from Moscow:

Today's selection of approved Communist Party candidates provided a dramatic reminder of the Kremlin's ability to manipulate what have been billed as the most democratic elections in Soviet history. The [P]arty has managed to devise new electoral rules that guarantee it a virtual monopoly of political power behind the trappings of parliamentary democracy.[20]

The new system produced some multi-candidate elections for the seats that are not allocated to social organizations. The choice was limited, however, even for this section of the Congress. The newly amended laws guarantee representation to such organizations as stamp collectors, book-lovers, and "friends of cinema," but not to independent mass movements such as Memorial, which has been supported by millions of people.[21] Dobbs wrote from Moscow:

Last week's nominating session of the philatelists' association provided an excellent opportunity to see how the system works in practice. The meeting was called to choose candidates to fill the one seat in Congress reserved for the representative of the Soviet Union's 300,000 stamp-collectors. . . . In the case of candidates who have been endorsed by the [P]arty, all obstacles have a miraculous tendency to disappear. Unofficial candidates, by contrast, usually find that they are required to fulfill every exacting detail of the electoral law.[22]

This reflection is also true as far as non-allocated seats are concerned. The observation of the initial phase of the election process confirms that despite the attempts to portray the campaign as Western-style, its outcome on March 26, 1989, which gave 80 percent of seats in the Congress to the Communist Party, was easily predictable.

The actual casting of ballots was another element that in the past affected the democratic character of the socialist election process. The voter, before obtaining a ballot paper, had to identify himself and check his or her name on the list of voters. The Party propaganda claimed that the voter should cast a valid ballot simply by dropping it in the ballot box. This procedure was recognized as evidence of trust for the Party candidates who are located at the beginning of the list. In this case, even if the list had more candidates than seats allocated to this electoral district, the first candidates on the list were deemed voted on. The voting booths were usually located at the distant part of the electoral rooms. To vote secretly, the voter would have to pass by the whole room in the full view of Party representatives present.[23] The lack of trust in the elective practice (electoral rolls and the procedure for their compilation; counting votes in the electoral wards), created the atmosphere of futility and hopelessness that worked against the attempts to vote secretly. In addition, the Party's backstage propaganda discretely persuaded the voter to remember that the electoral behavior of the members of society would be carefully watched by the Party and would affect the assessment of individual contribution to the social well-being, a basic factor in the process of distribution of social goods. To illustrate this approach on the example of the Polish system of the mid-eighties (which *nota bene* provided for multiple-seat constituencies and recently was radically democratized), Dr. Wrobel wrote:

On September 26, 1985, just prior to the Seym "elections" Minister Miskiewicz announced, at a meeting of university chancellors, that the participation of Polish academic teachers in the "election" would be the criterion to judge whether or not these academics were in conformance with the constitutional principles of the Polish Peoples Republic. In practice, this meant that refusing to participate in "voluntary elections" could lead to the refusal to grant degrees, academic titles and even loss of job. From the perspective of Polish law, the minister acted criminally since according to Article 189.1 of the Polish Penal Code whoever by force, illegal threat, deceit or exploitation of dependency interferes with the free exercise of election rights is subject to the loss of freedom from six months to five years. Unfortunately, Polish law is treated instrumentally by the ruling group, as a tool serving exclusively to maintain power. The minister is free.[24]

It has to be admitted that as far as the elective mechanisms are concerned the reform was a major sign of the restructuring of the Soviet legal system. The pressure, described above, which always accompanied socialist elections was not eliminated but was significantly reduced. The first session of the convened Congress did not bring major surprises but demonstrated, however, that *perestroika* is a risky game and that Gorbachev is not clearly in control of the forces he unleashed.[25] Gorbachev easily won unanimous nomination of the Party and was elected President, facing only symbolic opposition of the Congress, 80 percent of which is still composed of members of the Communist Party.[26] In the voting, Gorbachev's word still prevails; however, the deputies voted down the government's candidates to the Supreme Soviet commissions.[27] Jeff Trimble wrote from Moscow that "when it came to talking, arguing, shouting, criticizing and insulting, this Congress bowed to no one."[28]

A reform of the legislative structures which was to shift power from the Party to the representative bodies was widely heralded as another major element of constitutional restructuring. A *Pravda* editorial declared:

The draft laws are the legal foundation for the reform. . . . The soviets of people's deputies proved powerless. The work of law enforcement organs weakened drastically. . . . The additions and amendments to the USSR Constitution and the new law on elections are extensive. They are aimed primarily at the democratization of our entire life and the return of power to the soviets of people's deputies, placing them above all other state institutions. It is essentially a case of full power for the people.[29]

The amended Fundamental Laws draw from the tradition of the first Constitutions (1918 and 1924) which provided for a double legislative body: the Congress and its nucleus Central Executive Committee, itself a bicameral body since 1924. The new Law vests the supreme power in the USSR Congress of People's Deputies.[30] The Congress consists of 2250 elected deputies who are comprised of the following: 750 territorial electoral districts with an equal number of voters: 750 from national-territorial electoral districts (thirty-two deputies from each of the union republics, eleven deputies from each autonomous republic, five deputies from each autonomous region, and one deputy from each autonomous area); and 750 deputies from all-union social organizations (CPSU elects 100 deputies, USSR trade unions elect 100 deputies, cooperative organizations elect 100 deputies, Komsomol elects seventy-five deputies, women's councils elect seventy-five deputies, organizations of war and labor veterans elect seventy-five deputies, associations of scientific workers elect seventy-five deputies, USSR creative unions elect seventy-five deputies, and other legally constituted social organizations elect seventy-five deputies).[31]

The reservation of a bloc of one-third of the seats for the CPSU and other social organizations was recognized as a controversial departure from western practice, and was abandoned once the new Congress was formed.[32]

The Congress elects its nucleus body, a 450-person, bicameral, USSR Supreme Soviet which is "the standing legislative, administrative and monitoring organ of the USSR state power.[33] The USSR Supreme Soviet has two chambers: the Soviet of the Union and the Soviet of Nationalities, which are numerically equal and possess equal rights.[34] The chambers are elected at the USSR Congress of People's Deputies by a general vote of the deputies.[35] The Soviet of the Union was elected from among the USSR people's deputies of the territorial electoral districts, and the USSR people's deputies were elected from the social organizations.[36] The Soviet of Nationalities is elected from among the USSR people's deputies, from the national-territorial electoral districts, and from the social organizations in accordance with the following norms: eleven deputies from each union republic, four deputies from each autonomous republic, two deputies from each autonomous region, and one deputy from each autonomous area.[37]

Elected by clear Party majority, the Supreme Soviet gave Gorbachev less control over the proceedings than was expected. The number of radical deputies, who occupied up to 30 percent of the seats in the Congress, was reduced to between 10 to 15 percent in the Supreme Soviet. Nonetheless, Gorbachev faced unexpectedly strong opposition against his nomination of Politburo member, Anatoly Lukyanov, as first deputy chairman of the Supreme Soviet, and in several votes on national minorities issues.[38]

Although the overall reaction of the Western media was favorable, it must be cautiously noted that the laws hardly introduced any new elements into the socialist constitutional framework. The functioning of the double legislative body composed of the huge Congress and a smaller, but still bicameral, nucleus organ (the Central Executive Committee or Supreme Soviet), was well-tested in the 1920s and 1930s. The Soviet practice demonstrated that the Congresses of several thousands of delegates are handicapped by their size and are typically more responsive to Party rhetoric. The organization of the Party Congresses proved that they may be prepared in advance and may be held in an atmosphere encouraging no symbolic or dissenting debate.

The observation of the recent Congress indicates how much changed in the Soviet political culture. In fact, using the disguise of a revolutionary reform, Gorbachev tried to reintroduce well-known legislative structures. This strategy was, however, only partially successful. Gorbachev still controls the Congress and the Supreme Soviet, but not effortlessly anymore. The evaluation of his personal position is, in this situation, extremely difficult. His nomination to the position of the President of the Supreme Soviet enhanced his power in light of the new constitutional law. The new law limited the tenure for this position to ten years (two five-year successive terms), but extended the functions of the President as a head of the state who chaired the powerful Defense Council and named candidates for the posts of Chairman of the USSR Council of Ministers, USSR General Procurator, Chairman of the USSR Council of Ministers, USSR General Procurator, Chairman of the USSR Supreme Court, and other high officials. The combination of the position of the General Secretary of the Party with the presidency and the announced combination of the equivalent positions on the local level could hardly favor the announced "revival of the absolute power of the soviets."[39]

On February 27, 1990, the draft law was approved and marked the further shift in power from the Communist Party and the Soviet legislature to the President. In March 1990, Gorbachev was elected to a four year term as President of the Republic (different from his previously help position as President of the Supreme Soviet) by the USSR Congress of People's Deputies. Henceforth, it was declared, election for a five-year term would be by nationwide popular vote.[40]

The new laws raise an array of concerns, especially in the northern republics of the Soviet Union. The widely heralded, but vaguely implemented, shift from the Party to the legislature was accompanied by restrictions on public demonstrations and the freedom of association.[41] The Tide of resistance to communism and to Russian domination swept among the Soviet captive nationalities in 1989 and put Gorbachev under tremendous pressure. By unanimous vote, Lithuania separated itself from the Moscow 'center'.[42] The Estonian Parliament voted on the controversial residence requirement (later suspended), in its new election law.[43] In spite of Moscow's warnings, the Lithuanians and Estonians followed East European countries and abolished the clause in their constitutions giving the Communist Party a leading position, in fact, a monopoly of power.[44]

Responding to the threat of a further disintegration of the Soviet Union, Gorbachev released in November 1990 his new "Draft Union Treaty" which is to be signed by all member states of the Soviet Union.[45] The Draft Union Treaty contains a lot of typical communist rhetoric: it denounces racism, chauvinism, nationalism and authoritarianism. It declares protection of culture and native languages of member states, primacy of human rights, freedom of religion, information, personal freedoms, and fundamental principles of democracy. The new Draft Treaty provides that the new union's membership will be voluntary but it does not give the member states the right to secede, which was clearly guaranteed by the Soviet Constitutions of 1977.[46] Instead, the Treaty declares that "Members of the union may raise the question of terminating membership in the USSR of a republic that violates the terms of the treaty and the commitments a republic has assumed."[47]

The Union would get wide powers over foreign policy, economic development, defense, trade, social policy, communication, transport education, public order, and protection against crime. The Draft Treaty states that "Republic legislation on the territory of the republics takes precedence in all questions with the exception of those which are ascribed to the union's jurisdiction."[48] Also, republics are entitled to challenge the USSR if it contravenes the public constitution and if it exceeds the powers of the union. The disputes are to be resolved by conciliation procedures or are passed on to the newly established USSR Constitutional Court. The Court was set up for monitoring the compliance of the USSR and republican laws with the union treaty and the USSR Constitution.[49]

It has to be noted that the new Draft Treaty vests the legislative power in the union in the USSR Supreme Soviet without any reference to the Congress. The USSR President is to be the guarantor of the observance of the union treaty, the commander-in-chief of the USSR armed forces and the head of the union state exercising supreme executive power. The USSR prime minister and the cabinet of ministers will be both subordinated to the USSR President and responsible to the USSR Supreme Soviet.[50]

The adoption of the new Treaty of the Union is to be preceded by the nation-wide referendum (on March 17, 1991) which will answer the question: "Do you consider it necessary to preserve the Union of Soviet Socialist Republic as a renewed federation of equal Soviet republics, in which the rights and freedoms of people of any nationality will be fully guaranteed?"[51] The anticipated affirmative response to this question by the majority of the population of the large Soviet republics alerted the Baltic states which held their own referenda to confirm the will of their people to live in "an independent and democratic republic."[52] Georgia and Armenia also declared that they have no intention of taking part in the national referendum.

In summary, we can say that, with all power vested in him, Gorbachev seems to be vulnerable and more exposed to the criticism of the Party's conservatives and the Soviet workers.[53] In light of his domestic distresses, the current legalization of the Ukrainian Uniate Church appears almost suicidal. An inevitable process of democratization and liberalization of religious life will undoubtedly contribute to the new tide of social ferment. What Gorbachev still does not seem to comprehend is that those who are feared a great deal are sometimes admired, but those who are feared a little bit are usually hated. He does understand, however, that *glasnost* has its limits; to survive he has to retain control of his crumbling empire and most likely to crack down on the rebelling national minorities, workers, and again on the Party's conservatives. In a tradeoff presented silently to the West, the East European freedom is offered as a price paid up-front for the tolerance to an inevitable upcoming domestic confrontation in the Soviet Union. These possible implications of *perestroika* must be well-analyzed in the West. In 1988, Sakharov claimed that so far the Soviet people face *"perestroika* only from above."[54] After one year of experimenting with constitutional restructuring it is quite clear that *perestroika* is now hardly controllable from above. The question remains, however, whether it is still reversible.

POLISH PEACEFUL REVOLUTION

The anti-communist upheaval in Poland was often characterized as "a peaceful revolution"[55] but it would be, perhaps, more accurate to speak about the series of events or to call the Polish transformation an "evolution" rather than to present it as a sudden and radical revolutionary change. The last attempt to throw off communist control and establish the first non-communist government took almost a decade in Poland. It took only months and sometimes even weeks to successfully spread the crisis of communism to the other countries of Eastern Europe. And, in fact, the Polish "revolution" did not begin in the eighties; it started with the establishment of the communist system after World War II and proceeded through the consecutive Polish upheavals of 1956, 1968, 1970, 1976 to end up with the Solidarity era of the 1980s.[56]

In 1985 General Jaruzelski resigned as prime minister although he remained the First Secretary of the Polish United Workers' Party. After the party-controlled elections in 1985 he was replaced by Zbigniew Messner. Messner's successive attempts to cure Poland's collapsing economy became a total failure and as result of a new tide of labor unrest in 1988, Messner resigned and the Party turned the government over to Mieczyslaw Rakowski who announced his support for ideas of political pluralism and declared readiness to hold discussions with the opposition.

The roundtable negotiations began on February 6, 1989 and culminated on April 5. Ernest Skalski, a prominent Polish journalist and one of the editors of Solidarity's new daily *Gazeta Wyborcza* (Electoral Gazette), reported:

> First of all, despite the shape of the table, the
> negotiations were really a bilateral affair between
> the authorities and the opposition represented by

Solidarity. There were three primary discussion "sub-tables," concerned with politics, economics and the trade union question. These dealt with issues ranging from mass media accessibility, the independence of the judiciary, and local self-rule to the creation of a new government body and the office of President. The proceedings at the sub-tables were reported in the press and on television, with the authorities' delegates underlining how much was accomplished and the similarities in the objectives of both sides. Indeed, the government needed to appear conciliatory; it wanted to give an impression that it is gaining the support of the challengers and that an entente is round the corner.[57]

In fact, however, the main decisions were taken in an isolated government building in *Magdalenka*, near Warsaw, where Walesa with his closest advisors met with the chief of the governmental delegation, Interior Minister Czeslaw Kiszczak.[58] After several successive deadlocks, a major breakthrough for the roundtable talks occurred when the regime's negotiators offered a real novelty: the establishment of a Senate, or Second Chamber in the Polish parliament that would be elected in a truly democratic election in which the party coalition would compete with opposition for all seats. Before the government had time to reconsider all consequences of the proposal it was accepted by Bronislaw Gieremek, one of the opposition delegation leaders. The deal was made.[59] "The opposition agreed to political pluralism in exchange for being permitted to participate in elections. This pluralism had meant the re-legalization of Solidarity, Rural Solidarity and the rebellious independent Students' Association--with the possibility of reviving various other organizations that were dissolved by the authorities after the imposition of martial law. The regime has also promised further liberalization of censorship and some independence for the judiciary--both to a degree that was difficult to determine.[60] It was decided that the provisions of the roundtable accords should be incorporated in the constitution in a way that would reflect Poland's democratic traditions.

The constitutional changes were adopted in great haste shortly after the roundtable accords were concluded. The Constitutional amendments provided that the National Assembly would consist of two chambers: the Seym (or Diet) and the Senate. Electoral liberty for the Seym (composed of 460 seats) was limited. The opposition could freely nominate candidates for thirty five percent of the legislative mandates. Placement on the ballot required three thousand voter signatures from a given province.[61] Sixty percent of the legislative mandates was to belong to the coalition of the Communist party (Polish United Workers' Party) and its satellite parties (Democratic Association and United Peasants' Party). Five percent of the mandates was allocated to pro-Communist Catholic groups.

The elections to the Senate were not subject to any limitation. The Senate was composed of one hundred senators, two from each of the forty seven national voidships and an additional six from the two largest agglomerations of Warsaw and Katowice.[62] To claim the mandates in the Seym and the Senate, the candidates had to receive more than one half of the valid votes. Otherwise a new round of elections would have to be held.[63]

The election to the Polish parliament in June 1989 gave Solidarity clear dominance in the new, freely elected Senate where the union captured ninety-nine of one hundred seats. Solidarity also won thirty-five percent, or 161, of the seats open to opposition candidates in the Seym. The Communists and their allies suffered a crushing rejection by voters in the first round of the election. All but two of the thirty-five Communist Party officials who ran unopposed on a so-called "National List"—including eight members of the Politburo—failed to win the fifty percent of votes necessary to claim the seats allocated to them. Two hundred ninety-five seats out of 299 left by the accords to the Communist allies had to be filled in the second round of elections. The morning after the vote General Jaruzelski was said to admit to his top aides, "Our defeat is total. A political solution will have to be found."[64]

Although Jaruzelski was elected to the Polish Presidency, his government, led by General Kiszczak, could not form a viable coalition. Walesa's negotiations with two minor parties resulted in a Solidarity-led coalition. On August 24, 1989 Tadeusz Mazowiecki, an editor of Solidarity's weekly newsletter, *Tygodnik Solidarnosc*, was made the new premier of Poland. On September 12, 1989 the Seym confirmed the coalition government's cabinet.[65] Poland's peaceful revolution was a fact.

Since the completion of the roundtable talks, the 1952 Constitution was amended five times, with three amendments introducing major changes and two marginal adjustments of the constitutional vocabulary.[66] While the most important amendment of April 1989 was to prepare the legal framework for the forthcoming election through restructuring the main organs of state power, the other amendments were to purge the Constitution of the remnants of its Stalinist legacy.

The consolidated text dropped the word "People's" from the official name of the state, which now is called "Polish Republic."[67] The new law struck out the whole preamble which focused on "the liberating ideas of the Polish working masses," "the historic victory over Fascism of the Union of the Soviet Republic which liberated Polish soil," "the Polish working people's fight against the bitter resistance of the remnants of the former capitalist-landlords system," etc. Poland ceased to be described as "a socialist state . . . implementing and developing a socialist democracy."[68] The term "socialist society" was substituted by the "citizens' society."[69] The entire Chapter Two on "Social and Economic System" disappeared from the new constitutional text.

In the new constitutional law Poland is described as "a democratic legal sate (state of law) that implements principles of social justice."[70] Art. 2 explains that "democratic" means that a sovereignty "is vested in the Nation" which "exercises its power through its representatives in Seym, Senate and People's Councils." It means also the introduction of elements of direct democracy in a constitutionally guaranteed system of referendums. "Nation" which as a subject of power replaced "the working people of town and country" is conceived, corresponding to Polish doctrine, not as an ethnic entity but as a political aggregate of all the citizens.[71]

The concept of a "legal state" or "state of law" is well known to the socialist theory which for decades viewed this idea as a relic of widely criticized legal normativism and positivism. In the Polish doctrine the concept of "legal state" means a variety of principles such as: a duty of strict observance of the law by every organ of State and every citizen, the rule that all the organs of State authority and administration work solely on the basis and within the boundaries of the law, the principle of a hierarchy of the law with the Constitution as the apex of the legal system, followed by the statutes and sub-statutory acts, the hierarchization of organs of state power and administration with the legislature as a supreme power, the wide catalog of citizens rights and extensive system of public control.

The meaning of "the principles of social justice" which the Polish Republic is supposed to implement is less clear. The Polish commentators explain that this pronouncement is a reflection of a post-socialist protectionism. The Polish Republic is not any more a socialist state but neither is it a market economy. The Polish new law eliminated the privileges of state property and guarantees an equal protection to all forms of ownership but, differently from the new Hungarian Constitution, it does not describe Poland as a market economy. In the opinion of the Polish constitutional experts an emphasis put on "the principles of social justice" means that the drafters of the Polish amendments believed that in the transitory period between non-market and market economy the Polish society needs a special protection against the brutal mechanisms of a capitalistic competition.[73]

The other important principle which was introduced into the Polish Constitution in 1989 is that of a political pluralism. The reform was the result of a severe parliamentary struggle and an intense social pressure which stimulated the fifteen members of the communist party political club in the Seym to submit, in August 23, 1989, the motion to eliminate from the Polish Constitution the Article 3 description of the "meaningful role of the Communist Party." The newly introduced Article 4 states that "political parties are organized on the basis of principles of voluntary and equal membership of Polish citizens and in order to influence in a democratic way the state's politics."

Despite numerous suggestions that the principle of division of powers does not mean their equality and is recognized also in parliamentary systems, the new amendments, regrettably, did not declare this most commonly recognized constitutional rule.[74] The reluctance to adopt this principle seems to be a typical legacy of the socialist theory of law which for years persuaded that the division of powers is incompatible with the principle of superiority of the legislature. For a long time it was argued incorrectly that in a typical parliamentary system, only the legislature is "an organ of the nation's power." Although one has to admit that the principle that "the Seym is a supreme representative of the will of the Nation"[75] has deep roots in the Polish constitutional traditions, there can be reasonable reservations that the words "supreme organ" or "superior representative" mean "exclusive representation." Simply, the concept of superiority does not rule out the right of other organs to exercise or share a legitimate power on behalf of the Nation.

The new laws provided for a bicameral legislature composed of the Seym and the Senate.[76] The Seym remained the supreme legislative body, while the new Senate was given legislative initiative and the right to review the legislation passed by the Seym. The changes introduced by the Senate in the laws that were passed by the Seym could be overruled by a two-thirds vote in the Seym with at least one half of all deputies present.[77] It was resolved that the Senate would participate on equal footing with the Seym in modifying and adopting the Constitution and in the election of the President of the Republic.[78]

The constitutional amendments introduced the office of the President. The initial changes of April 8, 1989 provided that the President would be elected for six years by the joint session of the National Assembly (the Seym and the Senate). The Amendment of September 27, 1990 shortened the tenure of the President's office to five years and resolved that Presidents elected directly by the Nation could be reelected only once (*Dienuik Ustaw* Nr. 67, October 2, 1990). The President has legislative initiative and signs laws. His refusal to sign a statute may be overridden by a two-thirds vote of the Seym in the presence of at least half of its members.[79] The President can also submit the statute to the Constitutional Tribunal for the review of its constitutionality.[80] The President was given the power to proclaim martial law for a period of 3 months in case of serious danger to the state or a natural catastrophe. He can dissolve the Seym when the legislature is unable to establish a new government within a period of 3 months after it fails to adopt a budget; or when the legislature takes steps which encroach on the President's constitutional prerogatives.[81] The President is commander-in-chief of the Polish army and presides over the Committee of National Defence. He nominates the Prime Minister and can submit to the Seym a motion for his dismissal.[82] The right to approve or call the government and the members of the Council of Ministers is reserved to the Seym.[83] The executive acts of the President require countersignature by the Prime Minister. As the head of the state the President is not parliamentary or politically accountable to the Seym but is constitutionally accountable and can be impeached for a violation of the Constitution before the Tribunal of State by a decision taken by two-thirds of all the members of the National Assembly (the Seym and the Senate).

As the Polish model of administrative and constitutional judicial review was well established by the Statutes on the Supreme Administrative Court of 31 January 1980 and on the Constitutional Tribunal of April 29, 1985,[84] the changes introduced by the Amendments were relatively minor. The new laws resolved that independence of the judiciary was safeguarded by a National Judicial Council composed of judges delegated by a General Assembly of the Supreme Court, the High Administrative Court, and District Courts.

The other institutional changes terminated the existence of the Council of State, the duties of which passed over to the President. The laws introduced an organ of Ombudsman (*Rzecznik Praw Obywatelskich*) and eliminated the office of the Procurator General (until recently accountable to the Council of State) whose functions were taken over by the Minister of Justice.

To sum up, we can say the Polish elections of 1989 were "free" in a specific way. Some Polish observers noted that pre-electoral contact did not pluralize the Polish system. The "round-table" accords did not guarantee the proportional representation of all or even major political groups. They replaced monopoly of one party by a bipolar system in which the Communist block of parties was to compete freely with Solidarity for the seats in the Senate. The distribution of seats in the Seym was set up in advance.[85] The multi-seat electoral districts were maintained. Altogether there were 108 electoral districts: 9 two-seat districts, 27 (8.3 percent) three-seat districts, 34 (25 percent) four-seat districts, and 38 (35.2 percent) five-seat districts.[86] Hence, in each district the voters had a choice of 1-3 Solidarity candidates running against 1-4 candidates of the party block. In fact, however, what really counted for the election results was not the political personality of candidates but the support of either of the two blocks (in Solidarity case, namely, Walesa's personal recommendation).[87]

The constitutional reform was an important element in Solidarity's strategy to take over power from the communist party. The amendments changed substantially the Stalinist profile of the Polish political system but still they have a provisional character. As W. Sokolewicz wrote, "The April Constitutional amendments were not the realization of a consciously planned long-term project of a constitutional reform and still they have to be melted in an entirely new constitution."[88]

HUNGARY: REFORM "FROM WITHIN" AND "FROM WITHOUT"

The post-war history of the Hungarian People's Republic does not differ significantly from other countries of the Soviet bloc. The Yalta conference in February 1945 recognized the Soviet "liberation" of Hungary but called for a cooperation of the communists with other non-communist parties. At the time of the adoption of the first communist constitution, in May 1949, this cooperation was already a fiction and the communists fully controlled the government.

Following the pattern of communist "reconstruction," Matyas Rakosi, the leader of the Hungarian Worker's Party, introduced in the early fifties the program of a typical Stalinist industrialization and collectivization.[89] The attempts to collectivize economy and society caused widespread discontent and resulted in the adoption of the so-called "New Course" in 1953.[90] The new Prime Minister, Imre Nagy, put more emphasis on the economic sector producing consumer goods, and discontinued some of the projects which were focused on the increase of the heavy industry potential of the Hungarian economy. In the result of the power struggle between Nagy and Rakosi, Nagy the forerunner of the Hungarian "new deal," was ousted from his post and Rakosi and his successor Erno Gero tried to reintroduce a "proper" Stalinist course.[91]

Stalin's death resulted in the attempts to reassess the significance of communism in the Soviet bloc. Thousands of political prisoners were released from labor camps; the Hungarian communists had enough time to realize that some mechanisms of the system were obsolete and needed rapid modernization. "De-Stalinization," no matter how serious its concessions, undoubtedly stimulated widespread discussion over the theory and practice of communism. Stalin's death and Khrushchev's attack on the alleged "sanctities" of Stalinism deepened the process of the intellectual disintegration of Marxism-Leninism and initiated the relatively long stage of denunciation of the fallacies of communism. It started with the revolt of East German workers in 1953, turbulence in Siberian camps soon afterwards, and upheavals of Hungarian and Polish workers three years later.

The demonstrations of the students in Budapest in 1956 provoked the split in the Hungarian party. The conservative faction with Gero called for Soviet intervention, while the reformist faction with Nagy demanded Hungary's withdrawal from the Warsaw Pact and the recognition of its neutral status.[92] In November 4, 1956, the Soviet tanks entered Budapest and after several weeks of bloody fighting, the pro-Soviet government with Janos Kadar was installed. Imre Nagy was executed and Hungary remained an obedient Soviet Satellite.[93]

> Following the revolution of 1956—wrote Renee de Nevers—the new party leader Janos Kadar implemented a policy designated to heal the wounds inflicted by the crushing of the revolt. He tolerated all but outright hostility to his regime, using as his

slogan "He who is not against us is with us," and launched an economic policy which, by favoring consumer goods over the development of heavy industry, paid more heed to domestic needs than had the earlier Stalinist model. These steps gradually gained the regime a measure of credibility with the population, who recognized that the leadership was exploring the limits of Soviet patience with these cautious reforms. In time, Kadar's government gained more popularity than any other in Eastern Europe. It also came to be viewed in the West as being as legitimate and independent as was possible for a member-state of the socialist community; the result was that it gained relatively favorable trade terms.[94]

In the long run, Kadar's policy, however, turned out to be only partially successful. On the one had, it calmed down public dissatisfaction and through decentralizing measures gained some recognition and support from the West, but, on the other hand, it decreased the integration of the Hungarian economy with the highly centralized system of other CMEA (Council of Mutual Economic Assistance) countries.[95] In the 1980s the Hungarian economy deteriorated badly.[96] Especially in 1985 and 1986 the Hungarian GNP did not show any growth and the foreign debt was close to $20 bn. by 1989. It was the highest external debt per capita in the Soviet bloc.[97] There was a widespread conviction in the Hungarian Socialist Worker's Party (HSWP) that Kadar's regime was blocking a more thorough reform. The initiative of further reform came "from within" the communist party. It again called for adoption—by the healthy core of the party—of recent social and political trends. On 22 May 1988 Karol Grosz the representative of a moderate reformist group in the party, was appointed as General Secretary of the HSWP and he promised to sponsor a series of political and economic reforms in Hungary.

The further split in the HSWP occurred over the issue of 'socialist pluralism'. The new party leaders nominated to the Politburo, such as Imre Poszagy and Rezso Nyers, believed that further pluralization of the Hungarian political life was inevitable. The moderate conservatives, led by Grosz, tried to hamper the steps toward a multi-party system. Finally the Hungarian Parliament's new law, adopted in January 1989, established a legal basis for the creation of independent political parties. In February, the HSWP conference decided to relinquish its constitutionally guaranteed position as "a leading and guiding force" of Hungarian society. On May 2nd, 1989, Hungary—as the first socialist country—began to tear down its part of the Iron Curtain, the barbed wire on the border with Austria.[98] In Fall of 1989 Hungary decided to honor its commitments under the Helsinki Act, which proscribed forcible repatriation of foreigners to their home countries. The Hungarian government allowed East Germans who were passing through Hungarian territory to go to the West.[99] This exodus accelerated the fall of communism in Eastern Germany.

At the Party Congress in October 1989 the Hungarian Socialist Workers' Party was dissolved. A new party which emerged was named the Hungarian Socialist Party (HSP). It was led by a new Prime Minister, Miklos Nemeth, and such leaders as Reszo Nyers and Imre Pozsagy. The opening of the political system sped up also the mushrooming of opposition parties, at least 40 of them emerging immediately on the Hungarian political arena. The strongest political groups were: the Hungarian Democratic Forum, the Alliance of Free Democrats, the Union of Young Democrats, the Independent Smallholders' Party, the Social Democrats, and the Greens. Some HSWP members joined two small conservative groups: the Ferenc Munnich Society and the Janos Kadar Society (reportedly inactive in early 1990).[100]

The issue of the presidential election in Hungary caused a major collision between the opposition which favored a presidential election to follow free parliamentary elections, and the leadership of the Hungarian Socialist Party which opted for the idea of an early, and 'ad hoc' organized presidential election. The opposition view prevailed narrowly in the referendum, and the election that was held in April 1990 gave the victory to the Hungarian Democratic Forum which was joined in an alliance in the 386-member Parliament by the Independent Smallholders Party. The isolated Alliance of Free Democrats scored 24 percent of votes and the Hungarian Socialist Party received only 8.3 percent. The Prime-Ministry was turned to the leader of the Hungarian Democratic Forum, Josef Antall, and the initiative in the process of political and economic transformation passed over to the non-communist bloc.

Although the Hungarians did not adopt a new constitution, the amendments introduced in 1989 and 1990 to the Constitutional Act XX of 1949 were the most thorough constitutional transformation in the Soviet bloc.[101]

Accordingly, in the new constitutional text Hungary changed its official name from the Hungarian People's Republic to the Republic of Hungary. It is no longer declared that Hungary is a socialist state in which all power belongs to the working people, and that their leading force is the Marxist-Leninist party. The Republic is described as "a constitutional state implementing a multi-party system, parliamentary democracy and social market economy."[102] The constitutional amendments emphasize that the Republic of Hungary draws from the achievements of both western-type democracy, and traditions of democratic socialism. With the exception of this introductory statement the word "socialism" was carefully wiped from the entire constitutional text. The typical statements of the socialist constitutions on "the process of building of socialism,"[103] "elimination of the exploiting classes,"[104] and on "the dependence of the rights of citizens on the interests of socialist society,"[105] are totally omitted in the new text.

The constitution does not guarantee anymore a privileged status to "all forms of social ownership."(106). The amendments declare that "the economy of Hungary is a market economy" and give equal rights and protection to forms of public and private ownership.[107] The new text recognizes within the constitutional limitations the expropriation of property only for the reasons of public interest, and the right to free competition; and the text guarantees the right of inheritance.[108]

The constitutional amendments did not change a form of the state which is still described as a parliamentary democracy with the parliament as "a supreme organ of state power and popular representation." The Parliament has still vast powers to elect the highest executive and judicial officials of the state such as the members of the Council of Ministers, the Constitutional Court, the Commissioners of Citizens' Rights, The Presidents of the State Audit Office, the National Bank and the Supreme Court, and the Chief Public Prosecutor. The term of the Parliament was shortened, however, from five to four years and its right to declare a state of war, and to pronounce states of exigency and emergency, was reserved to the decision of a qualified, two-thirds majority.[109] The amendments imposed also new checks on the power of the Parliament through the elimination of the collegiate head of the state, the Presidium of the Hungarian People's Republic, and the creation, instead, of a separate office of the President of the Republic. The amendments introduced also the elements of direct or plebiscitary democracy through adding the provisions on a national referendum.[110]

The introduction of the office of the President of the Republic signifies an important step in the process of the evolution of the socialist model of parliamentary democracy into the presidential system. The amendments of 1989 and 1990 still seem to have only a temporary character. After the numerous attempts to stipulate that the President will be elected directly by the Hungarian people, the current Act still declares that he is elected for four years by the Parliament with only one chance for re-election. The nomination for the post of the President requires a valid support of at least fifty Members of Parliament with each Member having only the right to support one candidate.[111] The election can take place in several rounds. In the first two the President can be elected only by a qualified majority of two-thirds; in the third round, in which only two candidates remain, a plurality suffices for election. The President cannot be recalled by the Parliament but all measures taken by him require countersignature by one of the Ministers; Ministers are elected and dismissed by the Parliament.

The Presidency is still not a fully independent power. The President is a senior statesman who is an intermediary between the Parliament and the Prime Minister. After consultation with the leaders of the Parliamentary Panels, the President gives the Prime Minister "the mandate to form a Government"[112] but the final approval of the governmental program and the composition of the Council of Ministers is vested in the Parliament. The President appoints and dismisses only Parliamentary Undersecretaries, the Vice-Presidents of the National Banks and university professors.

The President represents the Hungarian state and is the commander-in-chief of the armed forces.[113] The President can be impeached upon the motion of one fifth of all the Members of Parliament supported by the vote of two thirds of the Members of the Parliament. The impeachment shall be considered by a Council of Judgment composed of twelve persons elected by Parliament from among its Members.

The President does not have a constitutional right to veto the legislative acts. He can, however, ask the parliament to reconsider the Act and eventually submit it to the Constitutional Court for the review of its constitutionality. If the Constitutional Act is not declared unconstitutional by the Court, the President has to sign it within five days. The President may dissolve the Parliament if it withdraws confidence from the Council of Ministers at least four times within twelve months or is unable to appoint the Council of Ministers. The provision that the President can dismiss the Parliament only twice during his tenure has recently been dropped by the newest constitutional amendments.

The introduction of the new Constitutional Court, composed of fifteen members elected by two-thirds of the Parliament and vested with the right to annul unconstitutional laws, is another remarkable change. However, with all the importance of the process of the development of the constitutional review in Hungary, one has to observe that the Constitutional requirement that the character of the Court be unpolitical is at least unusual and unrealistic. It can be expected that the provision that the Members of the Court should not be members of any political Party will have to be reconsidered and the rationale of this requirement submitted to wider discussion.[114]

The major changes were introduced into Chapter XII, which is on Fundamental Rights and Duties. The economic rights that, for their propaganda value, were put into all Stalinist constitutions at the forefront of the Chapter, gave way to the declaration of human rights to life and dignity, and the due rights of citizens to proper criminal procedure; all these, though guaranteed by most of the Western constitutions since the French Declaration of the Rights of Man and the American Bill of Rights, were omitted by the socialist constitutions. The Hungarian Constitution guarantees now due rights against unlawful criminal prosecution: the right to liberty and personal safety; the right to compensation for victims of unlawful arrest and detention; the presumption of innocence; the right to defence; the principle *nullum crimen sine lege* which means that no person shall be convicted or punished for an action that, at the time of commission, did not qualify as a criminal offence under the law.

The list of the civil-rights and freedoms is also more impressive and includes the right to freedom of thought, conscience, and religion; the free expression of opinions; the liberty of the press; the right to freely create organizations or communities; and the right to strike. The Constitution does not state anymore that the exercise of the rights is inseparable from the duties of citizen, although it enumerates several basic duties in its concluding articles, such as: duty to defend the country and the duty to contribute—in proportion to income and property circumstances—to public expenditures, or the duty of parents to take care of the education of their minor children.

To sum up, the Hungarian constitutional amendments, although they still require some further refinement, created a solid framework for further economic and social restructuring. The reform initiated from within the Party was undertaken by the non-communist elements and is continuing without losing its momentum. The grassroots support for political reconstruction, and the flexibility of the competing political forces, gained Hungary some credit in the West which was already facilitating the country's progress toward marketization and privatization.

CONCLUSIONS: TOWARDS A NEW CONSTITUTIONAL MODEL FOR CENTRAL AND EASTERN EUROPE

Is the constitutional reform a major sign of the reconstructing of the legal system of former "People's Democracies"? Given the kaleidoscopic political changes sweeping the Soviet Union, the definite answer hardly may be rendered at this moment. With the Soviet empire dissolving and crumbling rather than reconstituting, each change begets some unpredictable change, and requires evaluation of upcoming events. As far as it concerns the more advanced former Soviet satellite countries such as Poland or Hungary, the well-balanced assessment of the constitutional changes is more feasible although the application of the changes in practice still requires time and numerous constitutional adjustments. So, does this situation allow the further emergence of a new constitutional model applicable to the countries of Central and Eastern Europe? Given the diversity of traditions, national problems and ethnic aspirations, this task seems to be not only possible but necessary. "Of course," writes Timothy G. Ash, "there is a kaleidoscope of new parties, programs, and trends, and it is little short of impudence to subsume them into one 'message'. Yet, if you look at what these diverse parties are really saying about basic questions of politics, economics, law and international relations, there is a remarkable underlying consensus."[115] This statement is equally applicable to the constitutional transformations.

1. A new constitutional model is surfacing although the process is still far from completion. Until recently, no country of the former Soviet bloc adopted an entirely new constitution although all of them introduced remarkable changes into their basic laws and several of them declared already that the new constitutions are in process. The Soviets still seem to have only a vague concept of political reconstructing and their economic reforms are losing momentum, but even they seem to comprehend at this moment that *glasnost* is a distress signal within their system. At the moment they conclude that they do not need a "conservative revolution" but a radical and thorough *perestroika*, they will have to draft a new constitution.[116] The preamble of the amended Hungarian Constitution of 1949 states

that the parliament lays down the current changes "until enactment of a new Constitution." Bulgaria announced that a new constitution will be adopted in 1991. As far as Poland is concerned, the Constitutional Commission is already working on a project of a new constitution and its President declared that it will be submitted to the Seym in early Spring to be adopted in the bicentennial of the Polish first Constitution, on May 3, 1991.[117]

2. There is a strong tendency to emphasize that former communist states are in the process of transformation into liberal democracies. It is quite clear that the new constitutions will describe their countries not as "socialist democracies" but as parliamentary democracies. It means that all the power in these states will not be vested in the working classes as represented by their communist parties but in "people" (like in Hungary) or in "nation" (like in Poland). The parliamentary character of these democracies means the same as in the West, that the people exercise their sovereignty indirectly through elected representatives. Representative or indirect form of democracy will prevail although it already can be expected that the forms of direct participation of people in power (through referenda or plebiscites) will be better developed in new constitutions.

Communism managed to poison numerous basic principles of Western constitutionalism, the concept of division of powers included. The observer of the process of the development of constitutionalism in Central-Eastern Europe has to admit that the reluctance to experiment with the idea of checks and balances as practiced in the United States or even in a limited way in Western Europe is widespread in the former socialist countries. The reservations to the concept of balance and division of power stem equally from the interwar parliamentary experiences of Central European countries, the Polish legacy of "seymocracy," and from the idea of socialist parliamentary superiority which did not function in practice but was forcefully inserted into socialist constitutional theory. All these factors taken into account, it can be expected that forthcoming constitutional acts will favor the parliamentary form of government with elements of the presidential system tested cautiously and introduced gradually via the track of further amendments.

3. There is a tendency to describe the state as a "democratic constitutional state" (like in Hungary) or "democratic legal state" (like in Poland). Both concepts put an emphasis on legality (without an adjective "socialist") of state actions, which means (1)

observance of the law and working on the basis of the law by every organ of state, (2) the hierarchic character of legal acts with the basic laws recognized as an apex of the legal system, (3) the hierarchic character of state organs subordinated to the supreme legislative bodies, and (4) extended protection for human rights.

4. The new constitutions will show no clear preference for a bicameral or unicameral legislature. In the socialist legal theory of law, the second chamber was recognized usually as unnecessary with the exception made only for the countries with a federal system, like the Soviet Union or Czechoslovakia. As K. Grzybowski wrote, "The Senate is either antidemocratic or unnecessary."[118]

The creation of the Senate in a unitary state such as Poland responded to the demands of the revolutionary times and was expected to create a framework for further pluralization of the political system.[119] In the period of the disputes of "the round table," it was noted that sometimes the second chamber was conceived as an equivalent of "the chamber of labor" and was expected to represent trade unions or self-governmental institutions as in the Yugoslavian system. Some of the Polish commentators opted for a more democratic electoral system in which one senator would be elected by one million electors and not by the artificially set 100 electoral districts, two of each voidship. Some others argued that a weaker position of the Senate in comparison with the Seym undermines the rationale of this institution. To sum up, one has to admit that the emergence of bicameral legislative bodies in unitary states has to be reconsidered and that it can be expected that in a new constitutional model there will be room for the second chamber only as a federal component of the representative body.

5. The new constitutions will incorporate the principle of political pluralism among basic constitutional rules. One of the discernible trends in the new constitutions is the attempt to recognize a multi-party system as an element of well-functioning constitutional government. The drafters of the constitutional amendments showed already some sensitivity on this issue as well as the concern that some functions and public offices should be reserved only to people who are politically neutral. Although it can be expected that the last mentioned requirement will be dropped from the new basic laws the general tendency for guaranteeing a constitutional protection for a multi-party system will most likely prevail in the next round of constitutional works in Central-Eastern Europe.

6. It is still not clear which electoral system will prevail in the new constitutions. Poland traditionally favored the system of plurality

which recognized as elected candidates those who received the majority of votes in their constituencies. The Electoral Law of April 7, 1989[120] introduced two rounds of elections, the first one demanding the electoral victory and absolute majority of more than fifty percent of votes and the second round demanding only a plurality. This system worked properly in the transitory time when only two political blocks, that of Solidarity and that of the governmental coalition, competed for power. With the further pluralization of Polish political life, this system might require some adjustments. In the Hungarian election rules, *nota bene* one of the most complex in the world, the plurality system was combined with the principle of proportionality. About half the seats in the parliament were fixed on the basis of votes cast for individual parties.[121]

The drafters of the new constitutions have to realize that the plurality model was traditionally favored by the countries with a two-party system, while the proportional system prevailed in the multi-party democracies. It can be expected that if the multi-party system is going to gain the upper hand in a new constitutional model, it will have to be linked to the further introduction of the principle of proportionality into the electoral laws of the countries of East-Central Europe.[122]

7. There is a clear tendency to incorporate into the new constitutional model some elements of the presidential system. The collegiate heads of state (Councils of State or Presidiums) were eliminated and their functions passed on to the executive Presidents. Although at this moment there is a clear difference between the roles played by the bearers of the presidential offices in the new European democracies, it can be already expected that these posts will become a basic engine of further transformation in this region. The role of the Presidents in the new democracies will inevitably grow. Although it can be observed that Jaruzelski, the former leader of the Polish Communist Party, kept a relatively low profile as the President, while the Soviet or Czech Presidents are clearly conductors of domestic and foreign policies of their countries, it is certain that Lech Walesa, who was elected the new Polish President in December 1990, will not be a figurehead.

At this moment there are no symptoms that the new Eastern European constitutional model will evolve toward the American presidential system. The prevailing opinion is that the new model should maintain a dual executive system, with presidents as heads of state playing roles of "senior statesmen" or "supreme arbitrators" and the prime ministers, as heads of government functioning as politically accountable chief executive officers.[123] The observers believe that the new constitutional system may evolve either toward a German type of "chancellor's democracy" or a French presidential system.[124] In fact, an evolution either in the direction of French or German models depends a lot on the political personalities of future Presidents and Prime Ministers and at this moment one has to admit that the presidential prerogatives in the Soviet Union, Poland and Hungary are closer to the model which was worked out in socialist Czechoslovakia than to any of the West European types.

Some presidents, currently in office, still were elected by the representative bodies. This system is going to undergo a major change and it can be expected that the successive bearers of the presidential offices will be elected directly by the people.[125] The presidents will have a suspensive right of veto (or a right to deny the signature on the legislative act) which can be overruled by a qualified majority of the parliaments. It can be expected that the right to appoint ministers and other top officials will be returned to the presidents with the right to dismiss them reserved for parliaments. The presidents will not be politically responsible but can be impeached by the parliaments for constitutional violations. They will be commanders-in-chief of their countries and will be vested with a prerogative to impose martial law for a limited period in cases of grave danger to the state or a natural catastrophe. In sum, their positions will be by no means ceremonial and it can be expected that their prerogatives will grow.

8. As far as economic system is concerned the direction is quite plain. The constitutions will present the new democracies as market economies although the market system may be described as a "social" one.[126] "Social" will mean a widespread support for the still large role played by the state in a relatively egalitarian distribution of the wealth.

9. It can be expected that the catalogs of fundamental rights in the new constitutions will be relatively long and exhaustive. On the one hand, the current constitutional lists of rights will be supplemented by important political and civil rights and due rights in criminal prosecution; on the other hand, the provisions on economic, social and cultural rights will be moved behind the declarations of political rights, but these rights still will maintain constitutional protection.

10. Last but not least, the enforcement mechanisms will be built into the new constitutional texts. They will guarantee independence of the judiciary and will introduce the system of judicial

review of the constitutionality of legislative acts. It is predictable
that the new democracies will adopt a so-called "centralized" or
Austrian model, which reserves the right to constitutional review to
one special judicial organ (the Constitutional Court or the
Constitutional Tribunal). This system favors "abstract review" which
is initiated before the special court by special State organs or officials
in special proceedings in which constitutionality of the normative
act is the principle matter being reviewed, independently of any
pending case.

In sum, it seems important to note that the new East-Central
European model will be an embodiment of features commonly
recognized as essential for Western constitutionalism: parliamentary
and liberal democracy, limited government, open society providing
a broad coverage for human rights, legality or the rule of law,
enforcement of the constitutional principles, and guarantees for the
private ownership and market mechanisms. The question, however,
of how this model will function remains open. Those who study the
mechanisms of constitutional engineering should bear in mind that
practice can depart considerably from the best constitutional theory.
The legacy of socialist constitutionalism makes this reflection
especially fresh and instructive. Hence, the practical value of the
new constitutional model will be a function of many variables: the
applicability of Western constitutional ideas in a new post-totalitarian
political environment, their compatibility with socialist and pre-
socialist Eastern European traditions, and the social and political
compromise embodied in the new constitutions. The durability of
the new constitutional model will depend both on the coherence of
its essential components and on the political culture of the people
who will apply constitutional principles in practice. The new
constitutional model will be as good and firm as the will of the people
to protect it and to observe its basic provisions. How mature this
will actually is remains still to be seen.

NOTES

1. See *Legal System Cyclopedia* supra note 42, p. 418.
2. See E. Carr, *The Interregnum*, 1923-1924, p. 257 (1960).
3. In 1964 Mikoyan rose to the rank of President of the
Presidium of the Supreme Soviet but the following year he resigned
this office for reasons of ill health. In 1964 Kosygin was elevated to
the Premier position. He resigned in 1980 for the same reasons as
Mikoyan.

4. "Demokratizatsiya nashay zhizni" (Democratization of Our Country), *Pravda*, Oct. 25, 1988, p. 1.

5. *Tass*, Dec. 1, 1988 extracted in Constitutional Amendments Approved, FBIS-SOV-88-231, Dec. 1, 1988, pp. 46-47.

6. *USSR Law on Amendments and Additions to the USSR Constitution* (Fundamental Law), reprinted in Pravda, Dec. 3, 1988, pp. 1-2 (1st. ed), translated and extracted in Law on Constitutional Amendments, FBIS-SOV-88-233, Dec. 5, 1988, pp. 48-58 [hereinafter Constitutional Amendments]

7. *Id.*, p. 50.

8. USSR Law on Elections of USSR People's Deputies reprinted in Pravda, Dec. 4, 1988, pp. 1-3 (1st ed.) translated and extracted in Law on-, FBIS-SOV-89-233, Dec. 5, 1988, p. 35 [hereinafter Deputy Elections of Deputies Elections of Law].

9. *Id.*, art. 15, p. 37.

10. See *Democratization in Our Time*, supra note 196.

11. A. Vyshinsky, *The Law of the Soviet State*, p. *vii* (1948).

12. *Id.*, p. 722.

13. See Dezso, "Socialist Electoral Systems and the 1983 Hungarian Reform," in *Yearbook on Socialist Legal Systems* 45-46 (W. Butler ed. 1986).

14. Konst. SSSR of 1977, art. 100.

15. See Constitutional Amendments, supra note 139, art. 100; Deputy Elections Law, supra note 141, art. 24.

16. "Strogii Examen" (Strict Examination), *Pravda*, Oct. 18, 1988, p. 1.

17. A. Vyshinsky, supra note 203 p. 724.

18. See Dobbs, "Party Still Holds Key to Soviet Elections," *Wash. Post* Jan. 11, 1989, p. A15, col. 5.

19. *Id.*

20. *Id.*

21. *Id.*

22. Dobbs, "Sakharov Seeking Stamp of Approval," *Wash. Post*, Jan. 23, 1989, p. A14, col. 2.

23. *Id*; see L. Schapiro, supra note 48, p. 458.

24. J. Wrobel, "The Drama of Polish Education Continues," *Studium Papers*, Ja. 1987, p. 3.

25. Trimble, "Reform is Risky Business," *U.S. News & World Report*, June 19, 1989, pp. 27-28.

26. Remnick, "Sakharov Sees Gorbachov at Risk," *Wash. Post*, June 22, 1989, p. A34, Col. 1.

27. *Id.*

28. Trimble, supra note 227, p. 28.

29. *Democratization in Our Time*, supra note 196.

30. Constitutional Amendments, supra note 198,art. 108.

31. Deputy Elections Law, supra note 200, arts, 15, 17, 18. For the full text of article 18, see *Pravda*, Dec. 4, 1989, p. 1.

32. Dobbs, "Gorbachev Appeals for Political Reforms," *Wash. Post*, Nov. 30, 1988, p. A34, col. 1.

33. Constitutional Amendments, supra note 198, ch. 15.

34. *Id.*

35. *Id.*

36. *Id.*

37. *Id.*

38. Dobbs, "Soviet Reformers Suffer Broad Defeat in Key Legislature Vote," *Wash. Post*, May 28, 1989, p. A-1, col. 1.

39. *Tass*, Oct. 22, 1988, extracted in "Changes to Enhance Democracy," FBIS-SOV-88-2-5, Oct. 24, 1988, p. 50.

40. Remnick, "Presidential Bill Passes in Moscow: Gorbachev Prevails After Angry Debate Over 'Dictatorship'," *Wash. Post*, Feb. 28, 1990, p. A-1, col. 6; Clines, "Gorbachev Forces Bill on Presidency Past Legislature," *N.Y. Times*, Feb. 28, 1990, p. A-1, col. 3.

41. See Remnick, "Angry Estonians to Discuss Changes in Constitution," *Washington Post*. Nov. 4, 1988, p. A 30, Col. 1.

42. See Keller, "Lithuania Declares Annexation by Moscow Void", *N.Y. Times*, Oct. 6, 1989, p. A5, col. 1.

43. See Fein, "Estonia Suspends Part of Disputed Vote Law," *N.Y. Times*, Oct. 6, 1989, p. A9, Col. 1.

44. Remnick, "Multi-Plan Adopted by Lithuania," *Wash. Post*, Dec. 8, 1989, p. A 1, col. 6.

45. *Pravda*, Special Supplement, "Draft Union Treaty" Nov. 24, 2990; translation after 1990, The British Broadcasting Corporation Summary of World Broadcasts, Nov. 26, 1990, a S:U/0931/C3/1.

46. See 1977 Constitution, art 72.

47. Art 1, Draft Union Treaty, *op. cit.*, p. 3.

48. Art 9, Draft Treaty of the Union, *op. cit.* p. 5.

49. *Ibid.*, Art 16.

50. *Ibid.*, Art 15 p. 7.

51. "Gorbachev Appeals to Nation to Preserve Union", *Wash. Post*, February 7, 1991, A 16.

52. *Ibid.*

53. Shlapentokh, "Gorbachev's Real Foe - The Soviet

Workers," *Wash. Post*, Nov. 26, 1989, p. C2, col. 1.

54. Lee, "Sakharov Sees Threat to Reform," *Wash. Post*, Nov. 8, 1988, p. A1. col. 1; Kirkpatrick, "Sakharov's Fears, " *Wash. Post*, Nov. 7, 1988, p. A23, col. 4.

55. See *Washington Post*, December 24, 1989 A21-25.

56. For more profound analysis of the collapse of communism in Poland see Rett R. Ludwikowski, *Crisis of Communism*, Washington, D.C., 1986.

57. E. Skalski, "After the Round Table Poland Turns to the Polls," *The New Leader*, April 3-17, 1989, p. 6.

58. *Ibid.*, p.7.

59. J. Dieh, "Polish Side Agrees on Freely Elected Senate" *Wash. Post*, March 10, 1989, A1.

60. E. Skalski, *New Leader*, supra note, p. 7.

61. Electoral Law, April 11, 1989, art 41, *Rzeczypospolita* (Republic), April 11, 1989, p. 2.

62. Skalski, *New Leader*, supra note, p. 7.

63. *Electoral Law*, supra note, p. 3.

64. "Solidarity's Stunning Win," *Newsweek*, June 19, 1989, p. 42.

65. Four ministers (agriculture, justice, environment, and health) were accorded to the United Farmers Party; commerce and technical development ministers were allocated to The Democratic Association; defense, the interior, transport, and foreign trade were assigned to the Polish United Workers' Party. Solidarity took over major economic ministers: communication, labor, central planning, country planning and building, industry, finance, and also culture & art and education. The Ministry of Foreign Affairs was taken over by an independent Polish scholar.

66. The most significant amendments were adopted in April 7, 1989 (published in *Dziennik Ustaw* - Official Gazette, Nr. 19, April 8, 1989); in December 29, 1989 (*Dziennik Ustaw* Nr. 75, December 31, 1989; and in September 27, 1990 *Dziennik Ustaw* Nr. 67, October 2, 1990). Two less important changes were introduced by the Statutes of March 28, 1990 (*Dziennik Ustaw*, of March 19, 1990) and of April 11, 1990 (*Dziennik Ustaw* Nr. 29 of May 7, 1990).

67. Current Art. 1.

68. Former Art. 1 and 7.

69. Current Art. 85.

70. Current Art. 1.

71. See W. Sokolewicz, "Rzeczpospolita Polska -

demokratyczne panstwo prawne" (Polish Republic - a democratic legal state), *Panstwo i Prawo* (State and Law) Vol. IV, April 1990, p. 19.

72. See S. Zawadzki, "Nowa konstytucyjna definicja polskiej panstwowosci" (A New Constitutional definition of the Polish state), *Panstwo i Prawo* (State and Law), Vol. V, May 1990, p. 17; also J. Zakrzewska, "Nowa Konstytucja Rzeczypospolitej" (A new Constitution of a Republic, *Ibid.*, pp. 3-11.

73. W. Sokolewicz, "Rzeczypospolita Polska-," supra note, at 14; S. Zawadzki, "Nowa konstytucyjna definicja," supra note, p. 20.

74. A. Zawadzki spoke in favor of the introduction of the principle of division of powers in the article quoted above: "Nowa konstytucyjna definicja," supra note, 17-18; against this idea is clearly P. Sarnecki, "Zalozenia konstytucji" (Fundamental constitutional principles), *Panstwo i Prawo* (State and Law), Vol. 7. July 1990 p.8; also W. Sokolewicz, "Rzad w przyszlej konstytucji" (The Government in a future constitution), *Panstwo i Prawo* (State and Law), Vol. 7. July 1990, p. 15.

75. Current Art. 20 #2.

76. Chapter III of the amended 1952 Constitution.

77. The current Art. 27 #1 & 2.

78. Current Art. 32a #1.

79. Art. 27 #5.

80. Art. 27 #4.

81. Current Art. 30 #2. The provision of the amendment of April 7, 1989 on the Presidential prerogative to dissolve the Seym if it fails to adopt a long-term, economic plan was dropped by the amendment of December 29, 1990 altogether with the provision which obliged the Seym to adopt long-term and annual economic plans (former Art. 24 #1 and 3).

82. Current Art. 32f #6.

83. Art. 37 #1.

84. See R.R. Ludwikowski, "Judicial Review in the Socialist Legal System: Current Developments," *The International and Comparative Law Quarterly*, Vol. 37, 1988 pp. 96 and 100.

85. See S. Gebethner, "Wybory do Sejmu i Senatu 1989r" (Elections to Seym and Senate in 1989), *Panstwo i Prawo* (State and Law, XLIV/8 August 1989 p. 4. See also J. Kropownicki, "Liczyl sie Tylko Stepel Walesy" (Everything which Counted was a Stamp of Walesa), *Gazeta Wyborcza* (Electoral Gazette), Nr. 24 June 9-11, 1989 p. 5.

86. Gebethner, *ibid.*, p. 7.

87. In the first round of elections 62.32 percent of electorate participated; in the second round only 25.11 percent (*Ibid.*, at 12).

88. W. Sokolewicz, "Kwietniowa Zmiana Konstytucji" (April Constitutional Changes), *Panstwo i Prawo* (State and Law), Vol. 6, June 1989 p. 6.

89. John Lukacs, "Budapest 1945: The Year Zero," *The Wilson Quarterly*, Vol. XIV, No. 2, p. 41, Spring 1990.

90. *Ibid.*, p. 41.

91. *Ibid.*

92. *Ibid.*

93. *Ibid.*

94. Renee de Nevers, "The Soviet Union and Eastern Europe: The End of an Era," *Adelphi Paper*, Nr. 249, March 1990, pp. 28-29.

95. See Karen Dawisha, *Eastern Europe, Gorbachev and Reform. The Great Challenge*, 1990, p. 176.

96. R. de Nevers, "The Soviet Union and Eastern Europe," supra note, p. 29.

97. K. Dawisha, *Eastern Europe, Gorbachev and Reform*, supra note, p. 177.

98. See Stepen E. Deane, "After the Bloc Party," *The Wilson Quarterly*, Vol. XIV, No. 2, Spring 1990, p. 48.

99. See R. De Nevers, "The Soviet Union and Eastern Europe," supra note, pp. 32-33.

100. K. Dawisha, *Eastern Europe, Gorbachev and Reform*, supra note, p. 298.

101. A uniform structure of the Constitutional Act XX of 1949 and its amendments was published in *Magyar Kozlony* (The Hungarian Official Gazette) in August 24, 1990. The English version is quoted from the official translation of the constitutional text, which was sent to the author by the Hungarian Embassy in Washington, D.C.

102. Preamble to the Constitution of 1949 as amended.

103. Former Art. 5.

104. Former Art. 6.

105. Former Art. 54 #2.

106. Former Art. 6 #2.

107. Current Art. 9 #1.

108. Current Art. 9 #2, 13 and 14.

109. Amended Art. 19 #4.

110. Current Art. 19 #5.

111. Art. 29 B#1.

112. Art. 33 #3.

113. Art. 30A #1.

114. Practice worked out various mechanisms to neutralize political background and even to dissociate judicial officials from the interests of their home countries. The best example is the procedure of the European Court of Justice which requires the complete independence of its members. To protect the judges against national pressure the court always issues its decision without any separate concurring or dissenting judgments. The system works perfectly. See T.C. Hartley, *The foundations of European Community Law*, 1988 at 50-51.

115. T. G. Ash, "Eastern Europe: The Year of Truth," *The New York Review of Books*, February 15, 1990, p. 21.

116. For more comments on the idea of "conservative revolution" in the Soviet Union, see R.R. Ludwikowski, *"Glasnost as a Conservative Revolution," The Intercollegiate Review*, Fall 1989, pp. 25-32.

117. The most recent news from Poland indicates that the adoption of a new Constitution was postponed.

118. Separately published brochure, "Senat albo niedemokratyczny albo niepotrzebny" (Senate either antidemocratic or unnecessary), 1946; see also Z. Jarosz, Problem drugiej izby parlamentu - Zarys Koncepcji (Problem with the second chamber of Parliament - Outline of the Concept), *Panstwo i Prawo*, (State and Law), Vol. XLIV/1, January 1989, pp. 16-28.

119 W. Sokolewicz, "Kwietniowa Zmiana Konstytucji" (April Constitutional Change), supra note, pp. 3-19.

120. *Dziennik Ustaw*, Nr. 19 of April 8, 1989.

121. Blain Harden, "Centrist Parties Surge in Hungarian Voting," *Washington Post*, March 27, 1990, pp. A1 and A20.

122. S. Zawadzki, "Nowa konstytucyjna definicja polskiej panstwowosci," (A new constitutional definition of the Polish statehood), *Panstwo i Prawo*, Vol. 5, 1990 p.19.

123. W. Sokolewicz, "Rzad w Przyszlej konstytucji," supra note, pp. 12-27.

124. Some commentators believe, however, that in Central-Eastern Europe (especially in Poland) there is no conducive political environment for the development of a "chancellor's system." See P. Sarnecki, "Zalozenia konstytucji," supra note, p. 10.

125. See "Law of the Union of Soviet Socialist Republic On Establishing the Post of the President of the U.S.S.R.," March 14,

1990 *Current Digest of the Soviet Press*, Nr. 42/14 1990 pp. 22-23, 32; "Ustawa o Zmianie Konstytucji Rzeczypospolitej Polskiej" (The amendment to the Constitution of the Polish Republic), of September 27, 1990, *Dziennik Ustaw*, Nr. 67, of October 2, 1990, p. 933.

126. The Preamble to the Hungarian Constitution of 1949 as amended in 1989 and 1990. See also S. Zawadzki, "Nowa konstytucyjna definicja," supra note, p. 21.

PART III

TOWARDS FREEDOM AND CHOICE: SPAIN, TAIWAN, THE PHILIPPINES

CHAPTER IX

ALFONSO X'S IMAGE OF ENLIGHTENED RULE: NATURE, SOCIETY, AND POLITICS IN THE LAW PROLOGUES

ROBERTO J. GONZÁLEZ-CASANOVAS

This paper examines, according to rhetorical and cultural historicist models, the prologues to Alfonso X the Wise's books of laws in Castilian: *Fuero Real* (1255), *Espéculo* (circa *1256-60)*, *Sietepartidas (1256-65)*, and *Setenario* (circa 1275-84, with Laws 1-10 as prologue). Its aim is to establish the bases for authority (legal, political, social, and moral) in these official texts that serve as interpretative frames for the laws. In particular, it is important to consider the authority of natural law and the type of social utopia that emerge from the law books. As part of the process of reading these legal texts as cultural codes, it is necessary to determine their proper contexts: on the one hand, they reflect a renaissance of Roman law and Greek natural philosophy that takes place in the twelfth and thirteenth centuries; on the other hand, they constitute responses to opportunities and problems associated with the Christian Reconquest of half of Iberia from the Moors in 1212-52.

In order to investigate the foundations of royal power and the rationale for enlightened rule in the law prologues, three critical tasks need to be attempted: (1) to relate the ethical rhetoric to legal models (Roman, Islamic, papal, and imperial) of the times; (2) to link the political propaganda of the laws to the didactic function of all the Alfonsine prologues (historical, scientific, legal, courtly, and devotional); and (3) to analyze the underlying premises of the discourses of authority, seen as problems of human nature, society, and government, through a historicist reading of the legal prologues as they evolve over twenty years of the ambitious yet frustrated reign of the Wise King.

Alfonso X's legislation must be placed in its juridical, clerical, and cultural contexts: Roman traditions of written, codified law, as taught at the University of Bologna; national, royalist "constitutions" promoted by imperial chanceries, like the *Constitutions of Malfi* (1231) promulgated by Frederick II in Sicily; encyclopedias of canon law, undertaken by the Dominican Ramon

Peflafort in his *Summa de casibus poenitentiae* (1222-29) and *Decretales Gregorii IX* (1230-34); and Arabic reinterpretations of Greek natural philosophy, such as Averroist commentaries on Aristotle.

Beyond the legal traditions dominant in the thirteenth century, the most decisive influence on the models of authority in Alfonso's laws comes from the development of royal power in relation to the expanded frontier areas of New Castile, Extremadura, Andalucia, and Murcia. During his reign (1252-84), the frontier was the central phenomenon of existence and civilization: the physical frontier included a variety of territories, landscapes, and settlements that encompassed the whole range of urban and rural life in the Mediterranean; the cultural frontier contained a diversity of peoples, languages, and religions whose heterogeneity made it necessary to redefine traditional concepts of human nature and society. Both frontiers stimulated a renaissance in all aspects of life that is reflected in the encyclopedic and utopian works written at Alfonso's court. This renaissance served to reinterpret biblical, classical, scholastic, and Oriental ways of thinking about nature and society, which royal administrators applied to repopulating and governing the semi-developed and unassimilated frontier areas. It is in these geographic, historical, cultural, and ideological contexts that Alfonso X's law prologues, as enlightened codes of royal authority and power, must be read.

Furthermore, it is necessary to examine Alfonso X of Castile's use of courtly language to explain, apply, and extend the chivalric ideals of virtue and service as the basis of the new system of laws for the whole nation. This sociolinguistic code defines and elaborates the model of the Christian state for the wise lawgiver: for it projects the king's authority in relation to his responsibilities to his subjects, at the same time that it exemplifies, on the interpersonal level of aristocrat and commoner, the nobility of character and the bonds of concord which will guarantee justice.

A question arises, however, regarding the changing emphases that Alfonso X places during his reign on royal authority, political utility, rational ethics, and Christian morality. The variations in the rhetoric of the courtly code become manifest when a comparison is made between the three most important prologues to the Alfonsinse law codes: the prologue to the *Espéculo,* a preliminary draft of the laws (c. 1256-60), and two manuscript versions of the prologue to the complete laws in the *Sietepartidas* (c. 1260-65 in the British Museum [BM] and the Biblioteca Nacional [BN]). The king's difficulties in balancing his chivalric ideals with the nation's realities are revealed over the years in significant modifications in the intent, argument, and application of his model.

The prologue to the *Espéculo* stresses the divine foundations of Alfonso's reign, which it contrasts with the human disorder of regional laws and local customs (the various *fueros*). It goes on to establish the king's objective in the courtly metaphor of the mirror: the laws will reflect the noble's code of virtue, but in such a way as to provide exemplary images of justice for all the people in the land. Although the rhetorical structure is similar in the other two prologues, and certain passages are almost identical in the BM manuscript, it is clear that the *Espéculo* represents the most royalist and least courtly pronouncement of policy: it is the only one that includes all of Alfonso X's titles and it bases its appeal on the supremacy of the king's personal power as derived directly from God ("We, Alfonso, by the grace of God king...').

The prologue to the *Siete partidas* in the BM manuscript soon departs from the opening lines of the *Espéculo* in order to refer to the obligations that all rulers have in common as part of their *oficio* and *estado*. Alfonso X here appeals, rather than to the grace of God and his particular suzerainties, to the powers, rights, and obligations of all earthly kings. This version includes a more courtly image of the ruler, not as the one divine agent and viceroy of the land, but as one of many faithful servants and champions of God among the aristocratic ruling class of his day. Accordingly, what Alfonso here underscores is the courtly code of service "for the common good:" the king offers his people protection and example in their own efforts to lead virtuous lives. As a good and wise ruler, he upholds only those laws that represent the best of local justice, while seeking to establish a norm of behavior that will benefit all peoples.

The third prologue, in the BN manuscript of the *Siete partidas,* expands further on the moral authority of the laws by basing them on claims of divine Reason and examples of courtly Virtue. Once again, Alfonso presents a model of chivalry that extends to all rulers worthy of their estate: their exercise of power must correspond to their social obligations and should inspire a similar fulfillment of roles and duties among their loyal subjects. The metaphor from the *Espéculo* of the lawbook as mirror is here reintroduced, but with reference, not to the peoples, but to the king's reflection in it. For the king, as a good lord and courtier, serves as embodiment, propagandist, and interpreter of the code which he attempts to enforce.

The sociolinguistic functions of the code of aristocratic virtue, courtesy, and service emerge in these three prologues as keys to the understanding and enforcement of the laws that follow. On the rhetorical and ideological planes, the courtly model determines the changing emphases chosen by Alfonso X in the evolution of royal lawgiving throughout his eventful reign. One only has to recall his efforts over seventeen years to become Holy Roman Emperor, or his struggle with a rebellious brother and son, to appreciate the urgency which underlies the increasingly idealistic and chivalrous language that he employs: if his present reign has not enjoyed as much peace and justice as he desires, perhaps his successors and their noble companions will be persuaded, through the courtly code of the *Espéculo* and *Siete partidas,* to practice the virtues traditionally associated with their office and estate.

Although all the prologues to the Alfonsine laws deal with an ideal representation of nature and society as a basis for justice, each underscores a different aspect of the model. For the sake of comparing rhetorical terms, which involves a certain simplification of the philosophical concepts and political contexts upon which they are based, it can be said that the prologues to the Alfonsine laws are to be distinguished as follows: the *Fuero Real* opposes, according to royalist and scholastic codes, a good social order to a bad human nature; the *Espéculo* projects a hierarchical model of society that is governed according to an enlightened and enlightening image of human nature as found at the royal court; the *Siete partidas,* in the British Museum [BM] manuscript, equates the functions and effects of royal legislation and natural law so as to guarantee a just social order and at the same time ratify an absolutist political regime; the *Siete partidas,* in the Biblioteca Nacional [BN] manuscript, promotes royal lawgiving as the proper and full "knowledge" (i.e. the quasi-divine understanding, experience, and control) of both human nature and society; and the *Setenario* associates law, in symbolic and exemplary terms, with good counsel in such a way as to relate human nature and society to a divine scheme of order or great chain of justice.

The juridical system established by Alfonso X in his various written law codes was never enforced during his own reign, but rather began to be applied, only in part, under his descendant Alfonso XI almost one hundred years later. Nevertheless, given the significance of such a vast undertaking in the politics of the emerging national monarchies (as with the parallel efforts by Philip IV of

France at the end of the same century), and given the influence of the royal statutes in the legal history of Spain and the New World (including Louisiana in what is now the United States), it is important to take seriously the utopian rhetoric employed by Alfonso in his prologues. As the "King of the three religions" in that expanded part of Iberia now controlled by Castile, and as pretender to the crown of the Holy Roman Empire during most of his reign, Alfonso saw the need to emphasize the common ethics of Jews, Christians, and Muslims, at the same time that he affirmed the divinely-sanctioned responsibility of the king-emperor as absolute judge of his people. The Wise King had grown up under the models of his father St. Fernando III, the magnanimous reconqueror of Seville, and of his uncle Frederick H, the autocratic reformer of Sicily; both monarchs were powerful and astute politicians, who deliberately cultivated images of enlightened courts so as to secure national consensus among a pluricultural people and promote international prestige for their ambitious courts. As someone brought up to seem and act as a wise king, Alfonso knew the political function and propaganda value of the rhetoric of justice. Therefore, for him natural reason and social order are as much a utopian dream of renaissance and reform, based on the restoration of Greco-Roman principles of justice and government (interpreted in complementary ways by Arabic philosophers and Italian jurists), as they are a pragmatic strategy based on the exercise of royal authority as interpreted by the king, mediated by his legal experts, and received by his heirs, elite, officials, and people. What the Averroist commentators of Aristotle and the Bolognese professors of civil law were advocating in theory Alfonso was attempting to accomplish in practice: the reordering of society in thirteenth-century Iberia, made possible and necessary by the Reconquest, called for a systematic rethinking of traditional law and a comprehensive program of royal reforms. In this way, the prologues serve as didactic codes for reeducating the ruling classes and the people alike; at the same time they constitute political acts that, as they redefine the very order of law and power, challenge all, rulers and subjects, both to enact and to expect justice.

APPENDIX

THE THREE PROLOGUES
IN ENGLISH TRANSLATION

Fuero Real

Since men's hearts are divided, therefore it is a natural thing that [their] understanding and actions are not in agreement as one, and for this reason there are many disagreements and many disputes among men. Hence it is proper for a king, in order to maintain his peoples in justice and law, that he make laws so that the peoples may know how they are to live, and the disagreements and quarrels [or lawsuits] that arise among them may be ordered in such a way that those who do wrong may receive punishment, and the good may live securely. And therefore, we, don Alfonso, by the grace of God king . . ., took counsel with our court and with those knowledgeable in law, and we gave [the town of Valladolid] the statute written in this book, so that men and women may be judged in common. And we commanded this statute to be kept forever, and that none dare to act against it (OL 2: 6).

Espéculo

We made the laws written in this book, which is a minor of the law, so that all in our kingdoms and dominion may be judged, and it is a light to all for knowing and understanding things pertaining to all deeds according to [their] benefit and harm, and to correct the deficiencies we have mentioned, and especially for judges, that they may know how to give judgment rightly and to preserve in its rights each party that comes before them, and to follow the established order in lawsuits as they ought to do (OL 1:1-2).

Siete Partidas (BM ms)

For it is proper for kings, who are to maintain and safeguard their peoples in peace and justice, to make laws, ordinances, and statutes, in order that the disagreement that men naturally have among themselves may be resolved by force of law. . . . The many statutes used in the towns and lands . . . were against God and against the law . . . (SP prol: 2-3 infra).

We made the laws written in this book to serve God and the common good of all in our dominion, so that they may know and understand with certainty the law, and know how to act according to it, and keep from doing wrong so as not to incur punishment. And we took them from the good statutes *[fueros]* and customs of Castile and León, and from the law that we found to be most common and beneficial to all persons throughout the world (SP prol: 4-5 infra).

Whosoever acts against this, we say that he errs in three ways: first, against God, who is the fullness of justice and truth, according to which this book is made; second, against his natural lord by scorning his action and command; and third, by showing himself to be proud and quarrelsome, since he is not satisfied with the law that is of common knowledge and benefit to all (SP prol: 6 infra).

Siete Partidas (BM ms)

Since men's understanding is divided in many ways, we could make them agree through a true and lawful reason in order first to know God . . ., who is lord over all, and then the temporal lords from whom [men] receive bounty in many ways, each according to his estate and merits. . . . All these things men could not do properly, unless each were to know what is his estate and what he ought to do in it, and what he ought to refrain from doing (SP prol: 3 supra).

It is very proper for kings, and especially for the ones of these kingdoms, to have a very great understanding so as to know things as they are. . . . The one who does not know this would not be able well and truly to do justice, which is to give to each what is proper to him and what he merits. . . . The kings, knowing the things that are true and lawful, shall do them themselves and shall not consent that others act against them, as King Solomon, who was very wise and very just, said . . . (SP prol: 4 supra).

For this reason we especially made this book of ours so that the kings of our dominion may look in it as in a mirror, and see the things they should correct and correct them, and that according to this they do the same among their own (SP prol: 4 supra).

Setenario

Through these seven letters [God] sent over us the seven gifts of the Holy Spirit . . ., with which to light our understanding and our will so that we may know the things that serve Him and understand what pleases Him most. And that we may always have good counsel to do it [Set, Ley 1: 7-8].

It was proper that this counsel be kept in writing forever, not only for those who live now, but also for those to come. And therefore he understood that the best and most fitting thing to do was to keep a written document *[escriptura]* in which to show them these things. . . . And that they make and keep this written document as if an inheritance from a parent, or a bounty from a lord, or a counsel from a good friend. And that they often hear what was placed in this book, so that they might learn to have good customs, and to trust and make use of them, as they let the good take root in them and remove the evil. And that they accept it as a statute and as a complete and certain law . . . [Set, Ley 10: 23].

The things they did not know made them not know God and not believe in Him or in their natural lord as they ought to do, and not to know how to honor or serve or fear him, or be grateful for the good he did to them. . . . Against reason they also trespassed much. . . . Against the nature of their lords [or dominions] they acted. . . . They did other evil things, disordered and against nature, in which they wronged God and all goodness [Set, Ley 10: 24-25].

Note: Quotations are from texts listed as primary sources in the bibliography; the translations are mine.

BIBLIOGRAPHY

A. Primary sources

Alfonso X. *El Espéculo o Espejo de todos los derechos,* in *Opúsculos legales,* I. Madrid: Real Academia de la Historia, 1836; 2 vols.
———— *[Estoria de Espanna],* or *Primera crónica general de España que mandó componer Alfonso X el Sabio.* Ed. R. Menéndez Pidal. Madrid: Gredos, 1955; rev. ed.; repub. 1978.
———— *Fuero Real,* in *Opúsculos legales,* 2. Madrid: Real Academia de la Historia, 1836; 2 vols.
———— *General Estoria.* Part I, ed. A. G. Soiaiinde. Madrid: Junta para Ampliación de Estudios e Investigaciones Cientiftcas/Centro de Estudios Histdricos, 1930.
———— *Setenario.* Ed. K. H. Vanderford. Buenos Aires: U. Buenos Aires/Inst. Filología, *1945.*
Sietepartidas. Madrid: Real Academia de la Historia, 1807; 3 vols;

repub. by Atlas, 1972.

B. Studies on Alfonso X's Laws and Politics

Alford, John A. and Dennis P. Seniff. *Literature and Law in the Middle Ages: A Bibliography of Scholarship.* New York: Garland, 1984.

Andrachuk, Gregory Peter. "Alfonso el Sabio, Courtier and Legislator," *Revista Canadiense de Estudios Hispanicos* 9, 3 (primavera 1985): 439-50.

Barragán, G. C. *La obra legislativa de Alfonso el Sabio.* Buenos Aires: Abeledo-Perrot, 1983.

Cesareo, Francesco C. "The Centrality of the King in the Thought of Alfonso X of León-Castile," *Kings and Kingship [ACTA* 11], 121-31. Ed. J. T. Rosenthal. Binghamton: SUNY/Center for Medieval and Early-Renaissance Studies, 1986.

Craddock, Jerry R. "Dynasty in Dispute: Alfonso X el Sabio and the Succession to the Throne of Castile and Leon in History and Legend," *Viator* 17 (1986): 197-219.

————— "How Many *Partidas* in the *Siete Partidas?*," *Hispanic Studies in Honor of Alan D. Deyermond,* 83-92. Ed. J. Miletich. Madison: U. of Wisconsin/Hispanic Seminary of Medieval Studies, 1986.

————— "The Legislative Works of Alfonso el Sabio," *Emperor of Culture,* 182-97. Ed. R. I. Burns. Philadelphia: U. of Pennsylvania Press, 1990.

————— *The Legislative Works of Alfonso X, el Sabio: A Critical Bibliography.* London: Grant and Cutler, 1986.

————— "Must the King Obey his Laws?," *Florilegium Hispanicum: Medieval and Golden Age Studies Presented to Dorothy Clotelle Clarke,* 70-79. Ed. J. S. Geary. Madison: U. of Wisconsin/Hispanic Seminary of Medieval Studies, 1986.

Escavy Zamora, Ricardo. "El contenido lexicográfico de las *Partidas,*" *La lengua y la literatura en tiempos de Alfonso X,* 195-2 10. Eds. F. Carmona and F. J. Hores. Murcia: U. de Murcia, 1985.

Estepa Diaz, Caries. "El 'fecho de Imperio' y la politica internacional en la época de Alfonso X," *Estudios alfonsles: Lexicografia, lirica, estética y politica de Alfonso el Sabio,* 189-205. Eds. J. Mondéjar and J. Montoya. Granada: U. de Granada/Fac. Filosofia y Letras, 1985.

Flores Arroyuelos, Francisco J. "El *Setenario,* una primera versin de los capitulos introductorios de las *Siete partidas,*" *La lengua y la literatura en tiempos de Alfonso X,* 169-79. Eds. F. Carmona and F. J. Flores. Murcia: U. de Murcia, 1985.

Fraker, Charles F. "Alfonso X, the Empire, and the *Primera crónica,*" *Bulletin of Hispanic Studies* 55 (1978): 95-102.

Garcia Gallo, Alfonso. "El *Libro de las leyes* de Alfonso el Sabio del *Espéculo* a las *Partidas,*" *Anuario de la Historia del Derecho Español* 21-22 (1951-52): 354-528.

————— "Nuevas observaciones sobre la obra legislativa de Alfonso X," *Anuario de la Historia del Derecho Español* 46 (1976): 609-70.

————— "La obra legislativa de Alfonso X: hechos e hipótesis," *Anuario de la Historia del Derecho Espanol 54* (1984): 97-161.

————— "La problemática de la obra legislativa de Alfonso X," *Boletin del Ilustre Colegio de Abogados de Madird5* (1984): 9-18.

González-Casanovas, Roberto J. "Courtly Rhetoric as a Political and Social Code in Alfonso X's *Siete partidas,*" *Motives and Motifs: Studies in Societal Change in Medieval Iberia.* Eds. J. Snow and D. Kagay. Kalamazoo: Western Michigan U./Medieval Institute [in press].

Iglesias Ferreirós, Aquilino. "Alfonso X, su labor legislativa y los historiadores," *Historia, Instituciones, Documentos* 9 (1983): 1-104.

————— "La labor legislativa de Alfonso X el Sabio," *España y Europa, un pasadojuridico común,* 277-99. Ed. A. Perez Martin. Madrid: Instituto de Derecho Comün, 1986.

Linehan, Peter. "The Politics of Piety: Aspects of the Castilian Monarchy from Alfonso X to Alfonso XI," *Revista Canadiense de Estudios Hispdnicos* 9 (1985): 385-404.

Lopez Estrada, Francisco. "El sentido utOpico de las *Partidas,*" *Las utopias,* 205-14. Madrid: Casa de Velázquez/IJ. Complutense, 1990.

MacDonald, Robert A. *Kingship in Medieval Spain: Alfonso X of Castile.* Diss., U. of Wisconsin at Madison, 1958.

————— "Law and Politics: Alfonso's Program of Political Reform," *Worlds of Alfonso the Learned and James the Conqueror,* 150-202. Ed. R. I. Burns. Princeton: Princeton U. P., 1985.

————— "Problemas politicos y derecho alfonsino considerados desde tres puntos de vista," *Anuario de la Historia del Derecho Español* 53 (1984): 25-53.

Montes, Eugenio. "Federico II de Sicilia y Alfonso X de Castilla," *Anejo de Revista de Estudios Pollticos* 10 (julio-agosto 1943): 1-3 1.

O'Callaghan, Joseph F. "Image and Reality: The King Creates His Kingdom," *Emperor of Culture*, 14-32. Ed. R. I. Burns. Philadelphia: U. of Pennsylvania Press, 1990.

Pérez-Prendes, José Manuel. "Las leyes de Alfonso el Sabio," *Revista de Occidente* 43 [extra. 11] (dic. 1984): 67-84.

Sabatino Lopez, Roberto. "Entre el Medioevo y el Renaeimiento: Alfonso X y Federico H," *Re-vista de Occidente* 43 [extra. 11] (die. 1984): 7-14.

Socarrás, Cayetano J. *Alfonso X of Castile: A Study on Imperialistic Frustration*. Barcelona: Hispam, 1976.

Seniff, Dennis P. "Introduction to Natural Law in Didactic, Scientific, and Legal Treatises in Iberia," *The Medieval Tradition of Natural Law*, 16 1-78. Ed. H. J. Johnson. Kalamazoo: Western Michigan Univ./Medieval Institute Publications, 1987.

Wolf, Armin. "El movimiento de legislación y de codificatión en Europa en tiempos de Alfonso el Sabio," *Alfonso X el Sabio: Vida, obra y época*, I: 3 1-37. Eds. J. C. de Miguel Rodriguez, A. Munoz Fernández, and C. Segura Graiño. Madrid: Sociedad Española de Estudios Medievales, 1989.

C. General studies on Alfonso X

Ballesteros Beretta, Antonio. *Alfonso el Sabio*. Barcelona: Albir/ Academia Alfonso X, 1984; 2nd ed. Bloom, Leonard. *The Emergence of an Intellectual and Social Ideal as Expressed in Selected Writings of Alfonso X and don Juan Manuel*. Diss., U. of Pittsburgh, 1967.

Burns, Robert I. "Alfonso X of Castile, the Learned: *Stupor Mundi Thought*, 60(1985): 375-87.

_____. (ed.). *Emperor of Culture: Alfonso X the Learned of Castile and His Thirteenth-Century Renaissance*. Philadelphia: U. of Pennsylvania Press, 1990.

————— *The Worlds of Alfonso the Learned and James the Conqueror: Intellect and Force in the Middle Ages*. Princeton: Princeton U. P., 1985.

Cárdenas, Anthony J. "Alfonso's Scriptorium and Chancery: The

Role of the Prologue in Binding the *Translatio Studii* to the *Translatio Potestatis*," *Emperor of Culture*, 90-108. Ed. R. I. Burns. Philadelphia: U. of Pennsylvania Press, 1990.

"The Literary Prologue of Alfonso X: A Nexus between Chancery and Scriptorium," *Thought* 60, 239 *(1985):* 456-67.

Catalán, Diego. "El taller histórico alfonsi: métodos y problemas en el trabajo compilatorio," *Romania* 84 (1963): 354-75.

Fradejas Lebrero, José. "Alfonso X, humanista," *La lengua y la literatura en tiempos de Alfonso X*, 211-18. Eds. F. Carmona and F. J. Flores. Murcia: U. de Murcia, 1985.

Hillgarth, J. N. *The Spanish Kingdoms, 1250-15 16*. Oxford: Clarendon Press, 1976; 2 vols.

Keller, John E. *Alfonso X, El Sabio*. New York: Twayne, 1967.

_____. and Richard P. Kinkade. *Iconography in Medieval Spanish Literature*. Lexington: U. P. of Kentucky, 1984.

Lomax, Derek W. "La lengua oficial de Castilla," in *Actele celui de-al XII -lea Congres International de Lingvistica si Filologie Romanica*, 411-17. Bucharest: Académie de R.S.R., 1971.

Lopez Estrada, Francisco. "Los maestros de la prosa medieval," *Introducción a la literatura medieval espanola*, 4 12-20. Madrid: Gredos, 1979; 4~ ed.

Maravall, José Antonio. *Estudios de historia del pensamiento espanol*, I: *Edad Media*. Madrid: Cultura Hispániea, 1983; 3rd ed.

Márquez Villanueva, Francisco. "The Alfonsine Cultural Concept," *Alfonso X of Castile the Learned King* [Harvard U. Symposium, 17 Nov. 1984], 76-109. Eds. F. Márquez Villanueva and C. Vega. Cambridge: Harvard U. Studies in Romance Langs., 1990.

Menéndez Pidal, Gonzalo. "Como trabajaron las escuelas alfonsies," *Revista de Filologia Hispdnica* 5 (1951): 363-80.

Menéndez Pidal, Ramón. "De Alfonso a los dos Juanes: Auge y culminaciOn del didacticismo (1252-1370)," *Studia Hispanica in honorem R. Lapesa*, I: 63-83. Madrid: Gredos, 1972.

Nepaulsingh, Colbert I. *Towards a History of Literary Composition in Medieval Spain*. Toronto: U. of Toronto Press, 1986.

——— "Notes for a Study of Wisdom Literature and Literary Composition in Medieval Spain," *Hispanic Studies in Honor of Alan D. Deyermond*, 2 17-22. Ed. J. Miletich. Madison: U. of Wisconsin/Hispanic Seminary of Medieval Studies, 1986.

Procter, Evelyn S. *Alfonso X of Castile, Patron of Literature and Learning*. Oxford: Clarendon Press, 1951.

Rico, Francisco. "En torno a Alfonso el Sabio," *El pequeno mundo del hombre,* 59-80 and 308-12. Madrid: Castalia, 1986; 2nd ed.

Romano, David. "Los judios y Alfonso X," *Revista de Occidente* 43 [extra. 11] (die. 1984): 203-17.

Roth, Norman. "Jewish Translators at the Court of Alfonso X," *Thought* 60, 239 (Dec. 1985): 439-55.

Rubio Garcia, L. "En torno a la biblioteca de Alfonso X," *La lengua y la literatura en tiempos de Alfonso X, 531-51.* Eds. F. Carmona and F. J. Flores. Murcia: U. de Murcia, 1985.

Valdeon Baruque, Julio. "Alfonso X y la convivencia cristiano-judio-islámica," *Estudios alfonsies: Lexicografia, lirica, estética y politica de Alfonso el Sabio,* 167-77. Eds. J. Mondéjar and J. Montoya. Granada: U. de Granada/Fac. Filosofia y Letras, *1985.*

D. Studies on Muslim Spain and Medieval Islam

Cantarino, Vicente. *Entre monjes y musulmanes.* Madrid: Alhambra, 1978.

Castro, Américo. *Espana en su historia: Cristianos, moros, judios.* Barcelona: Critica, 1984; 3rd ed. Chejne, Anwar G. *Muslim Spain: Its History and Culture.* Minneapolis: U. of Minnesota P., 1974.

———— "The Role of al-Andalus in the Movement of Ideas Between Islam and the West," *Islam and the Medieval West,* 110-33. Ed. K. Semaan. Albany: SUNY Press, 1980.

Daniel, Norman. *Islam and the West.* Edinburgh: Edinburgh U. P., 1966.

Kedar, Benjamin Z. *Crusade and Mission.* Princeton: Princeton U. P., 1982.

Menocal, Maria Rosa. *The Arabic Role in Medieval Literary History.* Philadelphia: U. of Pennsylvania Press, 1987.

Southern, R. W. *Western Views of Islam in the Middle Ages.* Cambridge: Harvard U. P., 1962.

Vernet Ginés, Juan. *La cultura hispanoarabe en Oriente y Occidente.* Barcelona: Ariel, 1978.

Watt, W. M. *The Influence of Islam on Medieval Europe.* Edinburgh: Edinburgh U. P., 1972.

———— *Islamic Political Thought.* Edinburgh: Edinburgh U. P., 1968.

————. and Pierre Cachia. *A History of Islamic Spain.* Edinburgh: Edinburgh U. P., 1965.

E. Other studies

Curtius, E. R. *European Literature and the Latin Middle Ages.*
Princeton: Princeton U. P., 1973.

Lerner, Ralph; Mushdin Mahdi (eds.). *Medieval Political Philosophy.* Ithaca: Cornell U. P., 1972.

Manuel, Frank and Fritzie. *Utopian Thought in the Western World.*
Cambridge: Harvard U. P., 1979.

Murray, Alexander. *Reason and Society in the Middle Ages.*
Oxford: Clarendon Press, 1978.

Sigmund, Paul E. (ed.). *St. Thomas of Aquinas on Politics and
Ethics.* New York: Norton, 1988.

CHAPTER X

CRITICAL THINKING AND DEMOCRATIZATION IN TAIWAN

MING-LEE WEN

Since Aristotle, there has been a wide consensus that there is an intimate relationship between critical thinking and democracy. Following Aristotle, such contemporary scholars as, e.g., Dewey (1915), Rawls (1972), Shor (1980), Gutmann (1987), Guyton (1988), Siegel (1988), Tran (1989), Weinstein (1989) and the scholars of the Frankfurt School are convinced that in critical thinking lies the foundation of democracy.

In this thesis, my argument will be that critical thinking could lead a country like Taiwan from a chaotic situation towards democracy when the people aspire thereto but do not know how rationally to respond. To justify my argument, first, I must point out the nature of critical thinking, and then indicate the relationship between the characteristics of critical thinking and rational democratization.

THE NATURE OF CRITICAL THINKING

In recent years many educators have become convinced that critical thinking is the key to educational reform. (Lipman, 1990, 1) Nevertheless, there is no consensus on the definition of critical thinking. (Martin, 1990, 4) Some consider critical thinking to be a skill for problem-solving, e.g., cognitive psychologists hold this; while others take critical thinking to include all forms of rational thinking, e.g., Robert Ennis and Harvey Siegel hold this. If we are to grasp the very nature of critical thinking and avoid sinking into confusions of definition, it might be helpful to take a look at the history of its development.

The developmental history of critical thinking is associated with the history of human problem-solving in its broadest sense. Although it has taken various forms, critical thinking has always been the most vital instrument for understanding the world and our place within it. There is much evidence to suggest that "Throughout history people have asked questions about the kind of world that we live in, such as whether it makes sense, or whether we can feel at home in it." (Sankey, Sullivan & Watson, 1988, 7) Searching for a better understanding of the world, in the belief that this will enhance the quality of life has been the hope of human beings.

I do not intend to repeat nor to explain in detail the history of critical thinking which I have dealt with it in my Ph.D. thesis (ch. 3); here I shall give a synopsis. In brief, parallel to the history of human problem-solving, whether in Western or Eastern countries, the development of critical thinking can be divided into four stages. They are: the pre-scientific stage, the enlightened scientific stage, the dialectic stage and the dialectic-critical stage. The nature of critical thinking in terms of its foci, purposes, methods, and cognitive styles can be seen in the following table:

TABLE OF THE CHARACTERISTICS OF CRITICAL THINKING

stage *dimension*	*I*	*II*	*III*	*IV*
focus of attention	supernatural	natural	"self-consciousness"	life-worlds
purposes	universality through ritual terms	universality in physical terms	universality through the spirit	rationality by "quasi-universality"
methods	intuition logic mathematics	logic, mathematics, empirical research	dialectic	all methods
cognitive styles	imagination with reason	natural-empiricism	consensus-dialectical development	category-construction

From the above table, the general characteristics of critical thinking can be analyzed as follows.

I. Working out an accepted answer to explain the enigma or mystery of the universe.

II. In thinkers establishing a universal law to justify systematically the previous truth in physical instead of ritual terms.

III. Focusing attention upon self-consciousness in order to

emancipate human beliefs from the domination of scientism via the dialectic movement of self-consciousness. With the dialectic method and its spirit, critical thinking reveals the characteristics of reflecting, correcting and developing/becoming.

IV. Concern not only for oneself, but also for society. All methods, e.g., intuition, logic, mathematics, phenomenology, dialectic, hermeneutics, and so on, could be used for an adequate rationality based on human interests and forming its science. Ultimately, the aim of critical thinking in this fourth stage is a democratic, autonomous society in which people possess communicative abilities with open-mindedness.

A tentative definition of critical thinking is needed in order to discuss its function as a means towards a rational democracy. Its definition, however, must remain open to revision in view of its specific character as becoming (developing), for critical thinking should be taken as a dynamic rather than a static system. A tentative definition is: a type of thinking promoting rationality in which one questions the authorities around one, with skepticism as its starting point and quasi-universality as its criterion, for the construction of a good life, including our rational "scientific" mode of operating and our moral and aesthetic life.

According to this definition, the characteristics of critical thinking are: a) emancipation, b) quasi-universality and c) reconstruction.

THE NEED FOR CRITICAL THINKING FOR DEMOCRATIZATION

These three specific characteristics make it possible to analyze how critical thinking is able to contribute to democratization. With Taiwan as an example, we shall try to work out the relationship between the characteristics of critical thinking and rational democratization.

Emancipation

The possibility of emancipation depends on the opportunity there is for freedom. Kant regards "freedom as an ability from which proceeds contradiction to the moral law." (Kant; Abbott tr., 1967, lix) Similarly, to a critical thinker, freedom is not only an ability but the spirit/attitude to question, to rebel against any irrationality surrounding one. More than that, Bréhier claims that "our freedom is a creation of ourselves; to be free is to do, not to become, but to do and doing, produce ourselves." (Bréhier; Baskin tr., 1969, 61) In this sense, freedom results from human will rather than from something extrinsic. Therefore, it is incumbent upon human beings to emancipate themselves from any ideology proposed as an eminent authority.

Generally, we do not question authority, partly because we do not recognize where the authority is, partly because we fear its threat. Psychologically, one reason for not questioning the authority could be that we prefer to live a stable life if only we can endure the status quo. As Brookfield analyses it,

> trying to shake off habitual ideas and behaviors so that we can try out alternatives are emotionally potent activities. They, of course, may well produce anxiety, fear, resentment and feelings of being threatened or intimidated. (Brookfield, 1987, 232)

Similarly, in Taiwan, the traditional ideas, e.g., harmony and order, constrain people from liberating themselves. The idea of harmony can be derived from the theory of *Yin-Yang* offered in the *I-Ching*:

> *Yang* meant the sunny side of a hill, while *Yin* meant shadow. More generally the pair of terms came to stand for a ceaseless alternation of opposites throughout all nature (including the human nature): day and night, sun and moon, summer and winter, male and female, (strong and weak). (Meskill, 1973, 33)

It can be inferred from the above quotation that "*Yin-Yang* separate, but each contains half of its opposite in a recessive state." (Ronam, 1978,162) According to *I-Ching*, they are formed into the *Gigantic Whole*, from which everything in the world comes. Quoting from *Hsun-Tzu*, a Confucian work, Meskill pointed out that "the events of Heaven and Earth followed a regularity quite independent of anything man does . . . a magic bond between man and gods was as the role man plays in the way of the universe." (Meskill, 1973, 28-29) The Chinese take Heaven as an ultimate authority; men must serve as a faithful messenger between Heaven and Earth. In this sense, all men can do is to follow every order from Heaven. Hence, in the *Analects* Confucius says that "obeying Heaven, we can survive; in contrast, rebelling against it, we will die." In a word, it can be shown from these quotations that the idea of authority has been ingrained in Chinese culture for more than two thousand years. Worse still, Chinese dare not question authority; it is useless to ask them to rebel against authority. Unfortunately, in education teachers have not enlightened students' minds; quite the contrary, they impose their ingrained ideas upon students.

Moreover, harmony appears distinctly in a book of Confucianism, *Chung-Yung:*

> Feelings of joy, anger, sorrow and delight which have not yet been expressed can be called *Chung*, but when these four feelings are expressed in just the right manner it is called *harmony*. Whereas *Chung* is the foundation of the world, *harmony* is the universal path. (*Chung-Yung*, ch. 1)

It is evident from this that harmony is another unchallenged authority in Chinese society due to its ultimacy and universality in terms of truth and morality.

In addition, *order* or rather morality appears in the *Great Learning*. There are eight steps in its progressive realization:

> After the thing has been investigated, human knowledge can be extended; after the knowledge has been extended, the will can be sincere; after the will has been sincere, the mind can be rectified; after the mind has been rectified, the personal life can be cultivated; after the personal life has been cultivated, the family can be regulated; after the family has been regulated, the nation can be in order; after the nation has been in order, the universe can be peaceful. (*The Great Learning*)

On a par with the *Yin-Yang* and *Chung-Yung*, order as a logical arrangement of things implies a moral rule which cannot be overturned or even questioned due to its orthodoxy. Like harmony, order is taken as an undisputed authority.

Following these two authorities, harmony and order, the Chinese characteristics are: obedience, forbearance, silence, conformance, conservation (adhering to old rules), proceeding according to logical order, and so on for two thousand years. As a result, what we called "good boys" or "good citizens" are those who do everything they are told and act as directed. This can be seen also in students in the classroom: all so-called good students are those who pay attention, who listen rather than speak, answer rather than question, conform rather than argue, obey rather than rebel, etc. For the Chinese, a good person is just a person without a mind or independent thinking, viz., without self-consciousness; instead that person has ingrained ideas, which could be false-consciousness.

Lindley quotes from Lewy (1982, *False Consciousness)* to point out the relationship between self-ideology and false consciousness. He says,

> ideology is a process accomplished by the so-called thinker consciously, it is true, but with false consciousness. The real motive forces impelling him remain unknown to him, otherwise it simply would not be an ideological process. Hence, he imagines false or seeming motive forces. (Lindley, 1986, 166)

In this case, the first step for emancipation would be enlightenment about the ideology, because "the enlightenment has always aimed at liberating men from fear and establishing their sovereignty." (Horkheimer & Adorno,1973, 3) Thus, a rational democracy is based on human emancipation from the strains of circumstances and human mind. Here, autonomy is identical with, rather than independent of, authenticity. Only under this circumstance can a rational democracy be possible because, as Haydon claims, an autonomous individual will best be himself and harmonize his life by using his powers of reason. (Haydon, 1989, 4) Democratic participation and responsibility for all is fostered by personal maturity with a decentralized ego and open, reflective communication. (Young, 1989, 23) Therefore, emancipation is the threshold of a rational democratization. It calls for an enlightened self-consciousness which in turn results from self-reflection based on skepticism and questioning and accompanied by open-mindedness, communication and responsibility. In a word, emancipation aims at an autonomous individual in society. This is of special functional significance for democratization in Taiwan.

Quasi-universality

The term "quasi-universality" is borrowed from Habermas' 'quasi-transcendental', which means a consensus resulting from communicative action in an ideal speech situation. (Habermas, 1984) It implies also that rationality should be established by communicative action, dialogue or discussion, rather than by an authority. In this way the consensus is based upon the majority instead of a super-authority. In other words, democracy as a system proceeds from bottom to top rather than from top to bottom. People establish various consensuses in view of the variety of the purposes which stem from their various human interests, and the variety of their social circumstances in time and space. This means that there can be no unique law: anyone who tries to unify or explain things in universal terms could be mistaken. Hence, the absolute universality revealed in Chinese society should be questioned.

For example, *loyalty is* one of the fundamental Chinese virtues. It results from the feudalistic system, which maintained social order by categorizing different powers by virtue of social status. Basically, it guaranteed the status quo and a harmonious relationship between the ruler and the ruled. On the other hand, this virtue could become a negative ideology once its function is transferred from maintaining the social order into the blind worship of an idol or an authority. Loyalty then becomes an omnipresent and unrivalled authority under which the ruler possesses not only political, but moral power in Chinese society. The ruler's words, behaviour and thoughts become the rules of society and the model for its people due not to his wise words or correct behavior, but to his social status. This excludes rebellion against the authority/ruler because it represents the authority of society or even of Heaven. Hence, Chinese people are encouraged and are even taught to obey the ruler and tolerate authority, rather than to question or rebel against it.

By the same token, in thought, Chinese irresistibly follow an orthodoxy decided by the ruler, authoritative person or government, e.g., Confucianism, KMT [the Kuomintang], etc. In education, Chinese students are encouraged to listen and to do what they are asked, instead of thinking and questioning; in a family children are requested to show their filial piety by unquestioningly obeying their parents. All these social phenomena imply that there is no concept of quasi-universality, but an absolute authority in Chinese culture. Chinese history thus simply replaced one authority by another. That is one of the essential reasons why for nearly forty years in Taiwan there has been no competitive political party. It is the reason too why our education cannot cultivate students who create original ideas, but merely those who reproduce all the materials which they are taught and retain them in mind.

Contrary to this, the concept of quasi-universality reminds us that there is by no means an absolute universality in the world. Everyone has to open his mind to hear others' opinions and vice versa. Furthermore, in order to escape systematic distortion, viz., negative ideology, the exchanges of opinions should proceed according to Habermas's notion of an ideal speech situation. Using the criterion of quasi-universality to escape negative ideology is at least a suitable, if not a perfect, means to reconstruct public and even private value because it calls on us to reflect not only others' ideology, but also our own by both expressing ourselves and examining others' opinions. In this process, consensus is established in a more or less reasonably democratic way which brings together various values.

Of course, we must inquire whether an ideal speech situation can really be attained and whether the consensus we reach could be distorted implicitly or explicitly by economic or political power, self-interests or culture. Communicative action can enlighten our own consciousness, especially self-reflection. It can reduce the sorts of distortions, caused by power, authority or ideology. In sum, the quasi-universality acquired from communicative action does not cling to any authority, but reflects the need for open-mindedness and communicative competence in rational democratization.

Reconstruction

After an old value has been destroyed, a new one must be constructed, otherwise, a chaotic situation can hardly be escaped. Thus, after emancipation, critical thinkers must reconstruct another quasi-universality. Emancipation, quasi-universality and reconstruction constitute a unified process of critical thinking which is continuous and developing. Quasi-universality is the criterion for both emancipation and reconstruction: while emancipation might lead to destruction, reconstruction realizes another new paradigm or rule. That is, as developing or becoming, the paradigm attained through emancipation and reconstruction could be destroyed again by another emancipation. This relationship of the individual-unity-whole can be shown as follows:

—>doubt—>question—>reflect—>*reconstruct—>doubt—>
quasi-universality

Let us take Taiwan's present social structure as an example. It has brought about astonishing changes since the government was forced to move to Taiwan in 1949. For example, it is among the top four in economic development among the Asian countries; education has been improved in quantity as well as in quality; people's living standards have been raised; and politically it has developed a multi-party system. In general, great progress has been made in Taiwan, particularly in the economy. However, a number of anomalies which cause skepticism are obvious. For instance, we would ask why the following problems have arisen: the sharp increase in crime; the monopolization of the market economic system by a few capitalists; the widening gap between the rich and the poor; the focus upon economic speculation reflecting the Chinese motto: "no pains, no gains," and looking instead for unreasonable rewards; the lack of political activity though a multi-party political system has been established for several years; the operation of the political power for the benefit of the leadership group rather than for the majority and so on.

From questioning these anomalies, the old paradigms or rules could be destroyed in rebelling against these irrational structures. Chaos results when an old value system is destroyed and a new one is not yet formed; at least a period of uncertainty will occur. This period provides a good opportunity to reconstruct a society, although it could also cause its disastrous collapse.

Thus, reconstruction plays a significant role in a chaotic society. Critical thinking bears the mission both of emancipation and re-construction on the ground of quasi-universality. The reconstruction of such a chaotic society as Taiwan will require critical thinking and education as a democratic society. First, we must clarify in which ways critical thinking functions for democratization before taking it as a means thereto. Namely, in which aspects can Taiwan's society be reconstructed towards democratization through critical thinking?

The following aspects should and must be reconstructed in order to progress towards rational democratization. First, communicative competence and open-mindedness must be cultivated in order to promote democratic argument. Communicative competence includes expressing oneself rationally, listening to others' opinions, responsibility, participation, discussion, decision-making, judgment and so on. Second, freedom of communication must be warranted in order to protect autonomous people; then the ideologies, e.g., powers, authorities and even false-consciousness, can be emancipated, for it appears that an adequate value system might be set up by autonomous people through reasonable communicative action. By the same means, the burden of culture and ingrained ideas could be shaken off and a divergent but harmonious interpersonal relationship could be established. More importantly, a rational value system could be regenerated from the chaos. In this way, a picture of rational democracy can be mapped out, even though it be a merely tentative picture.

CONCLUDING REMARKS

In a nutshell, these three fundamental characteristics of critical thinking: emancipation, quasi-universality and reconstruction are able to generate rational ways towards democratization. To be precise, at the very least critical thinking has created a move toward democratization: it questions authorities in society, reflects on self-ideology, institutes communicative action to grope for quasi-universality and to reconstruct rationality. First, critical thinking can be taken as a point of initiation for democratization by marking a social system with at least the following characteristics: "shared participation, discussion, decision-making." (Young, 1989, 123) Second, rationality based on quasi-universality gives direction to the value system; skepticism, rebellion and freedom are the strong sinews of emancipation from the negative ideologies, in particular, self-ideology. Finally, reconstruction facilitates the speed of the replacement of the old value with the new. We have emphasized that these three characters constitute a single unified whole.

All of them signal autonomy and democratization, but whether this reconstruction can succeed depends upon the progress of our own knowledge. To be precise, without abundant knowledge, reconstruction is far from rational, if not impossible. Analogously, the relationship between critical thinking and democracy is perplexing. For example, we can ask whether critical thinking facilitates democracy or vice versa? By and large, there is a reciprocal relationship between them; they are entwined. Nonetheless, it is hard to deny that reconstruction comes with the energy of emancipation as its sinew and with the rationality of quasi-universality as its criterion. With these, a society, like Taiwan, could go forward toward democratization.

If the above conclusion is correct, critical thinkers are needed in order for a country to establish a democratic society. How we cultivate critical thinkers should then be our next step. Optimistically, I would suggest that education should take this responsibility. Yet, as has been evident, education cannot work effectively unless politics and society back it up, for education cannot be isolated from society. Similarly, there seems to be another dilemma: do the achievements of education lead to democratic politics and society or do the circumstances of politics and society significantly influence education in practice? As in Nietzsche's *Will to Power*, or Foucault's will to truth, teachers and students as subjects of education, could be their own masters provided they are conscious of the crisis in their life-worlds and have the will to dissolve it. Becker claims that will is one of the spirits of Renaissance.

> Man is not made of mush; he has a will; train it, without fear of irresponsible willfulness. Man also has a deep, inborn conscience; cultivate it, and he will know self-control. Train an elite, cultivate excellence, and you will change the world. (Becker, 1967, 11)

Thus, education at the very least should and could light the fire of consciousness through the task of enlightenment. Obviously, that is indeed a hard *chronic* work, Popper terms it, piecemeal human-engineering.

In conclusion, the chaos of the moment in Taiwan constitutes a crisis and at the same time provides a vital chance for the reconstruction the society. Without critical thinking, however, and a negative response to this chaos rational democratization will not be possible. This reveals the importance for democratization of educating citizens with critical thinking. In the education of all citizens, the teaching of critical thinking should be implemented even if there is a lack of strong support for this from politics or society at this moment.

A Chinese motto for all educators reads: *take precautions after suffering a loss*. This means that it is never too late to begin once again.

*Reconstruction should include not only the renewal of the old *value but its* confirmation.

REFERENCES

Adorno, T.W. (1982), *Against Epistemology: A Meta-critique.* Oxford: Basil Blackwell.

Becker, E. (1967), *Beyond Alienation.* N.Y: George Braziller.

Bréhier, E., W. Baskin, trans. (1969), *Contemporary Philosophy Since 1850.* Chicago & London: Routledge and Kegan Paul.

Brookfield, S.D. (1987), *Developing Critical Thinkers.* Open University Press.

Chung-Yung [The Doctrine of the Mean].

Gutmann, A. (1987), *Democratic Education. N.J:* Princeton University Press.

Guyton, M. (1988), "Critical Thinking and Political Participation: Development and Assessment of a Causal Model" in *Theory and Research in Social Education.* Winter, XVI, 1, pp. 23-49.

Habermas, J., T. McCarthy, (trans.), *The Theory of Communicative Action: Reason in the Rationalization of Society.* Boston: Beacon Press, 1984.

Haydon, G. (1989), "Education for Democracy: Transmission or Creation of Value" (at press).

Horkheimer, M. & Adorno, T.W. (1973), *Dialectic of Enlightenment.* London: Allen Unwin.

Kant, I., T. K. Abbott (trans.) (1873[1] 1967[11]), *Kant's Critique of Practical Reason and Other Works on the Theory of Ethics.* London: Longmans.

Lindley, R. (1986), *Autonomy.* London: Macmillan Education Ltd.

Lipman, M. (1985), "Philosophy for Children and Critical Thinking" in *National Forum,* Winter, pp. 2-3.

_____. (1989), *Critical Thinking: Critical Issues.* Montclare, N.J.: Institute for the Advancement of Philosophy for Children.

Martin, D.S. (1990), *Thinking and Teacher Education.* Vol. 1:1, Washington D.C: Gallaudet University.

Meskill, J. (1973), *An Introduction to Chinese Civilization.* N.Y: Columbia University Press.

Popper, K. (1966), *Open Society and Its Enemies.* London: Routledge and Kegan Paul.

Rawls, J. (1972), *A Theory of Justice.* Oxford: Clarendon Press.

Ronam, C. (1978), *The Shorter Science and Civilization in China. An Abridgement of Joseph Needham's Original Text.* Cambridge University Press.

Sankey, D., Sullivan, D. & Watson, B. (1988), *At home on Planet*

Earth. Oxford: Basil Blackwell.

Schrag, F. (1988), *Thinking in School and Society.* London: Routledge and Kegan Paul.

Shor, I. (1980), *Critical Thinking and Everyday Life.* Canada: Black Rose Books.

Siegel, H. (1988), *Educating Reason: Rationality, Critical Thinking and Education.* Routledge and Kegan Paul.

Tran Van Doan (1991), *Reason, Rationality and Reasonableness.* Washington: Council for Research in Values and Philosophy.

———— *(1990), The Poverty of Moral Education.* Taipei: Sui-Ta Bookshop.

Weinstein, M. (1990), "Critical Thinking and Education for Democracy," in *The National Conference on Democracy and Education.* (unpublished)

Young, R.E. (1989), A *Critical theory of Education: Habermas and Our Children's Future.* London: Harvester Wheatsheaf.

CHAPTER XI

VARIATIONS IN VALUE ORIENTATIONS:
Their Implications for Freedom and Choice in Filipino Democracy

VIVIAN LIGO

THE FRAMEWORK OF KLUCKHOHN AND STRODTBECK

The Definition of Value Orientation

Value orientations are complex but definitely patterned (rank-ordered) principles, resulting from the transactional interplay of three analytically distinguishable elements of the evaluative process—the cognitive, the affective, and the directive elements—which give order and direction to the overflowing stream of human acts and thoughts as they relate to the solution of "common human" problems.[1] This definition introduces three key ideas: first, the principles that give order to human acts; second, the inseparable elements of the evaluative process; third, the notion of "common human" problems.

The minimal instinctive determinism among humans brings about these "common human" problems. These problems express the human need to construct a world. A value system functions as a sustaining and directing mechanism because it provides a sense of coherence and a basis for decision-making.

A value system, therefore, is indicative of a people's need to survive as a people and as human beings amid the continuous flow of events and experiences. Without it a people will lose a sense of shared coherence and shared direction. Thus a value system has a "conservative" element as it sustains through time what a culture considers as the way things should be. It also has a "revolutionary" element because it provides the perspective for decision-making and action as a people go through the vicissitudes of life.

Variations in Value Orientations. Through their intelligence and capacity for making decisions human beings undergo the highly complex evaluative process. The cognitive, affective and directive elements of the value system correspond respectively to the human capacity for thinking, for feeling and for acting. The cognitive element suggests a culture's definition of reality, of the way things are. The affective suggests, on the one hand, a people's emotional attachment to what they consider as the way things are and should be, and on the other, the feeling-and-attitude-content generated by their foundational beliefs about reality. The directive element impels them to prefer one particular course of action to others. It gives that course of action the weight of being normative, of being obligatory.

Therefore, value issues are moral issues. They involve decision-making. They involve norms. Value issues are also philosophical issues as they involve beliefs about the way things are. Value issues are religious issues as well because they deal with the direction to which collective human life is pointed. When such a direction is grounded on ultimacy, on the final destiny of a people beyond time, then the religious aspect of the value system is operative. Religion, in this respect, is understood broadly as that which roots a culture in the ultimate scheme of things. Insofar as value issues are taken to be part of the ultimate scheme of things, then these issues also become religious ones.

Value orientations. Kluckhohn and Strodtbeck theorize that human beings are oriented to finding answers to the following "common human" problems:

What is the character of innate human nature?

What is the relationship of human beings to nature (supernature)?

What is the modality of human activity?

What is the temporal focus of human activity?

What is the modality of the relationship of human beings to one another?[2]

From these questions are drawn five orientations that give order and direction to human life: human nature orientation; the human being-in-relation-to-nature (supernature) orientation; activity orientation; time orientation; and, relational orientation.

The Theory of Variation

Kluckhohn and Strodtbeck further propose that all cultures share the same "common human" problems, and therefore, the same orientations. Open to all cultures are three possible alternative solutions. These solutions are not limitless. They fall within a range of alternatives. Cultures differ from each other insofar as they rank these alternatives differently.

The subjugation-to-nature (supernature) alternative assigns powers to nature to which human beings succumb for the sake of survival. Cultures that opt for the harmony-with-nature (supernature) conceive of the universe as a principle of order with which human beings need to be at one. Mastery-over-nature (supernature) conceives of the world as being there for the service of human beings, as something to bend to suit human needs and desires.

As modality of human activity, the being alternative prefers those activities that are considered to be spontaneous expressions of the givens of the human personality. Kluckhohn and Strodtbeck liken this to the Dionysian description of the human personality. The becoming alternative is like the Apollonian personality in which the activity preferred is one that contributes to the natural development of the person. The doing orientation is the Promethean preference for measurable achievements that can stand apart from the acting person.

The temporal focus of human activity can be the past, i.e., the weight of tradition is more real than the immediacy of the present or the plans for the future. The present time orientation grants more realness to the now. The future time preference gives more emphasis on planning for tomorrow to make it better than the past and the present.

The lineal preference within the relational orientation puts first priority to one's relationship with one's elders or ancestors. Obedience to them is of prime importance. The collateral mode prefers a more horizontal reckoning of ties to the vertical. The individualistic preference grants primacy to the individual's option to arrange relationships according to the individual's needs.

All cultures have these alternatives. In terms of ranking, the first choice is considered the dominant alternative, the second is the variant and the third, the latent. Kluckhohn and Strodtbeck likewise theorize that the dominant, variant and latent alternatives create their own scheme of consistency so that a culture with a dominant subjugation-to-nature (supernature) orientation, is most likely to be being, past time and lineal oriented. A culture with the mastery over nature (supernature) orientation tends to be doing, future time, individualistic oriented. A whole host of factors explains why a culture has a particular scheme of consistency that differs from that of another, e.g., environmental factors, historical accidents and choices, a people's temperament.

Thesis on Change. Kluckhohn and Strodtbeck assume the dominant value system fulfills the maintenance-function of the social order. Both the variant and latent value systems are the carriers of change in a culture. Cultures exist within the inherent tension between self-maintenance and change. Change, no matter its painful side, and self-maintenance, no matter its resistance to change, are a culture's way of surviving as a culture. Its capacity for change lies in the strength of its variant value system. Its capacity for self-maintenance rests on the cohesive nature of the dominant system.

A Limitation of the Framework of Kluckhohn and Strodtbeck

Although Kluckhohn and Strodtbeck assume neutrality toward these alternatives within a given orientation, one realizes that the culture that has the mastery-over-nature (supernature)/doing/future time/individualistic orientations will have power over another culture with the subjugation-to-nature (supernature)/being/past time/lineal orientations. Mastery-over-nature can result in oppressiveness in the same way that subjugation-to-nature can create the ground for being oppressed. History, both ancient and recent, reveals the struggle between the oppressor and oppressed, between the mighty and the vanquished *within* a culture and *among* cultures. This fact has not been addressed at all. To our mind, this is one reason why the framework needs to be taken with some measure of reservation.

THE DOMINANT FILIPINO VALUE SYSTEM

Be that as it may, the framework functions as a way of appreciating the Filipino value configuration and its implications for freedom and choice in a democracy.

The Filipino Sense of Self

The Filipino human nature orientation and activity orientation are combined to make up the Filipino sense of self. *Loob* has been the holistic concept reflected on extensively by Leonardo Mercado,[3] Jose de Mesa,[4] and Dionisio Miranda.[5] Filipinos believe in the basic goodness of human nature although it is imperfect and prone to commit mistakes. Filipino identity is communal and hierarchic. One's identity is an extension of the identity of one's family members or vice versa. Addresses of respect are always attached to the person.

Such addresses dictate the terms of the social transaction so that their absence requires self-assertion to prove one's worth and to put the other in the other's proper place. Filipinos value those activities that are considered as spontaneous expression of the givens of a personality. One has to accept the other for who the other is. The person's reputation is given more stress than the quality of the person's achievements. Achievements are status symbols subsumed under the person's character.

The Filipino's sense of basic goodness may explain his *joie de vivre*. The Filipino is a happy creature, celebrative and fun-loving. Even in dire situations, he finds reason to laugh and to enjoy himself. Fun and joy are communal fun and joy. The Filipino stress on character has developed very markedly his sensitivity to his own feelings and those of others. He is a master of the unspoken side of communication. Eye language operates on different levels. The inflection of the voice and body posture say a lot about the level of acceptability accorded to another. Thus, *hiya* or *kaulaw* (lit., shame) is a very effective means of social control. The Filipino culture is said to be a shame culture rather than a guilt culture. The importance attached to enhancing one's reputation or protecting it is rooted in the cognitive, affective and directive elements of the Filipino sense of self. The three elements entail and explain each other.

The Filipino Sense of World

The dominant Filipino orientation toward nature (supernature) is one of subjugation. The Filipino believes that the world is inhabited by powerful beings who, for good or ill, influence his life. Evil is posited in the world, not in the self, so that should one commit sin, one is prone to explain it as a sign of weakness instead of culpability. One is not strong enough to battle against temptations that assail one from the outside. These powerful beings observe their own hierarchy. The one at the top is the Holy, the ones at the base are malevolent spirits that create havoc and bring about destruction to human life.

These spirits are directly involved in the day-to-day existence of Filipinos. There is no strict separation between their world and human world. The sacred/profane dichotomy is non-existent. The sacred is in the profane, the profane in the sacred. The direct influence of these spirits in the life of the Filipino explains why he is also a master of rituals and ceremonies that can cajole these spirits to be cooperative with the human enterprise. These rituals can be rituals of petition, appeasement, defense, thanksgiving or asking for permission.

The Filipino has a highly developed sense of the mysterious, the awe-inspiring, the thaumaturgic. His sense of the numinous leans more toward the *tremendum* rather than toward the *fascinosum*. His rituals are a way of assuaging his fears and his anxieties. His inability to distinguish between the sacred and the profane makes him take the symbolic too literally. His piety is marked by deep devotion to powerful objects, prayer gestures, holy men and women and, holy places. Once granted his wishes, the Filipino bursts into a celebration at once noisy and centered on partaking of a sumptuous meal.

The directive element of the Filipino sense of world is posited in his notion of *gaba*.[6] He may not transgress the sacred order with impunity. Derived from this worldview is the Filipino sense of time. Within the linear, as opposed to the cyclic context, the Filipino tends to focus on a past-present time orientation. The weight of the past is instilled by the force of tradition, the force of what has been ordained to be so and the force of the Filipino's sense of hierarchy. At the same time, he is also present-time oriented as his fun-loving side makes him extend the present moment *ad infinitum* if need be.

A brief analysis of the Filipino concept of *karon* or *ngayon* (lit., 'now') reveals that it is not measured in seconds, minutes or hours. *Karon* can mean right now, today, this month, this era. In contrast, the sense of the future, though extended, remains vague and subject to a lot of factors beyond human control. De Mesa's exploration of *Bahalana* (lit., 'it is in God's or fate's hands') indicates the close link between the Filipino sense of time, of the self and of the world.[7]

Furthermore, the Filipino sense of time is situational. The Filipino associates past events not with dates but with situations that have personal import to him. He has a selective sense of history. It is personal rather than objective. Since he tends to have a cyclic sense of time rather than the linear, he can be prodigal with time for it has a way of coming back. No opportunity is really lost. It will come back.

The Filipino Sense of Community

The dictum "no man is an island" is an unquestioned fact and a powerful norm. Thus, the Filipino family—as an extended clan—is as sacred as the numinous. The family is the foundational category for the Filipino's sense of community. Those outside the confines of this quite extended system of relationships are the real strangers, the *sila* ('they', 'apart from us') or *kamo* (plural 'you') in opposition to the *kami* (exclusive 'we') or *kita* (inclusive 'us').

As indicated by the structuring of the family system, the Filipino sense of community is hierarchic. Likewise the family is the depository of the social means of control. It is the social conscience of the members. Thus, the Filipinos have a deep sense of loyalty to the family. Interdependence is highly encouraged so that loneliness is one of the Filipino's greatest fears, and homesickness, the greatest heartache. The value placed on the family makes Filipinos maintain ties lineally and collaterally. They respect their elders and they feel they owe them a binding sense of gratitude. They also cultivate horizontal ties among peers both based on blood ties and ceremonial ties. Thus, they have highly developed social skills from the superficial level of maintaining *pakikisama* (smooth interpersonal relationship) to the deeper level of lifetime bonding in loyalty and trust.

The demands of *hiva* as *kataha* (as deferential attitude toward someone in authority) and *kaikog* (deferential attitude to an equal) as well as *utang na bob* or *utang kabubut-on* (debt of gratitude) help the Filipinos maneuver through the complexities of their social network. *Kataha* demands a certain distance from authority figures so as not to be too familiar with them. *Kaikog* prevents one from overstaying a welcome as those with whom one has collateral ties will feel obligated to be hospitable.

Utang na bob is the means of social control that sees to it that both the lineal and collateral ties last through time so that surviving together will always be insured. Once surviving together is insured, Filipinos tend to display a hesitancy to incur more *utang na bob* from others. Where avoidance of *utang na bob* operates, one can almost be sure that a possible relationship at hand is considered superfluous and therefore, not needed for survival. *Utang na bob* operates on the level of need, not on the level of want.

SOME THESES CONCERNING THE FILIPINO VALUE SYSTEM

So long as the Filipino was within the traditional *barangay* (the pre-hispanic political entity that was quite autonomous from other *barangays*), this complex of value orientations was really for his own good and survival with others. The directive elements of the values had placed the Filipino within a network of relationships that upheld and protected him. He, in turn, contributed to the maintenance of the given social order.

History has shown that this complex of value orientations did not protect that original *barangay* from the domination of foreign cultures with colonial and imperialist ambitions. The built-in hierarchical structure was now used to maintain a foreign structure. Alienation was created between the native hierarchy and its subordinates.

Thesis #1. *The Filipino Value System Has Always Been Under Strain and Is Still under Strain Right Now.*

Even with the purported Filipino independence in 1898, 1946, and then the "people power" revolution of 1986, the Filipino value system has been in confrontation with a dominating culture with the mastery-over-nature(supernature)/doing/future time/individualistic value orientations. This dominating culture is dictating the terms of the survival or eventual destruction of the present civilization. Its mastery-over-nature (supernature) orientation has given birth to science and technology which have redefined our view of reality. All taboos in the universe have been overcome. Only lately has there been a mellowing of this conquering spirit because of the ecological imbalances it has wrought in the world. The consequent doing and future time orientations have made this dominating culture dictate the terms of advancement. In order to survive, other cultures have to catch up. Its individualistic spirit has created conditions for individual initiative to pursue its ends regardless of the costs in human relationships. The individualistic spirit has contrived a way of living together that is not dependent on loyalty nor ties but on common agreement. Present democracies seem to move toward a form of government that is respectful of individual human rights rather than the demands of solidarity. Ironically, this dominating culture is also the original model for democracy. Even if the democratic ideals and structures have been transported to the Philippines, they have not put the two countries on equal political and economic terms.

Although the Filipino is no longer in a *barangay* but has been part of a nation, his *barangay* means of social control—*hiya, gaba, utang na bob*—have not evolved into a system of control applicable to the democratic running of a nation. *Hiva* ceases to have control in an impersonal context. Once it breaks down, and in the absence of an effective substitute, the Filipino loses his hold of his sense of self, his *amor propio*. Freedom in anonymity makes him undisciplined and dysfunctional.

Within personal settings, *hiya* makes the Filipino so conscious of what people think of him that he would rather keep his thoughts to himself rather than freely share them. Open participation is not straightforward. Rather it is often delicately couched in non-hurting terms. Communication is always a balancing act between idea and feelings.

In areas where technology has taken over the running of life, *gaba* has ceased to be a means of control. But it may still have a hold on the Filipino psyche in terms of his relationship to the supernatural. Filipinos are shifting to mastery-over-nature while retaining a subjugation-to-supernature orientation. As an example, we note how highly Westernized bank settings still have a place for the image of the *Sto. Niño* on their premises. We also note that the "people power" revolution was the coalition of non-violent political action and devotional religiosity. But after the euphoria, the political action ceased to be en masse and devotional religiosity for the most part receded into the homes and churches. Emerging Filipino democracy is nevertheless anchoring itself on a conscious effort of conscienticized circles to work on the political implications of the Christian faith. Democracy is not as much a right to claim as it is a responsibility to assume.

Old Filipino politics reveals the dysfunctional face of *utang-na-boob*. The mutual debt of gratitude became a ground for graft and corruption and for loyalties to unscrupulous political figures who have economically sucked the country dry. Placed in wrong settings, some values become dysfunctional. Placed under strain, values become distorted.

Thesis # 2. *Filipino Democracy, Like the Value System, is More of A Question Than An Answer.*

Survival under a strain requires change or accommodation to the stronger force in the strain. Thus, the question is raised as towards what value configuration the Filipinos ought to direct themselves in order to retain their identity as Filipinos and at the same time to meet present challenges.

Nostalgia for the past may not be an intelligent option. Nostalgia might be charming but it is hardly solid enough to carry a people through the next century. What is the nature of the change that the Filipinos need to take? Certainly, an uncritical appropriation of the dominating culture from the West is no solution. Filipinos may be adept at adaptation but this should never reach the point of losing their integrity as a unique people. A moral recovery program presumes unjustly that the Filipinos have simply gone wayward and all they need to do is to recover the right way that has always been there. Such a presumption not only thinks that value systems are static entities that do not change as the people change, but it also takes quite an authoritarian view of values education: We know exactly what the problem is; we have come up with the solution and therefore, we hand it to you for you to learn it. This "from me to you" kind of approach to values education is pretentious and ineffective.

Prior to even coming up with an answer is the posing of the question. If one starts from the premise that the Filipino value system is under strain, then awareness of this fact becomes the first step toward posing the question and the eventual answer. A people has to be given the chance to identify their problem and to own it so that together they may struggle toward coming up with a workable answer. To our mind, this important phase has been bypassed and we must wonder how effective the existing values education programs really are.

Thesis # 3. *The Question of Justice Has to Be Posed Side by Side With the Question of the Value System.*

Certain social arrangements tend to promote the upholding of certain values. A viable value system tends to create a particular social arrangement congenial to it. The *barangay* as economic, political and social institution was congenial to the Filipino dominant value system. When this institution was used as a tool to sustain the colonial past (and neocolonial present), the value system was also exploited right along with it. The Filipino people are a victim of injustice and therefore, the struggle for justice is part of the shaping of a value system that is their own but not dysfunctional in the present process of history making.

The inculcation of values that ignores the issue of justice is only addressing half the problem. One cannot demand that teachers, for example, uphold the nobility of the teaching profession, without also addressing the more fundamental question of their salaries and benefits. One cannot prevent graft and corruption merely by giving employees a seminar on values. Part of the problem of graft and corruption is economically based. One cannot separate the so-called immorality of prostitution from economic and political exploitation to which prostitutes are subjected. One cannot speak of a Filipino value system without addressing the fact that the Philippines is a Third World country beholden to the foreign powers that be. A values education that is also a justice education is a potent form of politicalization of a people.

One of the memories that has been associated with the "people power" event is that of a people taking charge of its own history. Since we are still close to that event, we find it hard to sift through layers and layers of propaganda for and against it. Yet the event is instructive of the process involved in claiming justice vis-à-vis the emergence of a functional value system. The Filipinos are in a state of flux. They are still in the process of shaping their contemporary identity as a people. The process is not a film clip that can be frozen in one photographic shot. They need to move on, conscious of their options and possibilities.

Thesis # 4. *The Variant Filipino Value System May Be An Indicator o te Emerging Value System.*

The variant Filipino value system is configured as the doing/mastery-over-nature (but subjugation-to-supernature)/present-future time/lineal-collateral orientations. The innovative side of the variant value system lies in its openness to science and technology. Achievements measurable by objective standards of efficiency and quality may prevail over mere stress on the givens of one's character as basis for self-expression. Subjugation-to-nature may give way to mastery-over-nature. More planning can be invested for the immediate future while enjoying 'fun' moments of the present may still hold.

The conservative side lies in the still powerful hold of the family and folk religiosity on innovative Filipinos. The innovative side is the one that responds to the need to catch up with the times. The conservative side keeps them from being overcome by the effort to the point of losing hold of themselves. The Filipino migrant workers are a good example of the variant Filipino personality.

The Filipino migrant workers are hardworking, efficient and capable of quality work. Their incursions in foreign countries have given them a sense of mastery of different situations. Yet their ties with the family and religion have been maintained. They have not become individualistic or agnostic. They already offer bits and pieces of the scenario of what a people could become in the future. Yet this is a possibility that is worth investigating further because of its ambiguity. Our personal experience has shown that although Filipinos abroad keep their ties with the family back home and although they still tend to congregate among themselves, they also manifest a marked sense of wariness toward other Filipinos. They exhibit the suspicion that their fellow countrymen and women are potential adversaries instead of allies.

Nevertheless, we can envision that the Filipino attachment to the family can be expanded into a deeper commitment to the nation. Furthermore, folk religiosity can continue moving from mere devotion to impersonal forces into devotion to the personal God of the Jewish-Christian tradition. In the process they need other means of social control beyond *gaba, utang na bob* and *hiya*. They need to build an effective government machinery that serves the task of nation building. This means politicalization. This means conscientization.

WHAT THEN OF FREEDOM AND CHOICE IN FILIPINO DEMOCRACY?

Filipinos tend to be more conscious of the inevitable than the possible. Freedom and choice are situated within the complex social network that they build around themselves. Individual freedom qua individual rights do not capture the imagination as much as shared freedom and shared rights. The Filipino version of democracy, which is still in its infancy, is quite close to the Latin American struggle against oppressive structures. It is marked more by a sense of solidarity than by individuality, a deep sense of religiosity and a resiliency of spirit that knows both the tragic and the comic side of existence. The rhetoric of American democracy, couched in the four freedoms, in suffrage, in participation in government, take on a very different nuance when employed by Filipinos. Filipinos are too personal and personable, too eager to please than displease, too loyal to ceremonial and blood ties to be American. Furthermore, the Filipino sense of nationhood is still so easily overcome by regionalism that the nationalist struggle seems to be constantly undermined while, in the meantime, developed countries are abandoning it for the sake of globalization. If there is a crisis of leadership in governing the country, half of the reason is the crisis of follower-ship. Filipino democracy may yet require more sacrifice and even perhaps more bloodletting.

And of course, there is the fact that we are in an unjust world. Metaphysical equality does not automatically translate into political, economic and social equality. The dream of democracy grows differently in differently soils. We still have to see the sapling grow into maturity in Philippine soils.

NOTES

1. Florence Kluckhohn and Fred L. Strodtbeck, *Variations in Value Orientations* (Wesport, Connecticut: Greenwood Press, 1961), p. 4.

2. *Ibid.,* p. 11.

3. Leonardo N. Mercado, SVD, *Elements of Filipino Theology* (Tacloban City: Divine Word Publications, 1975), pp. 50-66.

4. Jose de Mesa, *In Solidarity with Culture*, Maryhill Studies 4, 1987, pp. 43-67.

5. Dionisio Miranda, SVD, *Loob: The Filipino Within* (Manila: Divine Word Publications, 1989).

6. Lillian Garcia, "Some Observations on the *Gaba* Phenomenon," *Philippine Quarterly of Culture and Society*, vol. 4, no. 1 (March 1976), pp. 31-36.

7. Jose de Mesa, And God Said,"Bahala Na!", *Maryhill Studies* 2, 1979.1.

INDEX

L

M

COUNCIL FOR RESEARCH IN VALUES AND PHILOSOPHY
Members

THE COUNCIL FOR
RESEARCH IN VALUES AND PHILOSOPHY

PURPOSE

Today there is urgent need to attend to the nature and dignity of the person, to the quality of human life, to the purpose and goal of the physical transformation of our environment, and to the relation of all this to the development of social and political life. This, in turn, requires philosophic clarification of the base upon which freedom is exercised, that is, of the values which provide stability and guidance to one's decisions.

Such studies must be able to reach deeply into the cultures of one's nation—and of other parts of the world by which they can be strengthened and enriched—in order to uncover the roots of the dignity of persons and of the societies built upon their relations one with another. They must be able to identify the conceptual forms in terms of which modern industrial and technological developments are structured and how these impact human self-understanding. Above all, they must be able to bring these elements together in the creative understanding essential for setting our goals and determining our modes of interaction. In the present complex circumstances this is a condition for growing together with trust and justice, honest dedication and mutual concern.

The Council for Studies in Values and Philosophy (RVP) is a group of scholars who share the above concerns and are interested in the application thereto of existing capabilities in the field of philosophy and other disciplines. Its work is to identify areas in which study is needed, the intellectual resources which can be brought to bear thereupon, and the means for publication and interchange of the work from the various regions of the world. In bringing these together its goal is scientific discovery and publication which contributes to the promotion of human kind in our times.

In sum, our times present both the need and the opportunity for deeper and ever more progressive understanding of the person and of the foundations of social life. The development of such understanding is the goal of the RVP.

PROJECTS

A set of related research efforts is currently in process; some were developed initially by the RVP and others now are being carried forward by it, either solely or conjointly.

1. *Cultural Heritage and Contemporary Change: Philosophical Foundations for Social Life.* Sets of focused and mutually coordinated continuing seminars in university centers, each preparing a volume as part of an integrated philosophic search for self-understanding differentiated by continent. This work focuses upon evolving a more adequate understanding of the person in society and looks to the cultural heritage of each for the resources to respond to the challenges of its own specific contemporary transformation.

2. *Seminars on Culture and Contemporary Issues.* This series of 10 week crosscultural and interdisciplinary seminars is being coordinated by the RVP in Washington.

3. *Joint-Colloquia* with Institutes of Philosophy of the National Academies of Science, university philosophy departments, and societies, which have been underway since 1976 in Eastern Europe and, since 1987 in China, concern the person in contemporary society.

4. *Foundations of Moral Education and Character Development.* A study in values and education which unites philosophers, psycholo-gists, social scientists and scholars in education in the elaboration of ways of enriching the moral content of education and character development. This work has been underway since 1980 especially in the Americas.

The personnel for these projects consists of established scholars willing to contribute their time and research as part of their professional commitment to life in our society. For resources to implement this work the Council, as a non-profit organization incorporated in the District of Colombia, looks to various private foundations, public programs and enterprises.

PUBLICATIONS ON CULTURAL HERITAGE AND CONTEMPORARY CHANGE

Series I.	*Culture and Values*
Series II.	*Africa*
Series IIa.	*Islam*
Series III.	*Asia*
Series IV.	*W. Europe and North America*
Series IVa.	*Central and Eastern Europe*
Series V.	*Latin America*
Series VI.	*Foundations of Moral Education*

CULTURAL HERITAGE
AND CONTEMPORARY CHANGE

VALUES AND CONTEMPORARY LIFE

Series I. Culture and Values

George F. McLean,
ISBN 1-56518-022-4 (paper).

Vol. I.12   *Ethics at the Crossroads: Vol. 2. Personalist Ethics and Human Subjectivity,*
George F. McLean,
ISBN 1-56518-024-0 (paper).

Vol. I.13   *The Emancipative Theory of Jürgen Habermas and Metaphysics,*
Robert Badillo,
ISBN 1-56518-043-7 (cloth); ISBN 1-56518-042-9 (paper).

Vol. I.14   *The Deficient Cause of Moral Evil According to Thomas Aquinas,*
Edward Cook,
ISBN 1-56518-070-4 paper (paper).

Vol. I.16   *Civil Society and Social Reconstruction,*
George F. McLean,
ISBN 1-56518-086-0 (paper).

Vol.I.17   *Ways to God, Personal and Social at the Turn of Millennia The Iqbal Lecture, Lahore*
George F. McLean
ISBN 1-56518-123-9 (paper).

Vol.I.18   *The Role of the Sublime in Kant's Moral Metaphysics*
John R. Goodreau
ISBN 1-56518-124-7 (paper).

Vol.19   *Philosophhical Challenges and Opportunities of Globalization*
Obliva Blanchette, Tomonobu Imamichi and George F. McLean
ISBN 1-56518-1298 (paper).

Vol.I .20   *Faith, Reason and Philosophy Lectures at The al-Azhar, Qum, Tehran, Lahore and Beijing Appendix: The Encyclical Letter: Fides et Ratio*
George F. McLean
ISBN 1-56518-1301 (paper).

Vol.I.21   *Religion and the Relation between Civilizations: Lectures on Cooperation between Islamic and Christian Cultures in a Global Horizon*
George F. McLean
ISBN 1-56518-152-2 (paper).

Vol.22   *Freedom, Cultural Traditions and Progress: Philosophy in Civil Society and Nation Building: Tashkent Lectures, 1999*
George F. McLean

ISBN 1-56518-151-4 (paper).
Vol.24   *God and the Challenge of Evil: A Critical Examination of Some Serious Objections to the Good and Omnipotent God*
John L. Yardan
ISBN 1-56518-160-3 (paper).
Vol. 25   *Reason, Rationality and Reasonableness, Vietnamese Philosophical Studies, I*
Tran Van Doan
ISBN 1-56518-166-2 (paper).
Vol.26   *The Culture of Citizenship: Inventing Postmodern Civic Culture*
Thomas Bridges
ISBN 1-56518-168-9 (paper).
Vol.I.27   *The Historicity of Understanding and the Problem of Relativism in Gadamer's Philosophical Hermeneutics*
Osman Bilen
ISBN 1-56518-167-0 (paper).
Vol.28   *Speaking of God*
Carlo Huber
ISBN 1-56518-169-7 (paper).

CULTURAL HERITAGES AND
THE FOUNDATIONS OF SOCIAL LIFE

Series II. Africa

Vol. II.1   *Person and Community: Ghanaian Philosophical Studies: I,*
Kwasi Wiredu and Kwame Gyeke,
ISBN 1-56518-005-4 (cloth); ISBN 1-56518-004-6 (paper).
Vol. II.2   *The Foundations of Social Life: Ugandan Philosophical Studies: I,*
A.T. Dalfovo,
ISBN 1-56518-007-0 (cloth); ISBN 1-56518-006-2 (paper).
Vol. II.3   *Identity and Change in Nigeria: Nigerian Philosophical Studies, I,*
Theophilus Okere,
ISBN 1-56518-068-2 (paper).
Vol. II.4   *Social Reconstruction in Africa: Ugandan Philosophical studies, II*
E. Wamala, A.R. Byaruhanga, A.T. Dalfovo,
J.K. Kigongo, S.A. Mwanahewa and G. Tusabe

ISBN 1-56518-118-2 (paper).

Vol. II.5   *Ghana: Changing Values/Chaning Technologies:*
Ghanaian Philosophical Studies, II
Helen Lauer
ISBN 1-56518-1441 (paper).

Vol.II.6   *Sameness and Difference: Problems and Potentials in South African*
Civil Society: South African Philosophical Studies, I
James R. Cochrane and Bastienne Klein
ISBN 1-56518-155-7 (paper).

Vol. II.7   *Protest and Engagement: Philosophy after Apartheid at*
an Historically Black South African University,
South African Philosophical Studies, II
Patrick Giddy
ISBN 1-56518-163-8 (paper)

Vol.II.8   *Ethics, human rights and development in Africa:*
Ugandan Philosophical Studies, III.
A.T. Dalfovo, J. K. Kigongo, J. Kisekka, G. Tusabe,
E. Wamala, R. Munyonyo, A. B. Rukooko,
A.B.T. BYaruhanga-akiiki, M. Mawa
ISBN 1-56518-172-7 (paper).

Series IIA. Islam

Vol. IIA.1   *Islam and the Political Order,*
Muhammad Saïd al-Ashmawy,
ISBN 1-56518-046-1 (cloth); ISBN 1-56518-047-x (paper).

Vol.IIA. 2   *Al-Ghazali Deliverance from Error and*
Mystical Union with the Almighty: Al-munqidh Min Al-dalil
Critical edition of English translation with introduction by Muhammad
Abulaylah and Nurshif Abdul-Rahim Rifat
Introduction and notes by *George F. McLean*
ISBN 1-56518-153-0 (Arabic-English edition)
ISBN 1-56518-0828 (Arabic edition)
ISBN 1-56518-081-X (English edition)

Vol. IIA.3   *Philosophy in Pakistan*
Naeem Ahmad
ISBN 1-56518-108-5 (paper).

Vol. IIA.4   *The Authenticity of the Text in Hermeneutics*
Seyed Musa Dibadj
ISBN 1-56518-117-4 (paper).

Vol. IIA.5   *Interpretation and the Problem of*
the Intention of the Author: H.-G. Gadamer vs E.D. Hirsch

Burhanettin Tatar
ISBN 1-56518-121 (paper).

Vol.IAI.6   *Ways to God, Personal and Social at the Turn of Millennia*
The Iqbal Lecture, Lahore
George F. McLean
ISBN 1-56518-123-9 (paper).

Vol.I .7   *Faith, Reason and Philosophy*
Lectures at The al-Azhar, Qum, Tehran, Lahore and Beijing
Appendix: The Encyclical Letter: Fides et Ratio
George F. McLean
ISBN 1-56518-130-1 (paper).

Vol.IIA.8   *Islamic and Christian Cultures: Conflict or Dialogue:*
Bulgarian Philosophical Studies, III
Plament Makariev
ISBN 1-56518-162-X (paper).

Vol.IIA.9   *Values of Islamic culture and the experience of history,*
Russian Philosophical Studies, I
Nur Kirabaev, Yuriy Pochta.
ISBN 1-56518-133-6 (paper).

Vol.IIA.10   *Christian-Islamic Preambles of Faith*
Joseph Kenny
ISBN 1-56518-138-7 (paper).

Vol.IIA.11   *The Historicity of Understanding and the Problem of*
Relativism in Gadamer's Philosophical Hermeneutics
Osman Bilen
ISBN 1-56518-167-0 (paper).

Vol.IIA.12   *Religion and the Relation between Civilizations:*
Lectures on Cooperation between Islamic and
Christian Cultures in a Global Horizon
George F. McLean
ISBN 1-56518-152-2 (paper).

Vol.IIA.13   *Modern Western Christian theological understandings of*
Muslims since the Second Vatican Council
Mahmut Aydin
ISBN 1-56518-171-9 (paper).

Vol.IIA.14   *Philosophy of the Muslim World; Authors and Principal*
Themes
Joseph Kenny
ISBN 1-56518-179-4 (paper).

Vol.IIA.15   *Islam and Its Equest for Ppeace: Jihad, Justice and*
Education
Mustafa Köylü

ISBN 1-56518-180-8 (paper).

Series III. Asia

Vol. III.1 *Man and Nature: Chinese Philosophical Studies, I,*
Tang Yi-jie, Li Zhen,
ISBN 0-8191-7412-2 (cloth); ISBN 0-8191-7413-0 (paper).

Vol. III.2 *Chinese Foundations for Moral Education and
Character Development, Chinese Philosophical Studies, II.*
Tran van Doan,
ISBN 1-56518-033-x (cloth); ISBN 1-56518-032-1 (paper).

Vol. III.3 *Confucianism, Buddhism, Taoism, Christianity and
Chinese Culture, Chinese Philosophical Studies, III,*
Tang Yijie,
ISBN 1-56518-035-6 (cloth); ISBN 1-56518-034-8 (paper).

Vol. III.4 *Morality, Metaphysics and Chinese Culture
(Metaphysics, Culture and Morality, Vol. I)*
Vincent Shen and Tran van Doan,
ISBN 1-56518-026-7 (cloth); ISBN 1-56518-027-5 (paper).

Vol. III.5 *Tradition, Harmony and Transcendence,*
George F. McLean,
ISBN 1-56518-030-5 (cloth); ISBN 1-56518-031-3 (paper).

Vol. III.6 *Psychology, Phenomenology and Chinese Philosophy:
Chinese Philosophical Studies, VI,*
Vincent Shen, Richard Knowles and Tran Van Doan,
ISBN 1-56518-044-5 (cloth); 1-56518-045-3 (paper).

Vol. III.7 *Values in Philippine Culture and Education:
Philippine Philosophical Studies, I,*
Manuel B. Dy, Jr.,
ISBN 1-56518-040-2 (cloth); 1-56518-041-2 (paper).

Vol. III.7A *The Human Person and Society: Chinese
Philosophical Studies, VIIA,*
Zhu Dasheng, Jin Xiping and George F. McLean
ISBN 1-56518-087-9 (library edition); 1-56518-088-7 (paper).

Vol. III.8 *The Filipino Mind: Philippine Philosophical Studies II,*
Leonardo N. Mercado
ISBN 1-56518-063-1 (cloth); ISBN 1-56518-064-X (paper).

Vol. III.9 *Philosophy of Science and Education:
Chinese Philosophical Studies IX,*
Vincent Shen and Tran Van Doan
ISBN 1-56518-075-5 (cloth); 1-56518-076-3 (paper).

Vol. III.10 *Chinese Cultural Traditions and Modernization:*

Chinese Philosophical Studies, X,
Wang Miaoyang, Yu Xuanmeng and George F. McLean
ISBN 1-56518-067-4 (library edition); 1-56518-068-2 (paper).

Vol. III.11   *The Humanization of Technology and Chinese Culture:*
Chinese Philosophical Studies XI,
Tomonobu Imamichi, Wang Miaoyang and Liu Fangtong
ISBN 1-56518-116-6 (paper).

Vol. III.12   *Beyond Modernization: Chinese Roots of Global*
Awareness: Chinese Philosophical Studies, XII,
Wang Miaoyang, Yu Xuanmeng and George F. McLean
ISBN 1-56518-089-5 (library edition); 1-56518-090-9 (paper).

Vol. III.13   *Philosophy and Modernization in China:*
Chinese Philosophical Studies XIII,
Liu Fangtong, Huang Songjie and George F. McLean
ISBN 1-56518-066-6 (paper).

Vol. III.14   *Economic Ethics and Chinese Culture:*
Chinese Philosophical Studies, XIV,
Yu Xuanmeng, Lu Xiaohe, Liu Fangtong,
Zhang Rulun and Georges Enderle
ISBN 1-56518-091-7 (library edition); 1-56518-092-5 (paper).

Vol. III.15   *Civil Society in a Chinese Context:*
Chinese Philosophical Studies XV,
Wang Miaoyang, Yu Xuanmeng and Manuel B. Dy
ISBN 1-56518-084-4 (paper).

Vol. III.16   *The Bases of Values in a Time of Change:*
Chinese and Western: Chinese Philosophical Studies, XVI
Kirti Bunchua, Liu Fangtong, Yu Xuanmeng, Yu Wujin
ISBN 1-56518-114-X (paper).

Vol. III.17   *Dialogue between Christian Philosophy and Chinese*
Culture: Philosophical Perspectives for the Third Millennium;
Chinese Philosophical Studies, XVII
Paschal Ting
ISBN 1-56518-173-5 (paper).

Vol. III.18   *The Poverty of Ideological Education:*
Chinese Philosophical Studies, XVIII
Tran Van Doan
ISBN 1-56518-164-6 (paper.)

Vol.III.20   *Culural Impact on International Relations:*
Chinese Philosophical Studies, XX
Yu Xintian
ISBN 1-56518-176-X (pbk.)

Vol. IIIB.1   *Authentic Human Destiny: The Paths of*
    Shankara and Heidegger: Indian Philosophical Studies, I
    Vensus A. George
    ISBN 1-56518-119-0 (paper).

Vol. IIIB.2   *The Experience of Being as Goal of Human Existence:*
    The Heideggerian Approach: Indian Philosophical Studies, II
    Vensus A. George
    ISBN 1-56518-145-X (paper).

Vol. IIIB.3 *Religious Dialogue as Hermeneutics: Bede Griffiths's*
    Advaitic Approach Indian Philosophical Studies, III
    Kuruvilla Pandikattu
    ISBN 1-56518-1395 (paper).

Vol. IIIB.4   *Self-Realization [Brahmaanubhava]:*
    The Advaitic Perspective of Shankara:
    Indian Philosophical Studies, IV
    Vensus A. George
    ISBN 1-56518-154-9 (paper).

Vol. IIIB.5   *Gandhi: The Meaning of Mahatma for the Millennium*
    Indian Philosophical Studies, V
    Kuruvilla Pandikattu
    ISBN 1-56518-156-5 (paper).

Vol. IIIB.6   *Civil Society in Indian Cultures*
    Indian Philosophical Studies, VI
    Asha Mukherjee, Sabujkali Sen (Mitra) and K. Bagchi
    ISBN 1-56518-157-3 (paper).

Vol. IIIC.1   *Spiritual Values and Social Progress*
    Uzbekistan Philosophical Studies, I
    Said Shermukhamedov and Victoriya Levinskaya
    ISBN 1-56518-143-3 (paper).

Vol.1IIID.1   *Reason, Rationality and Reasonableness,*
    Vietnamese Philosophical Studies, I
    Tran Van Doan
    ISBN 1-56518-166-2 (paper).

Series IV. Western Europe and North America

Vol. IV.1   *Italy in Transition: The Long Road from the First to*
    the Second Republic: The 1997 Edmund D. Pellegrino Lecture
    on Contemporary Italian Politics
    Paolo Janni
    ISBN 1-56518-120-4 (paper).

Vol. IV.2   *Italy and The European Monetary Union: The 1997 Edmund*

D. Pellegrino Lecture on Contemporary Italian Politics
Paolo Janni
ISBN 1-56518-128-X (paper).

Vol. IV.3   *Italy at the Millennium: Economy, Politics, Literature and Journalism: The 1997 Edmund D. Pellegrino Lecture on Contemporary Italian Politics*
Paolo Janni
ISBN 1-56518-158-1 (paper).

Vol.4   *Speaking of God*
Carlo Huber
ISBN 1-56518-169-7 (paper).

Vol.5   *The Essence of Italian Culture and the Challenge of a Global Age*
Paulo Janni and George F. McLean
ISBB 1-56518-177-8 (paper).

Series IVA. Central and Eastern Europe

Vol. IVA.1   *The Philosophy of Person: Solidarity and Cultural Creativity: Polish Philosophical Studies, I,*
A. Tischner, J.M. Zycinski,
ISBN 1-56518-048-8 (cloth); ISBN 1-56518-049-6 (paper).

Vol. IVA.2   *Public and Private Social Inventions in Modern Societies: Polish   Philosophical Studies, II,*
L. Dyczewski, P. Peachey, J. Kromkowski,
ISBN 1-56518-050-x (cloth). paper ISBN 1-56518-051-8 (paper).

Vol. IVA.3   *Traditions and Present Problems of Czech Political Culture: Czechoslovak Philosophical Studies, I,*
M. Bednár, M. Vejraka
ISBN 1-56518-056-9 (cloth); ISBN 1-56518-057-7 (paper).

Vol. IVA.4   *Czech Philosophy in the XXth Century: Czech Philosophical Studies, II,*
Lubomír Nový and Jirí Gabriel,
ISBN 1-56518-028-3 (cloth); ISBN 1-56518-029-1 (paper).

Vol. IVA.5   *Language, Values and the Slovak Nation: Slovak Philosophical Studies, I,*
Tibor Pichler and Jana Gašparíková,
ISBN 1-56518-036-4 (cloth); ISBN 1-56518-037-2 (paper).

Vol. IVA.6   *Morality and Public Life in a Time of Change: Bulgarian Philosophical Studies, I,*
V. Prodanov, M. Stoyanova,
ISBN 1-56518-054-2 (cloth); ISBN 1-56518-055-0 (paper).

Vol. IVA.7 *Knowledge and Morality:*
Georgian PhilosophicalStudies, 1,
N.V. Chavchavadze, G. Nodia, P. Peachey,
ISBN 1-56518-052-6 (cloth); ISBN 1-56518-053-4 (paper).

Vol. IVA.8 *Cultural Heritage and Social Change:*
Lithuanian Philosophical Studies, I,
Bronius Kuzmickas and Aleksandr Dobrynin,
ISBN 1-56518-038-0 (cloth); ISBN 1-56518-039-9 (paper).

Vol. IVA.9 *National, Cultural and Ethnic Identities: Harmony*
beyond Conflict: Czech Philosophical Studies, IV
Jaroslav Hroch, David Hollan, George F. McLean
ISBN 1-56518-113-1 (paper).

Vol. IVA.10 *Models of Identities in Postcommunist Societies:*
Yugoslav Philosophical Studies, I
Zagorka Golubovic and George F. McLean
ISBN 1-56518-121-1 (paper).

Vol. IVA.11 *Interests and Values: The Spirit of Venture in*
a Time of Change: Slovak Philosophical Studies, II
Tibor Pichler and Jana Gasparikova
ISBN 1-56518-125-5 (paper).

Vol. IVA.12 *Creating Democratic Societies: Values and Norms;*
Bulgarian Philosophical Studies, II
Plamen Makariev, Andrew M. Blasko, Asen Davidov
ISBN 1-56518-131-X (paper).

Vol.IVA.13 *Values of Islamic culture and the experience of history,*
Russian Philosophical Studies, I
Nur Kirabaev, Yuriy Pochta.
ISBN 1-56518-133-6 (paper).

Vol. IVA.14 *Values and Education in Romania Today;*
Romanian Philosophical Studies, I
Marin Calin and Magdalena Dumitrana
ISBN 1-56518-134-4 (paper).

Vol. IVA.15 *Between Words and Reality, Studies on the Politics*
of Recognition and the Changes of Regime in
Contemporary Romania
Victor Neumann
ISBN 1-56518-161-1 (paper).

Vol. IVA.16 *Culture and Freedom;*
Romanian Philosophical Studies, III
Marin Aiftinca
ISBN 1-56518-136-0 (paper).

Vol. IVA.17 *Lithuanian Philosophy: Persons and Ideas*

Lithuanian Philosophical Studies, II
Jurate Baranova
ISBN 1-56518-137-9 (paper).

Vol. IVA.18   *Human Dignity: Values and Justice;*
Czech Philosophical Studies, III
Miloslav Bednar
ISBN 1-56518-1409 (paper).

Vol. IVA.19   *Values in the Polish Cultural Tradition:*
Polish Philosophical Studies, III
Leon Dyczewski
ISBN 1-56518-142-5 (paper).

Vol. IVA.20   *Liberalization and transformation of morality in*
post-communist countries: Polish Philosophical Studies, IV
Tadeusz Buksinski
ISBN 1-56518-178-6 (paper).

Vol. IVA.21   *Islamic and Christian Cultures: Conflict or Dialogue:*
Bulgarian Philosophical Studies, III
Plament Makariev
ISBN 1-56518-162-X (paper).

Vol. IVA.22   *Moral, Legal and Political Values in Romanian Cultur,*
Romanian Philosophical Studies, IV
Mihaela Czobor-Lupp and J. Stefan Lupp
ISBN 1-56518-170-0 (paper).

Series V. Latin America

Vol. V.1   *The Social Context and Values: Perspectives of*
the Americas,
O. Pegoraro,
ISBN 0-8191-7354-1 (cloth); ISBN 0-8191-7355-x (paper).

Vol. V.2   *Culture, Human Rights and Peace in Central America,*
Raul Molina, Timothy Ready,
ISBN 0-8191-7356-8 (cloth); ISBN 0-8191-7357-6 (paper).

Vol V.3   *El Cristianismo Aymara: Inculturacion o culturizacion?,*
Luis Jolicoeur
ISBN 1-56518-104-2 (paper).

Vol. V.4   *Love as theFoundation of Moral Education and*
Character Development
Luis Ugalde, Nicolas Barros, George F. McLean
ISBN 1-56518-080-1 (paper).

Vol. V.5   *Human Rights, Solidarity and Subsidiarity:*
Essays towards a Social Ontology

Carlos E. A. Maldonado
ISBN 1-56518-110-7 (paper).

FOUNDATIONS OF MORAL EDUCATION
AND CHARACTER DEVELOPMENT

Series VI. Foundations of Moral Education

Vol. VI.1   *Philosophical Foundations for Moral Education and
Character Development: Act and Agent,*
G. McLean, F. Ellrod,
ISBN 1-56518-001-1 (cloth); ISBN 1-56518-000-3 (paper).

Vol. VI.2   *Psychological Foundations for Moral Education and
Character Development: An Integrated Theory of
Moral Development,*
R. Knowles,
ISBN 1-56518-003-8 (cloth); ISBN 1-56518-002-x (paper).

Vol. VI.3   *Character Development in Schools and Beyond,*
Kevin Ryan, Thomas Lickona,
ISBN 1-56518-058-5 (cloth); ISBN 1-56518-059-3 (paper).

Vol. VI.4   *The Social Context and Values: Perspectives of
the Americas,*
O. Pegoraro,
ISBN 0-8191-7354-1 (cloth); ISBN 0-8191-7355-x (paper).

Vol. VI.5   *Chinese Foundations for Moral Education and
Character Development,*
Tran van Doan,
ISBN 1-56518-033 (cloth), ISBN 1-56518-032-1 (paper).

Vol. VI.6   *Love as the Foundation of Moral Education and
Character Development*
Luis Ugalde, Nicolas Barros, George F. McLean
ISBN 1-56518-080-1 (paper).

Series VII. Seminars on Culture and Values

Vol. VII.1   *The Social Context and Values: Perspectives of
the Americas,*
O. Pegoraro,
ISBN 0-8191-7354-1 (cloth); ISBN 0-8191-7355-x (paper).

Vol. VII.2   *Culture, Human Rights and Peace in Central America,*
Raul Molina, Timothy Ready,

218   *The Council for Research in Values and Philosophy*

ISBN 0-8191-7356-8 (cloth); ISBN 0-8191-7357-6 (paper).
Vol. VII.3   *Relations Between Cultures,*
John Kromkowski,
ISBN 1-56518-009-7 (cloth); ISBN 1-56518-008-9 (paper).
Vol.VII.4   *Moral Imagination and Character Development*
Volume I, The imagination
George F. McLean and John A. Kromkowski, eds.
SBN 1-56518-174-3 (paper).
Vol.VII.5   *Moral Imagination and Character Development*
Volume II, Moral Imagination in Personal Formation and
Character Development
George F. McLean and Richard Knowles, eds.
SBN 1-56518-181-6 (paper).
Vol.VII.6   *Moral Imagination and Character Development*
Volume II, Imagination in religion and social life
George F. McLean and John K. White, eds.
ISBN 1-56518-182-4 (paper).
Vol.VII.7   *Hermeneutics and inculturation*
George F. McLean, Antonio Gallo, Robert Magliola, eds.
ISBN 1-56518-184-0 (paper).
Vol.VII.8   *Culture, evangelization, and dialogue*
Antonio Gallo and Robert Magliola, eds.
ISBN 1-56518-183-2 (paper).
Vol. VII.9   *The Place of the Person in Social Life,*
Paul Peachey and John Kromkowski,
ISBN 1-56518-013-5 (cloth); ISBN 1-56518-012-7 (paper).
Vol. VII.10   *Urbanization and Values,*
John Kromkowski,
ISBN 1-56518-011-9 (cloth); ISBN 1-56518-010-0 (paper).
Vol. VII.12   *Freedom And Choice In A Democracy, Volume II:*
The Difficult Passage to Freedom
Robert Magliola and Richard Khuri, eds.
ISBN -56518-144-1 (paper).
Vol.VI I.16   *Civil Society and Social Reconstruction,*
George F. McLean,
ISBN 1-56518-086-0 (paper).

The International Society for Metaphysics

Vol. 1   *Person and Nature*
George F. McLean and Hugo Meynell, eds.
ISBN 0-8191-7025-9 (cloth); ISBN 0-8191-7026-7 (paper).

Vol.2 *Person and Society*
George F. McLean and Hugo Meynell, eds.
ISBN 0-8191-6924-2 (cloth); ISBN 0-8191-6925-0 (paper).
Vol.3 *Person and God*
George F. McLean and Hugo Meynell, eds.
ISBN 0-8191-6937-4 (cloth); ISBN 0-8191-6938-2 (paper).
Vol.4 *The Nature of Metaphysical Knowledge*
George F. McLean and Hugo Meynell, eds.
ISBN 0-8191-6926-9 (cloth); ISBN 0-8191-6927-7 (paper).
Vol.5 *Philosophhical Challenges and Opportunities*
of Globalization
Obliva Blanchette, Tomonobu Imamichi and George F. McLean
ISBN 1-56518-1298 (paper).

The series is published and distributed by: The Council for Research in Values and Philosophy, Cardinal Station, P.O. Box 261, Washington, D.C. 20064, Tel./Fax. 202/319-6089; e-mail: cua-rvp@cua.edu; website: http://www.crvp.org

Prices: -- Europe and North America: cloth $45.00; paper $17.50; plus shipping: surface, $3.50 first volume; $1.00 each additional; UPS, $5.50 first copy; air, $7.20. -- Latin American and Afro-Asian editions: $4.00 per volume; plus shipping: sea, $1.75; air, Latin America $5.70; Afro-Asia: $9.00.